MW01611703

MARCHING ON!

For my friend Bill Lizzott
Enjoy!
Robert W. Allen
Autumn 2002

MARCHING ON!

JOHN BROWN'S GHOST FROM THE CIVIL WAR TO CIVIL RIGHTS

by Robert Willis Allen

with a Foreword by Howard Coffin,
author of *Full Duty* and *Nine Months to Gettysburg*

Northfield, Vermont. Northfield News and Printery, 2000

Copyright ©2000 by Robert Willis Allen.

All rights reserved. No part of this book may be reproduced, stored, or transmitted in any form, by any process or technique, without the express written consent of the author.

Author's suggested CIP with LC subject headings for this publication:

Allen, Robert W. (Robert Willis), 1948-
Marching on!: John Brown's ghost from the Civil War to Civil Rights/ by Robert Willis Allen; with a foreword by Howard Coffin. —1st ed.
xviii,335p.: ill., maps; 25 cm.
Includes index.
Includes bibliographical references (p.313).
ISBN 0-9659326-2-1 (paper)
ISBN 0-9659326-3-X (cloth)
1. Harpers Ferry, W. Va.—John Brown Raid, 1859. 2. Brown, John, 1800-1859. 3. Slavery—United States—Emancipation. 4. Racism—United States. 5. United States—History—Civil War, 1861-1865—Songs and music. 6. Women Poets, American—Massachusetts. I. Title. II. Title: John Brown's ghost from the Civil War to Civil Rights.
E451.A45 2000
973.7'116—dc21

Published in the United States of America.

10 9 8 7 6 5 4 3 2 1

Dedicated to the memory of Rod Serling, 1924-1975.
His stories still inspire new generations to carry on
the struggle against racism and prejudice in America.

Foreword

Develop even a passing interest in Civil War history and you must, sooner or later, come to terms with John Brown. The encounter is never simple. Ralph Waldo Emerson likened him to Christ and Brown, himself, believed he was doing the Lord's work. Nathaniel Hawthorne, however, felt that no man was ever more justly hanged. Yet Henry Wise, the pre-Civil War governor of Virginia who pressed for Brown's trial on charges of treason, said after the South was defeated that Old Osawatomie was "a great man." Coming to terms with John Brown, even seven score years after he swung from a Virginia gallows on a blue sky Shenandoah Valley autumn day, is not easy.

I first encountered the John Brown legend in 1960 during a high school art history course in Woodstock, Vt., when I was introduced to artist John Steuart Curry's remarkable image of Brown. Curry, born in the Kansas once made bloody by conflict over slavery, gave us a John Brown of immense power. On his canvas a man far larger than life, feet firmly planted on the prairie earth, wields a rifle that he is, clearly, ready to use. Behind him a wagon train makes its way across the great plains, carrying not only the American dream, but the curse of American democracy—human bondage. Brown's fiery eyes are fixed on something above the earth as a prairie gale blows his hair and beard. He is shouting, surely some "battle cry of freedom," and a tornado funnel advances across the landscape, as if called forth by Brown in his rage against the enslavement of fellow human beings. A young black man kneels beside the abolitionist, his face betraying both hope and fear. Brown has sounded forth the trumpet and a mighty Civil War is about to be visited on the American landscape.

Another encounter with the legend came in 1999 at Harper's Ferry, in the little engine-house become a fort, hearing blow by blow from historian Dennis Frye of Brown's final battle against federal troops under Robert E. Lee. It became clear that when Brown rode in the night into that sleepy hamlet at the juncture of the Potomac and Shenandoah rivers, he never had a chance. Brown had come there to offer up his life to free slaves.

On a below zero winter night in North Elba, N.Y., I visited the quiet farmhouse where Brown lived for a decade before departing for Harper's Ferry. His famous body lies in a grave by an immense boulder in the front yard. I paused by the bronze statue of Brown in the company of a young black lad. On that clear and starry night the big dipper shone brilliantly to the north, the old drinking gourd escaped slaves were taught to follow on their perilous way toward freedom.

And I recall my friend Edwin Cole Bearss, who probably carries more Civil War knowledge in his head than any living human being, speaking of Brown early on in Ken Burns's monumental video *The Civil War*. Bearss leans close to the camera. "John Brown," he growls, then repeats the name for emphasis, "John Brown. A very important person in history… He becomes the single most important factor in bringing on the war." Bearss read Robert Allen's *Marching On!: John Brown's Ghost from the Civil War to Civil Rights* and gave it praise. So do I.

We learn from Allen that the song "John Brown's Body" was, most appropriately, born in Boston, that hotbed of abolitionism. Soldiers garrisoning a military fort in Boston harbor composed it and the marching song was first sung publicly on Boston Common by a Massachusetts regiment bound for war in Virginia. The lively tribute to Old Osawatomie became an immensely popular marching song during the Civil War. I well recall my joy on discovering that the Vermont Brigade had sung the old song when, in 1864, it marched through Charles Town, West Virginia, the scene of Brown's trial and hanging. Less than three years earlier, Julia Ward Howe, inspired by witnessing the Army of the Potomac on review, awoke in a Washington hotel room and penned new words. "John Brown's Body" became the "Battle Hymn of the Republic." Indeed, a case has been made for the inspiring song one day becoming the American national anthem, replacing the nearly unsingable "Star Spangled Banner." And we discover a verse of the "Battle Hymn" that Howe altered in the published version. It began:

In the whiteness of the lilies he was born across the sea
With a glory in his bosom that shines out in you and me.

Allen brings back to light some nearly-forgotten figures of the Civil War era. Among them are Vermont's distinguished Senator Jacob Collamer, the Green Mountain Socrates, who sought to get at the facts of Brown's Harper's Ferry Raid. We meet the Reverend Young, of Burlington, Vt., and experience the miraculous parting of the weather that allowed him to reach North Elba and preside at Brown's funeral. There's the noble Francis Pierpont who fought successfully to keep western Virginia out of the Confederacy and to make it the state of West Virginia. There's Brown's brave wife, and a daughter who ventured into the occupied Confederacy to teach freed slaves. And there's some of the mighty figures of the day, Lincoln, Howe, Lee, Jefferson Davis, and others, all in some way touched by Brown's deeds, or the music he inspired.

This book is a treasure trove of information, much of it previously obscure, that, skillfully assembled by Allen, becomes a book of history that has the remarkable coincidence of good fiction. It's a book almost impossible to put down.

In the end, what do I now make of this John Brown? Convinced that "the crimes of this guilty land will never be purged away but with blood," he willingly gave his life to bring on a conflict that would send 620,000 Americans to premature graves. Brown, indeed, gave his life to free slaves. Yet in the back of my mind there is ever the troubling thought of that dark night in Bloody Kansas when Brown and his boys hacked to death with swords five farmers. It was cold blooded murder. I wish he hadn't done it.

Of course the cost of ridding America of slavery was four astonishingly bloody years of civil war. Did that have to happen? Turn to Edmund Wilson's dated, but still impressive, *Patriotic Gore*, and after some one thousand pages you may agree with the author that the slave states would have collapsed, without war, failing under the weight of an unworkable, outdated economic system based on human bondage. Coming to terms with John Brown is never simple. But we all know that the trumpet was sounded, and retreat was never called until the Confederacy was bludgeoned into submission. John Brown, perhaps more than any other man, loosed the fateful lightning and changed the course of world history, one man, as Allen writes, "with a tormented soul which is still marching on."

Howard Coffin
Montpelier, Vermont
Summer, 2000

Author's Introduction

In Vermont, where I was born and raised, I was isolated from feelings of sectional and racial hatred until I was five. At that tender age, my uncle brought me to the State Capitol in Montpelier where he showed me Julian Scott's massive painting of the Battle of Cedar Creek. When I asked him about the painting, he said it had to do with a war between the "North and the South."

"Who won?" I asked.

"The North," he answered without hesitation.

I thought he was talking about a war between northern and southern Vermont. It was only many years later in middle and secondary schools that I came to an understanding that, between 1861 and 1865, Americans had fought each other over the issues of secession and slavery. As my teachers explained it, the war ended with the preservation of the Union and the freeing of black slaves who were then given all the rights of U.S. citizens. Nothing more was said, and I was left to believe that, since the close of the Civil War, African Americans were now accepted in our society, and that there were no more serious issues of concern over their welfare, especially as the United States government had recently passed antidiscrimination legislation which ended the so-called "Jim Crow" laws in the South and guaranteed black people the right to vote.

But my ignorance was not permanent. In the summer of 1968, a racially motivated shooting in Irasburg, Vermont, awakened me to the truth that something was wrong with the rosy picture of a tolerant America my teachers had painted. Much later, while I was living in Boston, I learned again that racial problems were still with us.

On December 11, 1974, I was working in an automotive parts plant in South Boston. That day, a black student at the newly integrated South Boston High School stabbed a white student. Angry South Boston residents armed with sticks attacked any black people they found in their neighborhoods. Blacks who worked at the factory had to walk home that night in a large group for protection.

I have asked myself a million times since then what motivated such violence. It was only in 1991 that I began finding answers. In

September of that year, Dolores Frascoia asked me to present a program on the songs of the Civil War for adult basic education students and tutors in Barre, Vermont. In the course of researching the songs, I discovered a large body of material about two songs in particular: "John Brown's Body" and the "Battle Hymn of the Republic." After studying various documents and histories concerning these songs, I came to the conclusion that I could only understand them if I knew more about John Brown and how the song written about him kept his memory alive during the Civil War. It has taken more than eight years to piece together the story of how these songs were used during and after the war, and what they meant to the American people, North and South.

For the purposes of avoiding unnecessary confusion, I have opted to use the original names of places mentioned in the text rather than their modern equivalents. In this manner, present day Harpers Ferry becomes Harper's Ferry, as it was written in 1859, and Charles Town, West Virginia, the place where John Brown was tried and hanged, reverts to its original name of Charlestown, Virginia.

Contents

MARCHING ON!

John Brown's body lies a-mouldering in the grave.
He will not come again with foolish pikes
And a pack of desperate boys to shadow the sun.
He has gone back North. The slaves have forgotten his eye....

"There is a song in my bones. There is a song
In my white bones...."

I hear no song. I only hear the roar
Of the Spring freshets, and the gushing voice
Of mountain-brooks that overflow their banks,
Swollen with melting ice and crumbled earth.

"That is my song.
It is made of water and wind. It marches on."

No, John Brown's body lies a-mouldering,
A-mouldering.

"My bones have been washed clean
And God blows through them with a hollow sound,
And God has shut his wildfire in my dead heart."

I hear it now,
Faint, faint as the first droning flies of March,
Faint as the multitudinous, tiny sigh
Of grasses underneath a windy scythe.

"It will grow stronger."

It has grown stronger. It is marching on.

—Stephen Vincent Benét
John Brown's Body: Book One

Prolog:

"I tremble for my country...."

I will not," said John Adams to Thomas Jefferson, his red-haired colleague. "You shall do it."

It was early June of 1776. The thirteen American colonies were in rebellion against their British masters. The war had been going on for nearly a year when delegates from North Carolina to the Continental Congress suggested that the colonies officially declare their independence. Congress debated the issue for nearly two months without resolution. But on June 7, Richard Henry Lee, a Virginia jurist, moved "that these United Colonies are, and of right ought to be, free and independent States." John Adams, a Boston lawyer representing Massachusetts, seconded the motion.

The next day, Congress placed Adams on the committee to draft a declaration of the colonies' independence, along with Roger Sherman from neighboring Connecticut, New York lawyer Robert R. Livingston, publisher and scientist Benjamin Franklin, and his friend Thomas Jefferson, the Virginian.

The committee first addressed itself to the question of who would write the draft of the document. Jefferson wanted Adams to do it, but Adams refused. When Jefferson asked him why he would not do it, Adams answered, "Reasons enough." "What can be your reasons?" Jefferson inquired.

"Reason first: you are a Virginian and a Virginian ought to appear at the head of this business. Reason second: I am obnoxious, suspected and unpopular. You are very much otherwise. Reason third: You can write ten times better than I can."

Jefferson finally agreed.[1]

The five men had much to consider. On November 7 of the previous year, the earl of Dunmore, then governor general of Virginia, had issued a proclamation declaring "all indented servants, Negroes, or others, [appertaining to Rebels,] free, that are able and willing to bear arms, they joining His Majesty's Troops, as soon as may be, for the more speedily reducing this Colony to a proper sense of their duty to His Majesty's crown and dignity."[2] The earl had abandoned his land base of operations, but he had taken many freedom seeking slaves with him.

On December 31, 1775, General George Washington responded to Dunmore's declaration with a forceful letter to the Continental Congress. The general had just been told by a committee from the Congress not to enlist blacks into the army. "As it is to be apprehended," he wrote, "that they may seek employ in the ministerial army, I have presumed to depart from the resolution respecting them, and have given license for their being enlisted. If this is disapproved of by Congress, I will put a stop to it."[3] Congress wrote to Washington on January 16, 1776, "That the free negroes who have served faithfully in the army at Cambridge, may be re-inlisted therein, but no others."[4] The pronouncement was ignored, and Washington allowed black soldiers, whether free or slave, to serve either in all-black regiments or alongside whites. Meanwhile, Dunmore sat with his fleet in the Potomac River. Before he left for England in August, he spirited away some three hundred fugitive slaves with dubious promises of freedom.[5]

As Jefferson pondered over the wording of the document, he contemplated an idea first proposed by John Locke in his essay *Concerning the True Original Extent and End of Civil Government.* Locke was a Puritan opposed to the aristocrat Sir Robert Filmer, who concocted the idea of the "Divine Right of Kings" during the English Civil War. Locke believed "that creatures of the same species and rank, promiscuously born to all the same advantages of Nature, and the use of the same faculties, should also be equal one amongst another," and "that being all equal and independent, no one ought to harm another in his life, health, liberty or possessions...."[6]

Ignoring Locke's statements on health and possessions, which American colonists did not regard as God-given rights, Jefferson condensed Locke's profound notions into a single statement: "We hold these truths to be self evident, that all men are created equal, that they are endowed by their Creator with certain unalienable rights, that among these are life, liberty and the pursuit of happiness."

Once these and other points were clarified, Jefferson listed the grievances against King George III. Borrowing again from Locke, who believed that forced bondage was a form of warfare, the Virginian noted among the grievances the institution of slavery, calling it a "cruel war against human nature itself." Twice, he referred to the African slaves subjected to its horrors as "MEN" in an attempt to include them in his statement about equality. In a reference to Dunmore's emancipation proclamation, Jefferson further accused the king of "exciting those very people [the slaves] to rise in arms among us, and to purchase that liberty of which he has deprived them, by murdering people upon whom he also obtruded them."[7] This grievance was removed because representatives from South Carolina and Georgia wanted the African trade to continue. Jefferson further noted that Northerners "felt a little tender under those censures" because they "had been pretty considerable carriers of [slaves] to others."[8]

This and other changes to the document worried Jefferson. Benjamin Franklin, who perceived the young Virginian's suffering, told him, "I have made it a rule, whenever in my power, to avoid becoming the draughtsman of papers to be reviewed by a public body." Franklin illustrated his "rule" with the story of a hatter who wanted a sign which read "John Thompson, Hatter, makes and sells hats for ready money." Thompson then showed the draft of his sign to several friends who objected to the wordiness of his effort, chopping out unnecessary words and phrases. "So the inscription was reduced ultimately to 'John Thompson' with the figure of a hat subjoined," Franklin concluded.[9]

Jefferson's equality idea did not meet with the same fate, surviving the harsh editing of the Congress and opening the way for the formation of what came to be called "free states" (i.e., states where slavery was abolished). Vermont was among the first of the northern states to write its own constitution during the American Revolution, and the first to abolish slavery in its state constitution ratified in July of 1777. The Vermonters believed that "all men are born equally free and independent.... Therefore, no male person, born in this country, or brought from over sea, ought to be holden by law, to serve any person, as a servant, slave or apprentice, after he arrives to the age of twenty-one years, nor female, in like manner, after she arrives to the age of eighteen years...."[10] Further provisions gave black men full citizenship and the right to vote.

Though there were only nineteen slaves in the state when the constitution was approved, many Vermonters took this position on slavery very seriously. One of them was Captain Ebenezer Allen, who was fighting against the British in New York in 1777. While patrolling

Lake Champlain with his men in November, he captured a black woman, Dinah Mattis, and her two-month-old child Nancy, along with some British troops. Since the Continental Congress had proclaimed that "all prizes belong to the captivators thereof," Captain Allen decided that Dinah and her child now belonged to him and his men. But Allen believed "that it is not right in the sight of God to keep slaves." Therefore, with the permission of his men, he gave Dinah and her child their freedom "to pass and repass any where through the United States of America with her behaving as becometh, and to trade and to traffic for herself and child as though she were born free, without being molested by any person or persons." The proceeding was recorded by the town clerk in Bennington, Vermont.[11]

Northern states with sizable slave populations usually opted for gradual emancipation of slaves. Pennsylvania passed such a law on March 1, 1780. Connecticut and Rhode Island followed suit in 1784. In 1785, New York passed a bill calling for partial gradual emancipation, later amending it to provide for complete manumission by 1827. New Jersey passed a gradual emancipation bill in 1786.

In Massachusetts, the state courts played a major role in converting that commonwealth to a free state. A young woman named Mumbet and other Massachusetts slaves sued for their freedom in 1781. When Mumbet and her fellow servants appeared in court, they posed a simple question to the judges. If the commonwealth's constitution, approved the previous year, declared that "all men are born free and equal," how could anyone in the state be a slave? The judges noted the discrepancy and declared slavery illegal in Massachusetts.[12]

New Hampshire never passed an ordinance banning slavery, but like Massachusetts, included a passage in its constitution adopted in 1783 declaring that "All men are born equally free and independent." The passage was interpreted to mean that slavery was abrogated in the state.[13]

Although his belief that all men are created equal had led to the formation of the free states, Jefferson was a Virginia slaveholder who, during the revolution, was ambivalent about slaves and their abilities. "Never yet could I find that a black had uttered a thought above the level of plain narration," he wrote in his book, *Notes on the State of Virginia*. He thought the slaves were fine musicians, but had never seen any evidence that they had ability in painting, sculpture, or poetry. "The improvement of the blacks in body and mind," he concluded,

"...proves that their inferiority is not the effect merely of their condition of life." To Jefferson, the dark color of the African skin and the slaves' seeming inferiority in mental abilities was "a powerful obstacle to the emancipation of these people."

Jefferson also had a horror of what might happen if Africans were allowed to intermarry or even have illicit sex with whites once they were freed. He also believed that the "deep rooted prejudices entertained by the whites" combined with the "ten thousand recollections, by the blacks, of the injuries they have sustained" would "produce convulsions which will probably never end but in the extermination of the one or the other race."[14] In a later passage, he wrote prophetically, "Indeed, I tremble for my country when I reflect that God is just: that his justice cannot sleep for ever: that considering numbers, nature and natural means only, a revolution of the wheel of fortune, an exchange of situation, is among possible events: that it may become probable by supernatural interference! The Almighty has no attribute which can take side with us in such a contest." To avoid race mixing and racial conflict, Jefferson hoped that all blacks would be emancipated and colonized either back in Africa or some other suitable continent or island.[15]

Jefferson sought every means possible to abolish slavery while he lived. As early as the spring of 1784, he attempted to get the Continental Congress to pass an ordinance which would provide for the elimination of slavery in newly settled territories after 1800. The measure, strongly opposed by the southern states, failed by only one vote; Jefferson and Hugh Williamson of North Carolina were the only Southerners who voted for it.[16] During his second term as president of the United States, he had better luck getting Congress to keep its obligation to end the African slave trade. At his insistence, Congress passed a law on May 2, 1807, providing for fines against persons who engaged in the trade or who knowingly purchased a kidnapped African after January 1, 1808.

But this was not enough to permanently end slave trading. By 1820, Congress was seeking stronger measures to inhibit importation, passing a bill declaring engagement in the African trade an act of piracy punishable by hanging. (The law was only enforced once, in 1862, when Captain Nathaniel Gordon was executed for kidnapping Africans with the intention of selling them in Cuba.[17])

After the American Revolution, Jefferson slowly changed his opinions of slaves' inferiority. Benjamin Banneker was a free black who had taught himself calculus and had managed to build a working clock with wooden gears without ever having seen one. In 1791, while Jefferson was serving as secretary of state, Banneker sent him an almanac. Jefferson praised the almanac as proof "that nature has given to our black brethren, talents equal to those of the other colors of men, and that the appearance of a want of them is owing merely to the degraded condition of their existence...."[18] He subsequently arranged for Banneker to obtain a post surveying the section of Maryland and Virginia making out the boundary of Washington, D.C., the nation's new capital.

During Jefferson's last days as president, he received from Henri Gregoire a volume of literature written by African Americans. Jefferson felt that Gregoire's book could not "fail to have effect in hastening the day of [the slaves'] relief...." The president freely admitted to Gregoire that he had harbored doubts about the "grade of understanding allotted to [blacks] by nature," but that "whatever be their degree of talent it is no measure of their rights."[19]

Some time after the first freed American slaves were unsuccessfully colonized to Liberia on the coast of western Africa, Jefferson wrote to Connecticut educator and clergyman Jared Sparks that African colonization as a means of liberating America's slaves would cost about 36 million dollars a year for 25 years. Instead, the former president favored colonization in the Caribbean, especially on the island of Santo Domingo where black people ruled. "Their Chief offers to pay their passage," Jefferson explained, "to receive them as free citizens, and to provide them employment." This would save considerably on the expense of freeing and then colonizing slaves.[20]

But already, forces were at work to prevent even this form of gradual emancipation from succeeding. With the advent of the cotton gin in 1793, slaves became highly valued property in America, and slavery, slowly dying before this period, had revived and spread into the growing number of southern states.

Jefferson also worried about the Missouri Compromise which allowed Maine to enter the Union as a free state and Missouri to come in as a slave state. "This momentous question," Jefferson wrote, "like a fire bell in the night, awakened and filled me with terror. I considered it at once as the knell of the Union.... I regret that I am now to die in the belief, that the useless sacrifice of themselves by the generation of 1776, to acquire self-government and happiness to their country, is to be thrown away by the unwise and unworthy passions of their sons, and that my only consolation is to be, that I live not to weep over it."[21]

In 1826, now dying and heavily in debt, Jefferson begged his creditors to allow for the manumission by will of five of his slaves. He also asked that these five be allowed to live and work in Virginia despite a state law prohibiting freedmen from remaining in the state any longer than 12 months, a measure Jefferson had fought against. The former president had already freed one slave, James Hemings, a chef, with disastrous results. Hemings, unable to hold a job for very long, eventually became an alcoholic. He had pleaded with Jefferson to allow him to return to Monticello, and ultimately committed suicide.

Jefferson died on July 4, 1826, at 12:50 p.m. In Boston on that same day, John Adams, the man who asked Jefferson to draft the Declaration of Independence, also lay dying. "Thomas Jefferson survives," Adams whispered on his deathbed. But Jefferson had already passed on, and before the day was over, Adams would join his old friend.[22]

Thanks in part to the railroad systems slowly spreading through the country, the America Jefferson left behind was quickly growing into a major economic world power. The Baltimore & Ohio line, which started construction in 1828, two years after Jefferson's death, helped passengers wishing to settle in the Northwestern Territory to reach their destinations. It also provided a vital transportation link to Harper's Ferry, an inland town built at the confluence of the Potomac and Shenandoah rivers at which George Washington had established an armory and arsenal in 1794.

President Washington reasoned that the armory would be safe from foreign invaders, but until the coming of the railroad, it was also a difficult place from which to ship goods. The train line had the capacity to move arms and other goods where they were needed at the rate of 20 miles per hour, much faster than the three-and-a-half mile an hour speed achieved by a horse drawn coach or freight wagon, or a barge.

The new trains lacked many safety features. The wrought iron rails sometimes broke and derailed an engine and the cars it was hauling. Passengers traveling in cars with a pot-bellied stove for heat and gas fixtures for light could be killed by fire in a train wreck. If one train became stalled on a line because of a break in a pipe or a boiler explosion, the train behind could hit it, causing all the cars on both trains to telescope into each other.

Safety on the rail lines increased after 1844, the year Samuel Morse invented the telegraph. The rail lines slowly caught on to the idea that Morse's clicking communications could be used not only to schedule trains, but also to warn of potential problems on a line, such as a washed out bridge or a stalled train. Telegraph operators armed with electromagnetic keys which could be rapidly hooked up to any telegraph pole soon became valued employees on rail lines. Operators riding on the trains doubled as baggage handlers when their services were not required.

The establishment of rail lines demanded a highly educated populace from which the railroad companies could hire surveyors to determine where the rail beds should go, and inventors and tool and die men to create and build the necessary equipment. They also needed people who could read and write to serve as telegraph operators. The North had a long-standing commitment to free public education, started by the Puritans of Massachusetts who had written the first laws for public education. They called the statutes "Old Deluder Laws" after "that old deluder, Satan," who wanted "to keep men from the knowledge of the scriptures."[23]

In the South, development of railroads proceeded more slowly due in part to a reliance on steam ships and more importantly to a lack of an educated populace. The southern economy was largely agrarian, based on the growing of cash crops like cotton, sugar cane, tobacco, rice, or indigo used for dyes. Any education received by slaves and other workers happened in the fields as they hoed weeds, pulled bugs off tobacco leaves, or planted rice.

Slaveowners made use of two basic systems to work their field hands: a "gang system" and a "task system." In the more common "gang system," the slaves were divided into work crews or "gangs." The driver of the gang kept the field hands at work all day until the setting sun made work impossible. Under the slightly more humane "task system," individual slaves were set to work at specific tasks. When they were done, they were dismissed from the field provided that the quality of their work was sufficient.[24]

Some slaves were trained in crafts such as blacksmithing, coopering, pottery, carpentry, stone masonry, and shoemaking. While they had the best chance of surviving as free people, their services were so prized that their owners were reluctant to manumit them. Others were used as house servants, cooks, and seamstresses. These domestic servants were also highly prized and were often treated like house pets.

The chattel slavery system, sometimes euphemistically referred to as the "peculiar institution" by its defenders and detractors, worked two ways. While the master wielded the power of life and death over his "chattels" and benefited from the work they performed, he was expected to provide them with the basic necessities of life: food, clothing, shelter, and medical care. None of the slaves on his plantation received an education beyond that needed for the work they were forced to perform. Very few could read and write. Many, especially field hands, suffered from cholera, typhoid, dysentery, tuberculosis, and malaria. Very few reached old age.[25]

Poor whites in the South fared little better in educational skills. Unlike the North, the South had no "Old Deluder Laws." The aristocrats of the plantation preferred to reserve all the benefits of higher education for themselves. They viewed free public education as incitement to rebellion. As early as 1671, Governor William Berkeley of Virginia, commenting on the lack of free public education in that colony, declared, "I thank God there are no free schools nor printing...; for learning has brought disobedience, and heresy, and sects into the world, and printing has divulged them, and libels against the best government. God keep us from both!"[26]

In 1831, Virginians found proof of the colonial governor's claims in a slave rebellion in Southampton County. Nat Turner, a slave trained in carpentry who also served as an itinerant preacher because he could read the Bible, led his followers on a bloody rampage, slaughtering every white person they found. After the rebellion was put down and Turner and his surviving followers were hanged, Virginians passed laws making it illegal for slaves to learn to read and write, or to hold religious services without a white man present.

These differing views on education between North and South had a profound influence on the development of music in America, thanks to the work of music educator Lowell Mason. As a young man, Mason had left his native Massachusetts to settle in Savannah, Georgia, where he worked in a bank. Since he was well-trained in music, he also conducted a church choir and wrote hymns for them to sing. But when the ambitious Mason wanted to publish his hymns, he found no backing in Georgia where plantation owners controlled all the money and there was very little free cash available for artistic projects of an educational or religious nature.

Upset over his lack of success, Mason showed the hymns to G. K. Jackson, an organist for the Handel and Haydn Society of Boston, a city that was rolling in money from overseas trade and railroad building, both of which fueled the development of an expanding middle class. Jackson recommended that the hymns be published by the Society. In 1827, Mason abandoned Savannah and the banking industry. He moved to Boston where he conducted three church choirs and became music director of the Handel and Haydn Society.

Boston's free education system became the target of Mason's next project, the introduction of music into the public schools. While running music instruction programs for children, Mason also trained teachers in his methods. He was so successful that, in 1838, he was named Boston's first city superintendent of public school music.[27]

As Mason's ideas spread through the North, the growing population, which had few amusements other than reading to each other in the evenings, added music to their household activities. The sale of pump organs and melodeons, a type of reed organ, increased. Pianos became more and more common in middle class parlors and church basements where choir practices were conducted. Communities also established singing clubs and town bands.

This rich soil demanded new music in abundance. Music from Europe was available, but people were more interested in popular songs written by American composers like George F. Root, a student of Lowell Mason, or Stephen Collins Foster, born in Pittsburgh, Pennsylvania, on the Fourth of July, 1826, the same day that Jefferson and Adams died.

The northern middle class also demanded musical entertainments. Sometimes this was achieved by towns swapping bands or singing societies, or holding competitions to see which town had the best music groups. More frequently, itinerant musicians filled the need. The performers included black-face minstrel shows like those of Dan Emmett or the Christy Minstrels, or singing families like the Rainer family from the Tyrolean Alps, or the Hutchinson Family Singers of New Hampshire.

The Hutchinson Family Singers, consisting of brothers John, Jesse, and Asa, and their young sister, Abby, began their career in the summer of 1842. These four young people had been raised to promote two things in life: melodious singing and radical abolitionism, the freeing of all chattel slaves. Their beliefs also embraced temperance (the outlawing of liquor and tobacco), and women's suffrage. They quickly discovered that song is a powerful way of communicating extreme political ideas. After a few years touring the country performing sensational songs like "The Madman" and "Ship on Fire," as well as abolitionist songs like "Clear the Tracks" and "The Liberty Ball," the brothers started their own families and set up their own separate "tribes" of the Hutchinson Family Singers.

Northern abolitionists, most especially those helping runaway slaves find freedom in Canada, were also spreading their ideas in print, thanks to the efforts of William Lloyd Garrison of Boston, and Harriet Beecher Stowe of Brunswick, Maine. Garrison founded an abolitionist paper called *The Liberator* in 1831, the same year that witnessed the bloody slave insurrection led by Nat Turner. In 1852, Mrs. Stowe published a book, *Uncle Tom's Cabin*, which condemned the inhuman treatment of slaves.

By the time Mrs. Stowe's book was printed, the country was seriously divided north and south over the issue of control of the U.S. Senate. The first major clash had come in 1819 when Maine attempted to enter the Union as a free state. At that time, there were eleven northern free states and eleven southern slave states. The northern states, however, had larger populations than the South, which would grow even larger once the rail lines were established. This gave the North control over the U.S. House of Representatives. If Maine came in as a twelfth free state, the North would control a majority of the Senate as well. Senator Jesse B. Thomas of Illinois proposed a compromise in which Maine would be allowed to join the Union as a free state in 1820, and Missouri would be admitted the following year as a slave state.

Thomas also wrote a measure into the proposal calling for the formation of free states above 36°, 30' of latitude (the line of Missouri's southern border), and slave states below it. Congress passed the bill, afterward known as the Missouri Compromise, on March 3, 1820.

For a time, the compromise worked. In the 25 years following its passage, the South added three new slave states (Arkansas, Florida, and Texas) while the North added only one, Michigan. But after 1845, the year that Florida and Texas achieved statehood, things started going downhill for the South. The North gained two new free states, Iowa and Wisconsin, before the end of the decade, setting the balance at 15 states for each side. And then California asked to join as a free state. A substantial portion of California territory lay below the 36°, 30' Missouri

Compromise line. Henry Clay, a Kentucky senator, worked out a measure known as the Compromise of 1850 which would allow California to become a free state and provide the South with a stronger application of the fugitive slave law.

While the battle over the 1850 Compromise was being settled, many Southerners placed their hopes for a new slave state on a Cuban adventurer and soldier, Narciso López. The Cuban organized an army of "filibusters"—from the Spanish *filibustero* meaning "pirate"—for the purpose of invading Cuba and turning the island into a U.S. territory. Since slavery was already legal in Cuba, this would give the South the advantage it wanted in the extension of slavery.

In May 1850, López sailed with his army to capture the port city of Cardenas, just 50 miles north of the Bay of Pigs. Spanish troops drove them back to their ships. López tried again in 1851, this time with southern soldiers led by William J. Crittenden of Kentucky. Spanish soldiers were waiting for them, and López and his army were captured. On September 1, López was publicly garroted in Havana. Crittenden and forty-nine other Americans were executed by firing squad.[28]

By then, Congress was discussing a concept which promised some hope for the extension of slavery: "popular sovereignty." Democrat Lewis Cass of Michigan proposed the idea during Senate hearings on the Wilmot Proviso in 1846, which attempted to eliminate slavery from land acquired from Mexico after the Mexican War. South Carolina Senator John Calhoun argued that the government could not limit slavery in new territories. Cass proposed that the settlers in a territory be allowed to decide the issue of slavery for themselves. Popular sovereignty was given its first real test in 1854 with the passage of the Kansas-Nebraska Act which provided for the settlement of land west of Missouri and north of the 36°, 30' line. The settlers would decide whether the territory would be free or slave.

The result was a blood bath. Armed Southerners, seeing this as their last chance to form a new slave state and restore the balance of power in the Senate, moved to the Kansas Territory. Armed Northerners who promoted the abolition of slavery did the same. For the next few years, pro-slavery and abolitionist forces fought each other, slaughtered unarmed civilians, and burned each other's towns. During elections, so-called "border ruffians" from Missouri crossed over into Kansas to vote in support of pro-slavery candidates. Northerners sent money and weapons to Kansas to support abolitionists fighting in the territory.

One such Northerner, Reverend Henry Ward Beecher, sent Sharps carbines to Kansas in wooden boxes labeled "Bibles." The carbines quickly became known among the Kansas abolitionists as "Beecher Bibles."

While this conflict continued, the Supreme Court, in 1857, handed down a decision in the case of *Dred Scott v. Sandford*. Dred Scott was a slave suing for his freedom because his master had brought him to live in a free state. Chief Justice Roger Taney of Maryland stated in his majority opinion that black people were "so far inferior, that they had no rights which the white man was bound to respect." Concerning the statement in the second paragraph of the Declaration of Independence about all men being created equal, Taney said "that the enslaved African race were not intended to be included, and formed no part of the people who framed and adopted this declaration."[29]

Senator Stephen Douglas supported the Supreme Court decision, stating that "all men are created equal" meant that "British subjects on this continent [were] equal to British subjects born and residing in Great Britain." Abraham Lincoln, then an obscure railroad lawyer and Douglas's political rival, strongly disagreed. "Why, according to this," Lincoln pointed out, "not only negroes but white people outside of Great Britain and America are not spoken of in that instrument. The English, Irish and Scotch, along with white Americans, were included to be sure, but the French, Germans and other white people of the world are all gone to pot along with [Douglas's] inferior races."[30]

Justice Taney not only proclaimed that Dred Scott could not be freed, he also declared the Missouri Compromise of 1820 to be unconstitutional and that Congress had no legal right under the Constitution to restrict or abolish slavery, even in free states. But the abolitionist settlers of Kansas were about to steal Taney's thunder.

On December 31, 1857, a pro-slavery convention in Kansas approved the Lecompton Constitution allowing slavery, and applied to the U.S. Congress for statehood. The pro-slavery men did not allow the people of Kansas to vote on acceptance of the constitution. Instead, they asked for a vote on a single measure which would allow slaves to be imported to the state.

Kansas abolitionists stayed away from the polls that day. The pro-slavery men, realizing that their efforts might not be approved without a public referendum, finally allowed a vote for approval of the entire constitution on January 4, 1858. The abolitionists rejected the document by an overwhelming majority. Later that year, the U.S. House of Representatives refused to admit Kansas as a state until the Lecompton Constitution was submitted again for approval. On August 2, the Kansas voters rejected it a second time.

The pro-slavery element in Kansas finally gave up the battle for statehood, but the battle for slavery in Kansas was far from over. Sporadic fighting continued as Kansas abolitionists fought Congress for the right to enter the Union as a free state, a struggle for statehood that would continue for nearly two years.

In the summer of 1859, a gray bearded man arrived at the factory town of Harper's Ferry, Virginia. He said he was Isaac Smith, a cattle rancher from New York intent on setting up a cattle business in the area. Some townspeople thought the man was a prospector because he carried surveying equipment. He was actually an abolitionist veteran of the Kansas fighting, and planned to lead a small troop of other Kansas veterans and abolitionists from other parts of the country against the U.S. arsenal and armory at Harper's Ferry, hoping to spark a war which would end slavery forever. His real name was John Brown.

Harper's Ferry as seen from Bolivar Heights looking down on the Potomac River bridge. This is most likely a post-war photograph, as the original railroad bridge was covered.

Part I

LEGEND OF THE GHOST

FROM A PHOTOGRAPH.

John Brown

1

"The bees will begin to swarm...."

When Frederick Douglass and his companion Shields Green arrived in Chambersburg, Pennsylvania, on August 19, 1859, they went to Henry Watson's barber shop to inquire how they might find "Isaac Smith."[1] The barber was more than happy to give Douglass and Green directions to the stone quarry where "Smith"—John Brown was spending the day fishing.

Realizing that Brown was well armed and wary of strangers, Douglass approached the quarry with great caution. But Brown, who had grown a beard to disguise his appearance, soon recognized his old friend Douglass and gave him a cordial welcome. "He looked every way like a man of the neighborhood," Douglass wrote afterward, "and as much at home as any of the farmers around there. His hat was old and storm-beaten, and his clothing was about the color of the stone-quarry itself—his then present dwelling-place." Douglass also noticed that there were no fish. Instead, the men now gathering at the quarry intended to discuss a bold plan for freeing the slaves of Virginia.

Although Douglass and Brown were nationally known abolitionists in 1859, both men had very humble beginnings. Douglass was born in Talbot County, Maryland, some time in February, 1817. This was as much as he would ever learn about his birth. As a slave for life, he was denied a formal education, but he did learn how to

---

John Brown, reviled by some as a villain, hailed by others as a saint. He was tormented by the notion that the United States was committed to the ideals of freedom while tolerating the enslavement of African Americans.

read and write. In this, he was largely self taught, taking his lessons informally from white friends whenever he could in the streets of Baltimore or in the shipyard where he worked.[2] On September 3, 1838, Douglass escaped to freedom in the North using papers borrowed from a free black seaman. He then became very active in the northern abolition movement and developed his talents for writing and public speaking. And in those circles of abolitionists, Douglass had met John Brown, the businessman with a passion for freeing slaves.

John Brown was born in Torrington, Connecticut, on May 9, 1800. He had moved with his father Owen, a stationmaster on the underground railroad, to Ohio at an early age and lived there for most of his life. He attributed his hatred of slavery to his companionship with a slave boy belonging to a United States marshal. The boy was, according to Brown, "fully if not more than [my] equal," and yet the lad was "badly clothed, poorly fed... & beaten...with Iron Shovels or any other thing that came first to hand."[3]

Young Brown's Bible also told him that slavery as practiced in America was sinful. Exodus 21:16 reads, "He that stealeth a man and selleth him, or if he be found in his hand, he shall surely be put to death." Every slave in America was the descendant of some ancestor kidnapped in Africa. He marked one set of verses in the fifth chapter of Jeremiah. The 26th verse said, "For among my people are found wicked men:... they set a trap, they catch men." The 29th verse told him, "Shall I not visit for these things? saith the Lord: shall not my soul be avenged on such a nation as this?"

As an adult, Brown ran a tannery in Randolph Township, Pennsylvania, with a hiding place for fugitives. In his free time, he fed his soul with Bible verses about God's punishment of wicked doers. He discussed these things with his wife and children, but made no public declaration of his feelings on the subject of emancipation until after the death of Elijah Lovejoy, an abolitionist from Maine.

Lovejoy, a graduate of Waterville College in Maine, had moved to St. Louis, Missouri, in 1827 where he set up a school and became a journalist. Some time later, he began publishing a religious newspaper called *The Observer* in which he declared his desire to see slavery gradually abolished. His pro-slavery neighbors took unkindly to his radical notions, and Lovejoy moved his presses across the Mississippi River to Alton, Illinois, where he continued his attacks on slavery.

In 1837, angry Missourians crossed the river and destroyed Lovejoy's presses. Lovejoy got new presses and kept on printing until the next attack. By November 7, 1837, Lovejoy's print shop had been destroyed several times, and he had had enough. On that night, when a pro-slavery mob arrived from Missouri intent on destroying his newspaper office yet again, Lovejoy and twenty supporters defended the presses. When the shooting stopped, the warehouse where the presses were kept was burning beyond salvation, and Lovejoy lay dead.

Later that month, Laurens P. Hickok organized a meeting in Hudson, Ohio, to commemorate Lovejoy's death. John Brown was seated in the back of the church as Hickok addressed the crowd. "The crisis has come," Hickok told them. "The question now before the American citizens is no longer alone, 'Can the slaves be made free?' but 'Are we free or are we slaves under Southern mob law?'" In the back of the church, Brown stood up and raised his right hand. "Here before God," he pledged, "in the presence of these witnesses, I consecrate my life to the destruction of slavery."[4]

The commitment was no idle one. While living in Franklin Mills, Ohio, in 1838, Brown and his family attended a revival meeting at the Congregational Church he had joined. Free blacks and runaway slaves who lived in the area were forced to sit in the back of the church during the revival. John was angered that such discrimination could exist in a house of God. He invited some of the blacks to sit in his family pew. The next day, deacons of the church warned Brown not to repeat the action, but Brown refused to bend to pressure. That night, he again led black people to his family pew.[5]

Brown suffered a long string of business failures and reverses all his life. His tannery in Randolph Township failed largely because of his perfectionist attitude. He refused to let any hide leave his tannery that was not completely dry. The tannery closed. He then got a contract to build part of the Ohio and Pennsylvania Canal which ran from Franklin Mills to Akron. This work made him certain that land in Franklin and Franklin Mills would some day be valuable. He and twenty-one other men invested heavily in the Franklin Land Company. They all lost their money in the financial crash of 1837. He tried breeding race horses, drove cattle from Ohio to Connecticut, and finally invested in sheep.

His interest in sheep brought him to the door of another sheep farmer and businessman, Simon Perkins of Akron. In June 1846, the two men went to Springfield, Massachusetts, and set up the firm of Perkins & Brown. They intended to act as agents for sheep farmers wanting to sell their wool to large manufacturing plants. But Brown graded all the fleece and placed a high price on what he considered high quality wool and a very low price on the lower grades. The manufacturers purchased all the low grade wool and ignored the more expensive piles. Brown also had a hard time keeping up with his ledgers and correspondence despite the fact that his son, John Jr., was helping him. The business was soon floundering under a mountain of debts and paperwork. [6]

In the late 1840's, Gerrit Smith, a wealthy abolitionist living in Peterboro, New York, gave away lots of land averaging about 40 acres in size in an area known as North Elba (present day Lake Placid) to free blacks residing in the state. Smith expected the new black landowners would help him obtain political office.

In April, 1848, Brown took time off from his wool business to go to Smith's Peterboro home with a proposal. "I am something of a pioneer," Brown told him. "I grew up among the woods and wild Indians of Ohio, and am used to the climate and the way of life that your colony find so trying. I will take one of your farms myself, clear it up and plant it, and show my colored neighbors how much work should be done; will give them work as I have occasion, look after them in all needful ways, and be a kind of father to them."[7] Since many of the free blacks wishing to settle the land had worked as waiters, coachmen, cooks, barbers, or in other trades, and knew nothing of farming, Smith was delighted with John Brown's offer.[8]

Brown arrived in North Elba with his family in May of 1849. He stayed at a farm he rented for $50 a year and immediately went to work sorting out the problems of his black neighbors.[9] Many had been given property on mountain slopes; others had tracts of land on low, swampy ground. One lot stretched between two separated islands in the middle of Lake Placid[10] Though Brown surveyed their land and helped his neighbors in any other way he could, his wool business was suffering from extreme financial difficulties. Brown returned to Springfield and later sailed to England in a futile attempt to open a European market for American wool. He was back in North Elba in November, 1849. In partnership with his sons Owen and Jason, he purchased 244 acres of land. Henry Thompson, Brown's son-in-law, built a house on the property in 1855.[11]

While he was waiting for the house to be built, Brown divided his time between his family in Ohio and what remained of his wool business in Springfield. During this period, the Compromise of 1850 was passed strengthening the fugitive slave laws. Brown responded by joining with African Americans living in Springfield and founding the United States League of Gileadites on January 15, 1851.

The organization was designed to protect free and fugitive blacks from southern slave catchers. "Nothing so charms the American people as personal bravery," Brown wrote in the group's charter. "Witness the case of Cinques, of everlasting memory, on board the 'Amistad.'"

Joseph Cinque or Cinques was a Mendi tribesman who was illegally sold into slavery in Cuba in 1839. Cinque and his companions had killed the captain and cook and driven off the two remaining crew of the Cuban coastal slaver *Amistad*. They kept two Cuban slaveholders alive and forced them to sail for Africa. The slaveholders tricked the Africans and sailed for America instead. The ship was captured off Long Island in New York and the Africans were jailed in New Haven, Connecticut. Their case eventually went to the Supreme Court where the Africans were declared free people who should be returned to Africa.

"The trial of life of one bold and ... successful man, for defending his rights...," Brown wrote of Cinque, "would arouse more sympathy throughout the nation than the accumulated wrongs and sufferings of more than three millions of our submissive colored population."[12]

When trouble began in the new Kansas Territory, Brown could not remain at home any longer. He left his family in North Elba, and in October, 1855, he arrived at Osawatomie, Kansas, the town where his sons had settled. He organized a company of men with himself as captain, and led them in the defense of abolitionist settlements all over the state.

Angered by a vicious attack of pro-slavery men on free state families in Lawrence, Brown traveled to Pottawatomie Creek where, on May 4, 1856, he ordered a night raid on the homes of pro-slavery advocates who had threatened the lives of free state settlers living along the creek. His men killed five people, hacking them to death with swords. After this, John Brown was sometimes called "Old Osawatomie."

Such atrocities were not limited to Brown's group alone. Both sides were engaged in bloody acts of attrition. On August 30, Martin White led a large group of pro-slavery men into Osawatomie. White's first act was to gun down the unarmed Frederick Brown, one of John Brown's sons. A battle ensued between the pro-slavery men and the abolitionists for control of the town. John Brown, who was camped with his men on the outskirts of the town, joined the fray in vain. By the end of the fighting, the town was ablaze.

"God sees it," Brown told his son Jason as they stood watching the town burn. "I have only a short time to live—only one death to die, and I will die fighting for this cause. There will be no more peace in this land until slavery is done for. I will give them something else to do than to extend slave territory. I will carry this war into Africa."[13]

John Brown spent the next few years traveling through the North, speaking both in public and private to sympathetic northern abolitionists about his special "Kansas business." He recruited fighting men for his company and gained support, financial and otherwise, from prominent men in the North, including Gerrit Smith, chairman of the Kansas Committee in Massachusetts George Luther Stearns, and Frederick Douglass.

Brown also recruited Hugh Forbes, a foreign adventurer who had fought unsuccessfully with Garibaldi in Italy. Forbes, who showed up destitute in New York City attached himself to Brown as a trainer of fighting men. But by 1858, the relationship between the two men had soured. Forbes kept demanding more money from Brown's backers, and when the funds were not forthcoming, he went to Washington to spread rumors about what Brown intended to do in the South.[14] These rumors made Brown's northern backers nervous. They asked him not to proceed with his plans until further notice. For the moment, Captain Brown was content to remain in Kansas near the Missouri border and continue to recruit soldiers for the eventual attack on the South. Because Forbes had deserted him, Brown turned over the training of his men to Aaron D. Stevens, who had fought in the Mexican War.

On December 20, 1858, one of Brown's men, George B. Gill, discovered a runaway Missouri slave who pretended he was a broom salesman. Gill brought the man to Captain Brown at Fort Snyder. The slave explained that he and his family were about to be sold, and begged John Brown to help liberate them. For Brown, this was the opportunity he needed to prove to his backers that he could carry out a strike on Virginia. That night, Brown and Stevens led separate attacks in Missouri on two slaveowners, liberating eleven slaves and taking two prisoners. In the months that followed, John Brown managed to get the runaways across several state lines in the dead of winter, evading posses and federal marshals.[15]

On March 11, 1859, Brown, Stevens, John Henry Kagi (one of Brown's Kansas recruits), and their party arrived in Chicago by boxcar at 4:30 in the morning. The runaways now numbered twelve, including a child born on the journey. They walked up Adams Street and banged on the door of the most prominent abolitionist and underground railroad agent in that city, Allen Pinkerton of the Pinkerton Detective Agency. Pinkerton's wife fed the fugitives while the detective made arrangements for their stay in Chicago.

On learning that Brown needed money to get the slaves the rest of the way to Canada, Pinkerton immediately requested a special railroad car. He then went to the hall where the Chicago Judiciary Convention was then in progress. "Gentlemen, I have one thing to do and I intend to do it in a hurry," he told the members of the convention. "John Brown is in this city at the present time with a number of men, women and children. I require aid and substantial aid I must have. I am ready and willing to leave this meeting if I get this money, if not, I have to say this. I will bring John Brown to this meeting and if any United States Marshal dare lay a hand on him he must take the consequences. I am determined to do this or have the money." The delegates sat in silence for a few moments. Then John Wilson, a prominent politician who later became a judge, walked to the front of the room and gave Pinkerton $50. Soon there was a stream of delegates coming forward and pouring money into Pinkerton's hat. He left the meeting with more than $500.

At four o'clock, Pinkerton, his son William, and Kagi gathered the runaways in a wagon and brought them to the train depot. While Brown was giving Pinkerton thanks and saying goodbye, he said, "Friends, lay in your tobacco, cotton and sugar because I intend to raise the prices." Fifteen minutes later, the fugitives were on board the special car.

"Look well upon that man, Willy," Pinkerton said to his son as the train pulled out of the station. "He is greater than Napoleon and just as great as George Washington." Six hours later, the train arrived in Canada.[16]

ar from reassuring Brown's northern supporters, the Missouri raid had only made them more nervous about Old Osawatomie's real intentions. In the summer of 1859, Brown may have entertained some doubts himself concerning the performance of his advance man, John E. Cook. Brown had sent Cook to the Ferry the previous year to scout out conditions in the town and surrounding area while keeping a low profile. At first, Cook had obeyed his instructions to the letter, working sometimes as a teacher and others as a lock attendant on the Chesapeake & Ohio Canal which ran next to the Potomac River opposite the Ferry. In his spare time, Cook studied the layout of the town and learned something of the town's social structure. But then he took up with a local woman, Mary V. Kennedy. He married her in April of 1859. That summer, she bore him a son.

Brown could never be sure what information Cook might have communicated to his wife, but Mary never revealed whatever Cook had told her. Cook wanted to spread broad hints to plantation slaves in the area about Brown's plans, but Brown forbade him to say anything.[17]

By the time Frederick Douglass and Shields Green met at the rock quarry in Chambersburg with Brown and Kagi, it had become

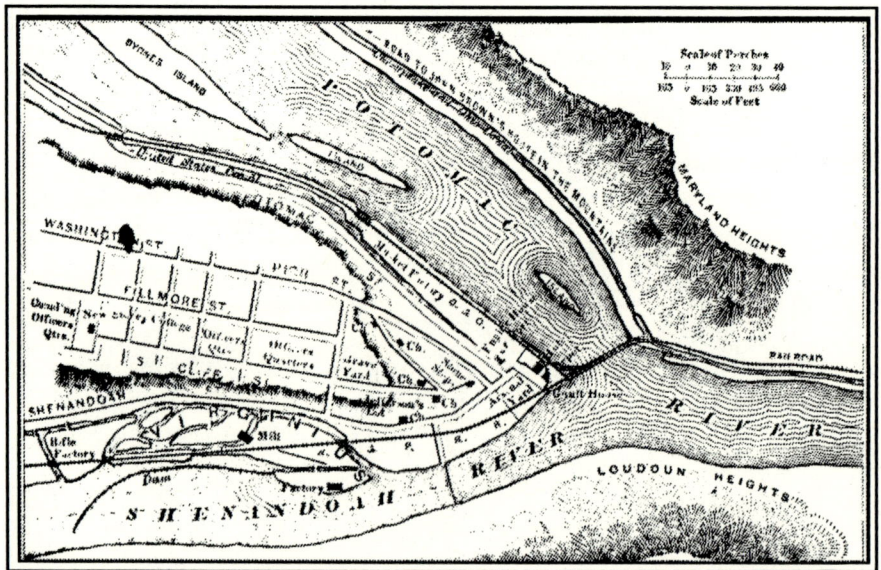

In 1794, George Washington selected Harper's Ferry as the site of a national armory and arsenal. John Brown thought this town was the perfect place to begin a war to free slaves.

obvious that Brown was abandoning his original plan of freeing slaves by striking villages and plantations from the mountains. The new plan was suicidal: a raid on the federal arsenal and armory at Harper's Ferry, Virginia. For two days the men argued. Brown expected Virginia and Maryland slaves to join him along with white settlers from western Virginia opposed to slavery. Douglass insisted that Brown would be "going into a perfect steel trap, and that once in he would never get out alive." Despite all of Douglass's arguments, Brown would not back down.

Douglass finally decided to go home. Brown put his arms around him and said, "Come with me Douglass; I will defend you with my life. I want you for a special purpose. When I strike, the bees will begin to swarm, and I shall want you to help hive them." The former slave turned abolitionist was moved by Brown's eloquence, but not enough to stay. Before leaving, Douglass asked Shields Green what he had decided. "I believe I'll go with the old man," Green stated. The conference in the rock quarry had ended, and Douglass would never see any of those men again.

It was nearly two months before John Brown decided that conditions were right for the raid. All that summer, men had been gathering at the Kennedy Farm on Maryland Heights where Brown had his headquarters. The farm was just five miles north of Harper's Ferry.

By late September, Brown had also amassed a formidable arsenal. He ordered and received 950 pikes from Charles Blair. With these crude double-edged blades mounted on long poles, he intended to arm slaves who knew nothing of firearms. For those slaves with some training, he had 200 Maynard revolvers. Unfortunately, he had not ordered caps large enough to make the revolvers useful. But he also had 198 Sharps Model 1855 carbines of the type called "capping breech-loaders," and they worked perfectly. These single shot carbines which took .577 caliber bullets in linen cartridges could be loaded and fired about six times a minute, giving them a distinct advantage over conventional long-barreled rifled muskets which could be loaded and shot only three times a minute. The short barreled carbines, however, lacked the long-distance accuracy of the muskets.[18]

Around the 30th of September, Brown sent John Cook down the Charlestown pike to scout out the conditions among the slaves and planters. Cook reported that the slaves would "swarm like bees" when they hit the Ferry.[19] Brown still did nothing for two weeks. Then on

THE CABIN ACROSS THE ROAD
FROM THE FARMHOUSE

SCHOOL-HOUSE GUARDED BY
JOHN E. COOK

THE HOUSE AT KENNEDY FARM, MARYLAND

John Brown used the Kennedy Farm as a gathering place for men who would participate in the raid on the Ferry. Brown's men intended to use the Maryland schoolhouse as a supply depot.

Saturday, October 15, three men arrived at the farm: John A. Copeland, Lewis Leary, and Francis Jackson Meriam who brought Brown $600 in gold. Brown decided at last that the time had come to strike.

The next day at dawn, he assembled his twenty-one recruits for a final worship service. Later that morning, he explained the plan to the newest recruits, and in the afternoon, he made assignments for specific parts of the overall plan. Owen Brown, Barclay Coppoc, and Francis

Meriam were ordered to remain at the farmhouse until the raid was well under way, then to move the guns and pikes stored at the farm to a schoolhouse near the Ferry. These weapons were to be distributed to the slaves of Maryland and any white abolitionists joining the revolt from southern Pennsylvania or western Virginia. The remaining eighteen men would follow Brown to the Ferry.

It was nearly eight o'clock in the evening before these arrangements were finished. By then a slight drizzle had started outside. Brown turned his gray eyes to his small army and said, "Men, get on your arms; we will proceed to the Ferry." The men put on black shawls, and each man armed himself with a Sharps carbine and a Maynard revolver. They marched out into the light rain as Brown climbed into a wagon loaded with pikes and other tools. Following the wagon, they marched up the hill and then turned left onto the long tree-lined, undulating road that led down to the Ferry.[20]

At the bottom of Maryland Heights, the road turned east with the Chesapeake & Ohio Canal and the Potomac River on the right. Brown's men could see lights from the town's streets and crude wooden buildings twinkling through the fog and mist on the opposite side of the river. Just beyond the town was the Shenandoah River which flowed into the Potomac. As the men approached, they could see the lights of the town shining on the Shenandoah, outlining the Potomac River bridge which connected the Ferry with Maryland Heights and the town of Sandy Hook. A second bridge extended across the Shenandoah from Loudoun Heights.

John Henry Kagi and Aaron Stevens arrived first, capturing William Williams, the night watchman on the Potomac River bridge. Shortly afterwards, Brown arrived with the wagon and his other men. John Cook and Charles Tidd broke ranks at the bridge to cut the telegraph lines east and west of the town. The remaining men, with Williams in tow, headed directly for the armory where they captured the armory night watchman, Daniel Whelan. "I came here from Kansas," Brown told Williams and Whelan, "and this is a slave state; I want to free all the negroes in this State; I have possession now of the United States armory, and if the citizens interfere with me I must only burn the town and have blood."[21]

Brown's men quickly took charge of the arsenal next to the Shenandoah River. Albert Hazlett and Edwin Coppoc were given responsibility for holding it, while Kagi and John Copeland were sent to take Hall's Rifle Works about half a mile from the armory on one of the islands in the Shenandoah. Brown also sent Aaron Stevens out with a group to take more hostages, especially Lewis Washington, the head of the town's militia. Washington, a great grand-nephew of George Washington, possessed a sword given to his great-great uncle by Frederick the Great. Brown had given his men specific instructions that Lewis Washington was to surrender this sword directly to Osborn Anderson, a black man.

Around midnight, Brown's carefully constructed plans began to unravel. Oliver Brown, guarding the Potomac River bridge, took a pot shot at Patrick Higgins, the man who was to relieve Williams at that hour. Higgins ran for the safety of the Wager House and started spreading the alarm that something was very wrong in the town. To make matters worse, an eastbound train arrived at the Ferry at 1:25 a.m. Higgins tried to convince the conductor, A. J. Phelps, not to attempt to cross the Potomac bridge. Unconvinced, Phelps walked out with Hayward Shepherd, a free black serving as the town baggage master, to investigate. Brown's men ordered them to halt, but the two men turned and ran back toward the station. A shot rang out and Shepherd was hit in the back. He managed to get to the train depot before collapsing.

The gunshot that downed Shepherd aroused the interest of a medical doctor, John D. Starry, who was lying awake in a room nearly opposite the Potomac bridge.[22] From his bedroom window, he could see two armed men wearing black shawls walking from the Potomac bridge to the armory. One of the men threatened some train passengers coming out from between the hotel and the train station, telling them, "The first man that fires at me I will shoot."

Starry quickly got dressed and grabbed his medical bag before heading out into the wet weather. At the train depot, he discovered Hayward Shepherd laid out on a plank set up between two chairs in the inner office. The doctor examined Shepherd and discovered that the bullet had passed just below Shepherd's heart before emerging from his chest. He realized that the baggage master would not survive his wounds. He dressed them and made Shepherd as comfortable as possible before leaving the depot to find out what these strange men were doing at the Ferry.

The doctor approached the armory first, trying to speak to one of the night watchmen. Brown's men told him there were no watchmen present. On returning to the train station, he was hailed by the men holding the Potomac bridge. They asked Starry if the train was going to cross the bridge. Brown had given permission for the train to leave, but Conductor Phelps feared a trap. Doctor Starry told the men he thought the train would not leave until morning. He then asked them what they were doing at the Ferry. One of them replied, "Never mind. You will find out in a day or two." The doctor asked if they intended to stay in the town that long, but he got no reply.

Starry continued to watch Brown's men until he could wait and watch no longer. It was dawn. Workers would be arriving at the armory and arsenal within the hour. They had to be warned. He ordered someone to ring the bell at the Lutheran church, and sent riders to alert the militia in Charlestown and Shepherdstown. One rider galloped to the Baltimore & Ohio Railroad office to prevent any more trains coming east. The doctor himself rode out to Virginius Island to warn workers at the mill and coopers' shop, then raced to the house of A. M. Kitzmiller, acting superintendent of the armory. His last stop was Bolivar Heights, after which he returned to the Lutheran church to help organize the citizens responding to the alarm bell. He discovered the townspeople had only a few squirrel rifles and shot guns to defend themselves. All other weapons in the town were in the hands of Brown's raiders.

Doctor Starry rode to Charlestown, to seek help from a Mexican War veteran, Captain John W. Rowan of the Jefferson County Guards. When he arrived, the alarm bells were already ringing. Men and boys carrying muskets, rifles, or squirrel guns assembled in the court house square.[23] The companies elected officers on the spot. At ten o'clock, they boarded the Winchester & Shenandoah train headed toward the Ferry six miles distant, disembarking on Bolivar Heights just west of the town. A company of civilians stayed in place on the Heights as the remaining troops marched north, crossing the Potomac. They then turned east following the Chesapeake & Ohio canal on the Maryland side as they advanced toward the Potomac River bridge—using John Brown's own invasion route. Their placements and maneuvers would box in Brown's men, thwarting escape.

The militia reached the Potomac bridge by noon and drove off Oliver Brown and the other raiders at that location. Before Oliver and his men could make it to the safety of the Engine House at the armory, Dangerfield Newby was shot, the first of Brown's men to die. Newby, a free black man, had joined the raid in an attempt to save his wife and children from being sold south. In anger and frustration, townspeople cut off Newby's ears for souvenirs and allowed pigs to rout on his body.[24]

Doctor Starry worked through the afternoon and evening on reversing the situation created by Brown's raiders. Some time around three o'clock, the doctor asked a man to lead a party of armed men to take Hall's Rifle Works before he went to his room to change into dry clothes. On his return, Starry discovered that the fight at Hall's was over. Two more raiders, John Henry Kagi and Lewis Leary, had been shot. John A. Copeland had been captured. The civilians in charge of Copeland were creating a rope of tied-together handkerchiefs with which to hang the man. Starry interposed his horse between Copeland and the civilians, until Copeland was safely in the hands of an officer.

It was too late now for John Brown to escape. Two earlier negotiations under a flag of truce had failed. His son Watson lay dying while the wounded Aaron Stevens and young Will Thompson had been captured and were under guard in the Wager House.

The bees had indeed swarmed, but these were not oppressed slaves longing to be free. They were angry Virginians fearful of another bloody slave insurrection like the one Nat Turner had led in Southampton County, Virginia, in 1831, slaughtering whole families down to the smallest babies. Many Virginians might long for a solution to the problem of slavery, but they didn't welcome it at such a bloody cost.

The crowd outside the Engine House, now thoroughly intoxicated because of the taverns which had stayed open during the raid, kept up a relentless gunfire directed toward the building. Earlier in the afternoon, one of Brown's men killed George W. Turner, a slaveowner and graduate of West Point. The death of Turner further angered the crowd.

Then Edwin Coppoc, who had been relieved of duty at the arsenal by Albert Hazlett and Osborn P. Anderson and was now defending the Engine House, committed an act guaranteed to cause the drunken mob outside to explode.

Fontaine Beckham, the stationmaster and mayor of the Ferry, grew concerned about the men who had killed Hayward Shepherd and were now interfering with the running of the trains. Around four o'clock, the mayor cautiously crept up to the armory wall near the front gate, just under the water tower. Edwin Coppoc saw him and drew a bead on him. His first shot missed, but the second downed the unarmed man.

Around the same time, Oliver Brown, sitting just behind a partially opened door, took aim at a man who was pointing his rifle toward the

Local and state militia fire on Brown's men at the Engine House.

Engine House. But before Oliver could fire, the man got off his shot, painfully and mortally wounding John Brown's son.[25]

Rain began pouring down. Drunk militiamen took refuge in the taverns. News of the mayor's death raced through the town. Henry Hunter, a grand-nephew of the dead mayor, and saloon-keeper George W. Chambers called together a band eager for revenge. At the Wager House they stormed the room where Aaron Stevens and Will Thompson were being held. Christine Fouke begged the men to leave Thompson to the law. Her cries fell on deaf ears.

The men grabbed Thompson by the throat and hauled him out into the street. "Though you may take my life," Will told them, "80,000 will rise up to avenge me, and carry out my purpose of giving liberty to the slaves."[26] Chambers and Hunter dragged him down to the edge of the Potomac bridge, and shot him in the head. The body was tossed into the river where it was used for target practice. The men then returned to the Wager House for Stevens, swearing they would kill him in like fashion. Finding him close to death, they instead returned to the streets, intent on killing any of Brown's men they could find.

John Cook and the men Brown had left in Maryland to take charge of a schoolhouse had heard gunfire from the Ferry late that afternoon.

Cook walked to the base of Maryland Heights to investigate.[27] Seeing that Virginia militia had surrounded the Engine House, he climbed up the embankment alongside the canal and, leaning against a tree branch, took aim and fired. The Virginia militia fired back. One lucky shot severed the tree branch Cook was leaning on. He tumbled down the hill toward the canal, badly scratched but otherwise intact. Cook limped back to the schoolhouse. On hearing Cook's report, Brown's Maryland contingent ran north toward the Pennsylvania border.

Toward evening the militia officer in charge, Colonel Robert W. Baylor, selected Samuel Strider, a citizen of the Ferry, to deliver a note asking the leader of the insurrection to surrender.[28] Strider carried the note to the building with an informal flag of truce made by tying a white handkerchief to his umbrella. Brown replied with a note asking that all his men be "delivered up to me with all their arms and amunition." He would then leave the town with his hostages. The note was signed "John Brown."

This note gave Baylor the first indication of who was leading this insurrection. Ferry residents thought Brown was Isaac Smith, a northern cattle dealer. But the militia were really facing the man who had ordered the Pottawatomie Creek massacre in Kansas and stolen slaves from Missouri. President James Buchanan had placed a reward of $250 for Brown's capture, and Baylor was not about to let such a valuable prize escape from his clutches.

Captain Thomas Sinn of Frederick, Maryland, arrived with his men late that afternoon some time after Baylor made his attempt to get Brown to surrender.[29] The captain crept as close as he dared to the Engine House. Brown hailed him and invited him to come in to negotiate. Sinn did not hesitate to enter the Engine House and talk with Brown, who was wearing the sword of Frederick the Great.

Brown repeated his demands for safe passage over the Potomac bridge and the release of his captured men, interweaving his terms with bitter accusations that his men, under flag of truce, had been shot down like dogs. Sinn replied that his men "must expect to be shot down like dogs if they took up arms in that way." Brown insisted that he would only fire on someone trying to shoot him. The captain related the circumstances of the unarmed Beckham's death. The bearded abolitionist seemed remorseful but maintained, "I fight only those who fight me."

Unsuccessful, Sinn withdrew into the night. He walked to the Wager House where he found young men teasing Aaron Stevens and threatening to shoot him. Sinn drove them out of the hotel, shouting, "If this man could stand on his feet with a pistol in his hand, you would all jump out of the window."

In the night, order gave way to chaos, as inebriated militia fired into the air and toward the Engine House. It would take a man of considerable authority and presence of mind to gain control of this situation, capture the raiders in the Engine House, and free the hostages. Fortunately, that man was already on his way. Lieutenant Colonel Robert Edward Lee would be arriving by train before the night ended.

2

"No man sent me here."

On the morning of October 17, 1859, while Doctor Starry was organizing townspeople in Harper's Ferry, Colonel Lee was at his home, a white house with Greek columns and round arched windows on a hill overlooking the nation's capital. Lee was making necessary repairs to the house which he hoped to complete before rejoining his regiment in Texas.

While the work continued, Lieutenant James Ewell Brown "Jeb" Stuart arrived with a message for Lee from a colonel at the War Department in Washington. The message ordered Lee to report at once to John B. Floyd, the secretary of war.[1] In the company of Stuart, Lee set out at once for Washington, not bothering to change out of his civilian clothes. The two men quickly covered the few miles separating them from Secretary Floyd's office and the White House.

Floyd explained that news had been received of a possible slave rebellion at Harper's Ferry and that U.S. troops and local militia companies were being sent to the besieged town. The secretary ordered Lee to take charge of all these troops using his brevet rank of colonel earned at the battle of Chapultepec during the Mexican War.[2] Then Floyd ushered Lee into the presence of President James Buchanan. The president and a military adviser drew up a proclamation Lee could use at his discretion depending on the magnitude and seriousness of the situation.

That afternoon, Lee and Stuart traveled by train to Relay House eight miles south of Baltimore where they would board a train for Harper's Ferry. Ninety marines under the command of Lieutenant Israel Green had been sent ahead of them. By that time, rumors were spreading that the number of insurgents who had taken Harper's Ferry numbered

Robert E. Lee wore civilian clothes when he took charge at Harper's Ferry.

between five to seven hundred men. Lee telegraphed orders that the marines were to get off the train at Sandy Hook, Maryland, just across the Potomac River from the Ferry, and await his arrival.[3]

Around ten o'clock that night, Lee arrived at Sandy Hook. He found the marines waiting for him with four companies of militia from Baltimore under the command of a state brigadier general, Charles C. Edgerton. The situation was very different from what Lee had expected. There were only a handful of raiders, and they had sought refuge in the Engine House at the armory. All bridges to the Ferry were open, but there were conflicting reports as to the identity of the leader of the insurgents. Some townspeople said the gray eyed, bearded man was Isaac Smith, but others reported that Colonel Baylor had received a note signed by John Brown, the abolitionist from Kansas responsible for the deaths of five pro-slavery men living on Pottawatomie Creek. Stuart had met Old Osawatomie while serving with the U.S. First Cavalry in Kansas. Could it be the same man?

Having discovered that the number of raiders had been greatly exaggerated and that he had command of more than enough men to end the crisis, Lee telegraphed orders to Baltimore: no more troops should be sent. He also set aside the president's proclamation and started organizing the marines for the night march into the Ferry. He left Edgerton's militia at Sandy Hook to decide how best to spend the night in the chilly air and rain-soaked sod at the bottom of Maryland Heights.

At eleven p.m., Lee, Stuart, and the marines crossed the Potomac bridge and surrounded the Engine House. He then drew up plans for storming the building in the morning. The assault would begin some time after dawn when it would be light enough to see. Stuart was to deliver a message to Brown calling for his surrender. When Brown refused, as Lee expected he would, Stuart would jump aside and three marines would attack the thick oak doors with sledgehammers. Once the doors were opened, twelve marines selected by Green would charge into the Engine House armed with unloaded rifled muskets fixed with bayonets. Lee didn't want the marines to shoot any of Brown's hostages by accident.

During the long night in the Engine House, Brown's son Oliver who had been severely wounded cried out for someone to shoot him. His father chastised him saying, "If you must die, die like a man." A little later, after a conversation with Colonel Washington, Brown called out to his son, but received no reply. "I guess he is dead," the old man commented.[4]

40

John Daingerfield, one of Brown's hostages, accused Brown of committing treason against the state of Virginia and the United States. Two of Brown's men, Jeremiah Anderson and Dauphin Thompson, told Brown they didn't want to fight anymore if Daingerfield was right. Brown told them that the hostage had spoken the truth.[5]

At dawn, Stuart approached the Engine House under a flag of truce. Brown allowed the doors to be opened a crack so that he could talk with the lieutenant, but did not let him in. Stuart recognized the leader of the raiders as the same Osawatomie Brown he had met in Kansas. He read Brown the formal note from Lee demanding that the raiders "peaceably surrender themselves" and reminding them that they could not escape and that Lee could not "answer for their safety" if they refused to surrender.[6]

Stuart then asked Brown if he was "ready to surrender, and trust to the mercy of the Government?" Brown replied, "No! I prefer to die here."[7]

THE STORMING OF THE ENGINE-HOUSE

Marines smashed in the doors of the Engine House using a ladder as a battering ram. Lieutenant Israel Green captured John Brown at the end of this assault.

At this point, under Brown's orders, John Daingerfield closed the doors and secured them with ropes. For added strength, some men pushed two fire engine wagons up against the doors.

The moment the doors closed, Stuart stepped to one side and waved his plumed hat. The three marines armed with sledgehammers ran to the doors and attempted to batter them in, while Brown's remaining men fired on them, creating a deafening thunder. The doors refused to yield. Lieutenant Green ordered his men to pick up a sturdy ladder nearby. Using the ladder as a battering ram, they managed to bash a ragged hole in one of the doors.[8]

Armed with a sword, Green led the way, as the twelve marines charged through the hole into the smoke-filled interior. Once inside, the lieutenant ran to the right of the fire engine in front of the door. Within a few seconds he was standing at the rear of the building looking at two men. One was Colonel Washington, who was standing beside an engine. Washington greeted Green and pointed at the other man who was kneeling down trying to reload a carbine. "This is Osawatomie," Washington said.

Green sprang at Brown and tried to run him through with his sword, but Green had left Washington, D.C., in such haste that he was carrying his dress sword and not his battle saber. It bent against Brown's leather belt. Green held the sword by the now-ruined blade and struck at Brown's head with the hilt. Brown fell, unconscious. Three minutes had passed since the moment Stuart had waved his hat until Green stood over the battered leader of the raiders.

Lee ordered that the raiders be brought out onto the armory lawn. Edwin Coppoc and Shields Green were unharmed. Dauphin Thompson and Jeremiah Anderson had been bayoneted to death while trying to surrender in the smoke and confusion of the assault. John Brown lay on the armory lawn, still unconscious, but he would live to be hanged.

A few hours after the storming of the Engine House, C. W. Tayleure, a reporter for a Baltimore newspaper, brought Watson Brown a drink of water. Watson was laid out on a bench and was using a pair of overalls for a pillow. "I remember how he looked," Tayleure recalled years later, "singularly handsome, even through the grime of his all-day struggles, and the intense suffering which he must have endured. He was calm, and of a tone and look very gentle. The look with which he searched my very heart I can never forget."

JOHN H. KAGI

A. D. STEVENS

OLIVER BROWN

WATSON BROWN

Four of Brown's men. John Kagi and Oliver Brown died before the fighting was over. Watson died after. Stevens survived his wounds and was hanged March 16, 1860.

As Tayleure watched over the dying man, he asked, "What brought you here?"

Watson replied weakly, "Duty, sir."

The reporter waited a moment before pressing Watson for an explanation: "Is it then your idea of duty to shoot men down upon their own hearth-stones for defending their rights?"

"I am dying," Watson answered. "I cannot discuss the question; I did my duty as I saw it."

Watson Brown died just a few hours after midnight.[9]

Later that morning, Lee ordered the Baltimore Greys, a Maryland militia company under the command of Colonel S. S. Mills, to proceed to a schoolhouse where Brown's men had been spotted.[10] They found arms at the site as well as Brown's papers. They recovered Colonel Washington's wagon and horses, but Brown's companions were gone.

On learning that Brown had used the Kennedy Farm on Maryland Heights as his base of operations, Lee sent Lieutenant Stuart with a detachment of marines to the site five miles away. They discovered that curious neighbors had already broken into the house. Documents were strewn all over the floor: marked maps, a provisional constitution, orders for his men, and a "Vindication of the Invasion." The lieutenant also found a carpetbag stuffed with letters. Many were from Kansas and New England friends innocent of any knowledge of Brown's plans. There were some from Frederick Douglass, the man who had spurned the raid. But this bag also contained letters from Brown's secret backers in the North, men who knew Brown's intentions.

Five hours after the end of the siege, Virginia Governor Henry Alexander Wise, the man who would decide John Brown's fate, arrived at the Ferry along with Senator James Murray Mason of Virginia and Company F of Richmond.[11] The governor—a pale, gaunt man with steel-gray eyes and a peculiar habit of chain-chewing tobacco, the juice of which stained his clothing with brown spots—looked like a walking corpse.[12] His cadaverous appearance was attributed to overwork and frequent illness, and it was said that he deliberately emphasized his bloodless complexion by wearing a white cravat.[13]

BRIGADIER-GENERAL HENRY A. WISE, C. S. A.,
EX-GOVERNOR OF VIRGINIA.
FROM A PHOTOGRAPH.

Although he condemned John Brown's raid, Governor Henry Wise came to admire Brown's courage. At the beginning of the Civil War, Wise arranged for Virginia militia to take the armory and arsenal at Harper's Ferry for Virginia and the Confederacy.

Like most prominent Virginians, Wise was a slaveholder who longed to emancipate all those in bondage, but wanted to colonize them once they were free. "Africa gave to Virginia a *savage* and a *slave*," he had said to the Virginia Colonization Society in 1838. "Virginia gives back to Africa a *citizen* and a *Christian*.... If this was not divine will, let those who object tell me, how came African slavery here?"[14]

Twice during his days representing Virginia in the U.S. Congress, Wise became involved in duels. In 1835, Wise wounded a political rival. Three years later, he acted as advisor to William J. Graves of Kentucky who killed his opponent, Jonathan Cilley, a Democrat from Maine.

While Wise's violent temperament did not bode well for John Brown's case, Wise's sterling reputation for fairness guaranteed that Brown would be treated fairly. Wise had once been asked to defend the rights of a man who had purchased a bowl of sugar at an auction. The widow who had put her goods up for sale had not intended to sell the sugar, only the bowl it was in. Wise stated that the sugar legally belonged to the man who had purchased the bowl. He then charged the man five dollars and gave the money to the widow.[15]

Wise looked on with great interest as Colonel Lee arranged for the politicians and newspaper reporters arriving at Harper's Ferry to interview John Brown on the afternoon of his capture. The interview took place in the paymaster's office at the armory where Aaron Stevens and John Brown rested on straw mats on the floor. Among the participants were Senator Mason, and U.S. Representative Clement Vallandigham of Ohio. Lee began by offering to exclude visitors from the room if the prisoners were uncomfortable. Brown replied that he was glad of a chance "to make himself and his motives clearly understood."[16]

Senator Mason began the questions: "Can you tell us, at least, who furnished the money for your expedition?"

"I furnished most of it myself," Brown replied. "I cannot implicate others."

Mason pressed Brown: "If you would tell us who sent you here—who provided the means—that would be information of some value."

Brown refused. "I will answer freely and faithfully about what concerns myself—I will answer anything I can with honor, but not about others."

Congressman Vallandigham pursued the question. "Mr. Brown, who sent you here?"

"No man sent me here," Brown stated. "It was my own prompting and that of my Maker, or that of the devil, whichever you please to ascribe it to. I acknowledge no man in human form."

Mason asked, "What was your object in coming?"

"We came to free the slaves," Brown said openly, "and only that."

The Virginia senator queried, "How do you justify your acts?"

"I think, my friend, you are guilty of a great wrong against God and humanity—I say it without wishing to be offensive—and it would be perfectly right in any one to interfere with you so far as to free those you willfully and wickedly hold in bondage.... I think I did right, and that others will do right to interfere with you at any time and all times. I hold that the Golden Rule, 'Do unto others as you would that others should do unto you,' applies to all who would help others to gain their liberty."

Lieutenant Stuart, who was present for this part of the questioning, commented, "But you don't believe in the Bible."

"Certainly I do," Brown protested.

The interview continued for three hours. Townspeople and politicians accused Brown of being a madman, murderer, and thief. Brown held forth that his sole object was to free the slaves and not to harm any person or to enrich himself.

Governor Wise warned, "Mr. Brown, the silver of your hair is reddened by the blood of crime, and it is meet that you should eschew these hard allusions and think upon eternity."

Brown responded, "Governor, I have, from all appearances, not more than fifteen or twenty years the start of you in the journey to that eternity of which you kindly warn me; and whether my tenure here shall be fifteen months, or fifteen days, or fifteen hours, I am equally prepared to go. There is an eternity behind and an eternity before, and the little speck in the center, however long, is but comparatively a minute. The difference between your tenure and mine is trifling and I want to therefore tell you to be prepared; I am prepared." Referring to the other slaveholders in the room, he continued, "You all have a heavy responsibility, and it behooves you to prepare more than it does me."

On the night after Brown's capture, a man residing at Pleasant Valley, Maryland, just three miles from the Ferry, heard a rumor that northern abolitionists and slaves were engaged in the massacre of the civilian population of Rohrersville a few miles north of him. He immediately rode his horse through Sandy Hook and down into Harper's Ferry spreading the alarm. The residents of Sandy Hook were so terrified of this new incursion that they fled across the Potomac seeking the safety of the local militia companies and U.S. Marines still stationed there. One of the refugees shouldered a half-grown hog and carried the squealing animal across the Potomac bridge.

Colonel Lee, who had been working on his final report, marched with Stuart, Green, and twenty-five marines to Rohrersville to investigate, but discovered only peaceful citizens going about their business. They marched back to the Ferry, and Lee continued work on his report. In the early morning hours of October 20, he and the other U.S. troops left Harper's Ferry by train for Washington.

On learning of Lee's departure, Governor Wise, who had arranged for Brown and his men to be tried in Charlestown by a Virginia court, protested the withdrawal of federal forces. From the correspondence collected at the Kennedy Farm, Wise knew that not all of Brown's men had been captured. Owen Brown, Albert Hazlett, John E. Cook, and three other men were still at large. (In the weeks that followed, only Hazlett and Cook would be arrested.) Wise also had questions about northerners who might have provided money and arms for the raid. Those men might mount a rescue attempt. The Virginia governor wanted those men identified and arrested as soon as possible.[17]

GEORGE L. STEARNS

GERRIT SMITH

FRANK B. SANBORN

T. W. HIGGINSON

THEODORE PARKER

SAMUEL G. HOWE

JOHN BROWN'S NORTHERN SUPPORTERS

3

"A comet dire and strange am I."

On the evening of October 18, 1859, Julia Ward Howe sat in the parlor of her home in South Boston reading the paper which had news of an insurrection in Virginia. "In what this insurrection consists," she read, "we are not as yet informed; but we are told that 'general terror' prevails in the vicinity of the outbreak, at Harper's Ferry...." She showed the article to her husband, Dr. Samuel Gridley Howe. "Brown has got to work," he concluded. This confirmed Julia's own impression of what was happening in Virginia.[1]

Some days later, they learned of Brown's capture. Howe immediately provided Brown with legal assistance. Some of Dr. Howe's friends had some inkling of what Old Osawatomie had intended to do in Virginia, and they were beginning to panic. For days after news of suppression of the raid reached Massachusetts, Franklin Sanborn, a Concord school teacher, sorted and burned his correspondence. Fearing arrest, he fled to Canada but returned after four days. Frederick Douglass made a voyage for England from Canada, leaving just a few days before federal marshals arrived at his door. In Peterboro, New York, Gerrit Smith had a nervous breakdown and was committed to an asylum. Unitarian minister Theodore Parker, who had advised Brown about possibilities for raiding the South and freeing slaves, was dying in Italy. He could afford the luxury of bravely stating that it was "a natural duty for the freeman to help the slaves to the enjoyment of their liberty, and as means to that end, to aid them in killing all such as oppose their natural freedom."[2] Thomas Wentworth Higginson, a Unitarian minister in Worcester, refused to burn his correspondence with Brown and defied anyone who wished to arrest him. Like Howe, he openly provided for Brown's defense. But he went Howe one better, secretly plotting with Sanborn to obtain Brown's release by force.

These six men had some idea of how John Brown planned to free southern slaves. None of them went to jail for supporting Brown's raid on Harper's Ferry.

Dr. Howe remained steadfastly in Boston during the period of John Brown's trial, but his legal counsel, John Andrew, led him to believe that he might be arrested and tried as one of Brown's fellow conspirators. Howe had been jailed once in Prussia. He dreaded repeating that experience.

Julia Ward first met her husband "Chev" at the Perkins School for the Blind in the summer of 1841. Her friends, Charles Sumner and Henry Wadsworth Longfellow, had invited the 22 year old aspiring poetess to visit the school, which was located at a seaside hotel in South Boston. Julia particularly wanted to meet Laura Bridgman, Howe's renowned deaf-blind student.

In her early childhood in New Hampshire, Laura had contracted scarlet fever. The disease ravaged her body for two years, robbing her not only of her sight and hearing, but also her sense of taste and smell. Howe had taken on the challenge of teaching her, something never successfully done before. The doctor's methods worked. Laura learned to read and write, and to communicate with other students using the manual alphabet.[3] Julia was astounded by Laura's ability to share her thoughts with her deaf-blind friend, Lucy Reed of Vermont.[4]

"While the two children were holding converse through the medium of the finger alphabet," Julia recalled years later, "Lucy's face was suddenly lit up by a smile so beautiful as to call forth from us an involuntary exclamation." Before leaving the institution, Sumner spied a bearded rider coming toward the school and called out, "Oh! here comes Howe on his black horse." Julia looked where Sumner was pointing and "beheld a noble rider on a noble steed.... He made upon us an impression of unusual force and reserve."

Howe was then 39, and had devoted most of his life to the promotion of worthy causes. In 1824, after completing his medical training at Harvard, he refused to settle down to the comfortable life of a Boston doctor. Instead, he chose to sail to Greece where he helped that embattled people gain its independence from Turkish rule. For his services, the Greek government conferred a knighthood on him, "Chevalier of the Order of St. Savior." He became known to his close friends as "Chev."

In 1831, he spent five weeks in a Prussian prison for attempting to provide aid to needy Polish people. The following year, back in Boston, he set up his school for the blind. And now that he had met Julia, the confirmed bachelor took up a new cause, trying to win the heart of the vivacious, red-haired woman.

The two met again the following spring at a farewell party for Charles Dickens.[5] They danced, and Julia, who had read Howe's book on the Greek revolution when she was 15, teased him about his military life. She even dared to ask if he had ever killed a man. The doctor was furious with her frivolity. He found her to be as fiery in temperament as her red hair. He also objected to her literary aspirations which he thought unbecoming in a woman.[6] But eventually the confirmed bachelor was won over by Julia's charm and grace. They became engaged sometime in February 1843, and were married on April 23.

The Howes' marriage was explosive and fraught with difficulties. Julia's literary pursuits frequently fanned the flames. When her first volume of poetry, *Passion Flowers*, was published in 1854, Howe was furious. Twice, they nearly separated, but Julia found Chev's conditions monstrous. He wanted two of the children. By 1857, the time of their last attempt to separate, they had five children, and Julia could not abide the thought of being separated from them. "Indeed, my trials are sometimes such that I would not endure them for a day, but for the children's sake," she wrote in an anguished letter to one of her sisters, "but these fits of perverseness come and go and there is generally something like peace between them."[7]

Julia frequently used her poetry to express her devotion to her children and her frustration with family life. In "The Heart's Astronomy," she wrote about walking "a weary mile" outside her house one evening for exercise. The children sat in the window and smiled at her each time she walked past.

> They watched me, as Astronomers,
> Whose business lies in heaven afar,
> Await, beside the slanting glass,
> The re-appearance of a star.
>
> Not so, not so, my pretty ones,
> Seek stars in yonder cloudless sky;
> But mark no steadfast path for me,
> A comet dire and strange am I.

Later in the same poem, she prays that "the laws of heavenly force/ Would help and guide the Mother star."[8]

Neither Julia nor her beloved Chev had been raised to accept abolitionist sentiments. Julia's father had insisted slavery must exist in the South. Once freed, the slaves would kill off their white masters, a fear based on the bloody Nat Turner rebellion of 1831.

Howe never gave the issue of abolition much thought until he traveled south in the winter of 1841. "Let a man be dropped from a balloon," he wrote to his friend Charles Sumner, "& he could tell in three minutes whether he were in a Slave State, or not: The very first sights, the very first sounds, the very first odours would attest the fact: the whites stand with their hands in their breeches pockets & the blacks are 'helping them do nothing': fences are down, doors ajar, filth is in the streets, foul odours in the air, confusion and neglect are every where."[9]

Howe's feelings against slavery were heightened in 1854 when a runaway slave in Boston was captured and held by federal marshals, an event which later generations would call the rendition of Anthony Burns. On the night of May 27, Howe's friend, Thomas Wentworth Higginson, made a botched effort to free Burns from federal marshals at the Court House in Boston. President Franklin Pierce responded to the violence by ordering federal troops to guard the Court House. Howe, who served on a vigilance committee which had sworn not to allow Burns to be extradited to Virginia, concluded that nothing more could be done.[10]

On June 2, thousands of Bostonians watched as United States soldiers marched Burns down to the wharf. Black edged American flags hung upside-down everywhere. Across from the old state house hung a coffin emblazoned with the words *Funeral of Liberty*. Howe stood near a young black girl who watched the procession with "clenched fists... and tears streaming down her cheeks." He tried to comfort her, saying that Burns would not be hurt. "Hurt!" the girl yelled at him. "I cry for shame he will not kill himself. Oh why is he not man enough to kill himself!"[11]

Some time in the mid 1850's, Howe told Julia about a man who intended "to devote his life to the redemption of the colored race from slavery, even as Christ had willingly offered his life for the salvation of mankind." In 1857, Chev reminded her again of their talk about the man who "wished to be a saviour for the negro race," and told her,

"That man will call here this afternoon. You will receive him. His name is John Brown."

That afternoon, Julia opened the door to "a middle-aged, middle-sized man, with hair and beard of amber color, streaked with gray. He looked a Puritan of Puritans, forceful, concentrated, and self-contained." She saw him one last time at her husband's office at the Perkins School.[12] She never knew what Brown told her husband about the Harper's Ferry raid, but after Brown's arrest and trial, she saw that Chev's involvement was deeper than she had known.

On Tuesday morning, October 25, just one week after Brown was captured, people gathered at the red brick Jefferson County Court House in Charlestown, Virginia, for the beginning of John Brown's trial. Governor Wise, worried over possible rescue attempts by northern conspirators, had insisted that Brown be quickly tried in Virginia by a local court. A grand jury had already been called and was still serving in Charlestown.

At 10:30 a.m., Sheriff James W. Campbell brought John Brown and his men under guard to the court house for a preliminary examination.[13] Brown and Edwin Coppoc were manacled together as they stood with Aaron Stevens, John Copeland, and Shields Green before the court.

When asked whether the prisoners had counsel, Brown replied, "If you seek my blood, you can have it at any moment, without this mockery of a trial. I have had no counsel. I have not been able to advise with any one. I know nothing about the feelings of my fellow-prisoners, and am utterly unable to attend in any way to my own defense.... But if we are to be forced with a mere form—a trial for execution—you might spare yourselves that trouble. I am ready for my fate.... I have now little further to ask, other than that I may not be foolishly insulted, only as cowardly barbarians insult those who fall into their power."

The court chose Charles J. Faulkner and Lawson Botts as counsel for the prisoners. Faulkner objected in part because of Brown's attitude, and also because he had himself been present at Harper's Ferry during the insurrection. Botts, however, had no objection. John Brown then made it clear that he had sent for his own counsel, his jailers having

THE PRISON, GUARD-HOUSE, AND COURT-HOUSE, CHARLESTOWN, WEST VIRGINIA
(The Prison is on the extreme left)

John Brown was tried here and found guilty of murder and treason. On November 2, he was sentenced to hang for his crimes.

allowed him to write to northern friends, but he was ambivalent about having counsel if he was not to have a fair trial. The attorney for the county, Charles B. Harding, insisted that Brown would have a fair trial.

"I am a stranger here," Brown told Harding; "I do not know the disposition or character of the gentlemen named. I have applied for counsel of my own, and doubtless could have them, if I am not, as I said before, to be hurried to execution before they can reach me. But if that is the disposition that is to be made of me, all this trouble and expense can be saved."

Harding was growing impatient and again asked Brown about Faulkner and Botts.

Brown said, "I feel as if it was a matter of very little account to me. If they had designed to assist me as counsel, I should have wanted an opportunity to consult them at my leisure."

A frustrated Harding gave up and asked Stevens and the others if they would accept Faulkner and Botts as counsel. They all readily agreed.

That afternoon at two o'clock, John Brown was brought before the Circuit Court, with Judge Richard Parker presiding. Newspaper reporters squeezed into the red brick building with white trim, hoping to catch sight of Brown and his accusers. Fearing that Brown might "put forth something calculated to influence the public mind, and to have a bad effect upon slaves," Parker ruled that newspaper reporters be kept from Brown.

At ten o'clock the next morning, Parker called the grand jury into session to bring indictments against Brown and his men. By noon, the jury returned a bill charging Brown with "conspiring with negroes to produce insurrection, ... for treason in the Commonwealth [of Virginia]," and "for murder." Brown had finally consented to allow Lawson Botts and his assistant William Green to act as his counsel. Through his counsel, Brown asked for a delay of two or three days to allow for the arrival of counsel from the North. But Parker refused to delay the trial for this reason.

That afternoon, when Brown was summoned to court, he said he was too ill. The jailers were ordered to bring him to court on his cot. For most of the afternoon, he lay in the courtroom with his eyes closed. By five o'clock, the twelve jurors were selected, and Brown got up from his cot and walked back to jail.

On Thursday morning, Botts and Green introduced into defense evidence a letter from A. H. Lewis of Akron, Ohio. "Insanity is hereditary in [John Brown's] family," Lewis wrote. "His mother's sister died with it, and a daughter of that sister has been two years in a Lunatic Asylum. A son and daughter of his mother's brother have also been confined in the lunatic asylum, and another son of that brother is now insane and under close restraint."

John Brown rose from his cot to address the court. "I look upon it as a miserable artifice and pretext of those who ought to take a different course in regard to me, if they took any at all, and I view it with contempt more than otherwise. As I remarked to Mr. Green, insane persons, so far as my experience goes, have but little ability to judge of their own sanity; and, if I am insane, of course I should think I know more than all the rest of the world. But I do not think so. I am perfectly unconscious of insanity, and I reject, so far as I am capable, any attempt to interfere in my behalf on that score."

Botts again asked for a delay of one day as he now fully expected northern counsel's imminent arrival. Parker refused any delay, and further maintained that an insanity defense required more than just one letter from an unknown and medically unqualified individual. The trial would proceed.

The judge then asked the attorneys for both sides to make their opening remarks. In his statement, Green brought up the subject of jurisdiction, stating that "crimes committed within the ... limits [of the armory at Harper's Ferry] are punishable by the Federal Courts.... Over murder, if committed within the limits of the Armory, the Court has no jurisdiction, and in the case of Mr. Beckham, if he was killed on the railroad bridge, it was committed within the State of Maryland, which State claims jurisdiction up to the Armory grounds."

Andrew Hunter, Harding's prosecuting associate, countered Green's remarks, stating that this was a matter "affecting State rights." He cited the case of an armorer in the rifle factory who, twenty-nine years earlier, had murdered the superintendent on the armory grounds. The armorer was tried, convicted, and hanged under the laws of the state of Virginia.[14]

"There was a broad difference," Hunter maintained, "between the cession of jurisdiction by Virginia to the Federal Government and mere assent of the State that the Federal Government should become a land-holder within its limits. The law of Virginia, by virtue of which the grounds at Harper's Ferry were purchased by the Federal Government, ceded no jurisdiction."

The trial proceeded with testimony from Dr. John Starry, Conductor Phelps and Colonel Lewis Washington, adjourning at seven o'clock.

The next morning, a young lawyer, George H. Hoyt of Athol, Massachusetts, arrived in Charlestown to act in John Brown's defense. Botts introduced Hoyt to the court and he was soon sworn in and joined co-counsels Botts and Green. Hoyt had been hired by John W. LeBarnes who was then acting in a conspiracy with Franklin Sanborn and Thomas Wentworth Higginson. LeBarnes had given Hoyt instructions to steal the carpetbag full of Brown's correspondence found at the Kennedy Farm, and to arrange for Brown and his men to escape.[15]

The attorneys for the state of Virginia completed their case that afternoon, and the defense began calling its witnesses. They did nothing more than confirm some earlier testimony and verify that Brown had taken good care of his hostages. The court adjourned for the day.

Samuel Chilton of Washington, D. C., and Henry Griswold of Cleveland, Ohio, were added to the counsel for the defense the following morning. Chilton was hired by John Andrew of Massachusetts. Griswold appeared in the case as a replacement for Judge Daniel R. Tilden, whom

Brown had asked for legal assistance. They were the last counsel for Brown to arrive and could do little about the testimony already given. The defense team concluded their evidence that evening, and only closing arguments remained. Fortunately they had Sunday to prepare.

The defense team asked Griswold to begin presenting the case for Brown. When the court opened on Monday, October 31, Griswold returned to the question of jurisdiction mainly because of the grand jury's charge that Brown had committed treason in Virginia. "We maintain that this prisoner was not bound by any allegiance to this State, and could not, therefore, be guilty of rebellion against it," he told the jury. "Is it to be supposed for a moment, I ask, now, when [Brown] is struck down to the earth, his few followers scattered or destroyed—now, when the fact is known that the South is alarmed and armed in every direction ready to repel any enterprise of this kind, is anything to be feared? No, gentlemen, there is not the remotest danger of your ever again witnessing in your State anything akin to that which lately occurred."

Chilton then took up the argument, stating that Brown could not be found guilty of treason against Virginia since he was not a citizen of the state. He also argued that John Brown was innocent of conspiring with slaves to foment insurrection or of murder because there was no such evidence presented.

Andrew Hunter's summation insisted that Virginia had jurisdiction, in part because the people murdered by Brown's men were not on the armory grounds. He accused John Brown of trying to make Virginia another "Hayti,"[16] and said that "the idea that Brown shed blood only in self-defense was too absurd to require argument.... If justice requires you by your verdict to take his life, stand by that column uprightly, but strongly, and let retributive justice, if he is guilty, send him before that Maker who will settle the question forever and ever."

The jury took only forty-five minutes to find Brown guilty on all counts.

On Wednesday, November 2, John Brown was to be sentenced. When asked if he had anything to say, he rose and spoke to the crowded room in a clear voice: "I see a book kissed, which I suppose to be the Bible, or at least the New Testament, which teaches me that all things whatsoever I would that men should do to me, I should do even so to them. It teaches me further to remember them that are in bonds as bound with them. I endeavored to act up to that instruction. I say I am yet too young to understand that God is any respecter of persons. I believe that to have interfered as I have done, as I have always freely admitted I have done in behalf of His despised poor, is no wrong, but right. Now, if it is deemed necessary that I should forfeit my life for the furtherance of the ends of justice, and mingle my blood further with the blood of my children and with the blood of millions in this slave country whose rights are disregarded by wicked, cruel, and unjust enactments, I say let it be done."

Judge Parker told the viewers that "no reasonable doubt could exist of the guilt of the prisoner." He sentenced John Brown to be publicly hanged on Friday, December 2.

Two days after the sentence, John Brown's wife Mary arrived in Boston. George Luther Stearns, Franklin Sanborn, and Howe arranged a reception for her at the American House hotel. Mary Brown had been seeking permission from Governor Wise and from John Brown to come to Charlestown, Virginia. Her husband didn't want her there, partly in fear of how she would be treated by Southerners, but also because he felt Mary's presence would distract from the image he was trying to project of a martyr suffering in solitude.[17]

Now that Brown had been condemned to death, Howe panicked and sought out his friend Stearns who was also involved with Brown's invasion of Virginia. Sanborn had been telling Howe that he felt flight was reasonable, and John Andrew had been telling him that, according to an 1846 statute, he and anyone else who had known Brown could be arrested as material witnesses.[18] Pacing nervously back and forth, Howe insisted that he would go crazy if he and Stearns did not leave immediately for Canada. The two men left sometime in the middle of November.[19]

Before leaving, Howe wrote a card printed in many newspapers across the country in which he tried to explain his friendship with Brown. "My relations with him," he wrote, "were such as no one ought to be afraid or ashamed to avow." He also criticized statutes "concealed as are the claws of the cat, in a velvet paw," which would allow unscrupulous slaveholders to arrest northerners as material witnesses and bring them by force to the South. Since the laws of Massachusetts could not protect him from such a procedure, Howe concluded that "each one must protect himself, as he best may. Upon that hint, I shall act; preferring to forego anything rather than the right to free thought and free speech."[20]

His wife Julia, who was then pregnant with their sixth child, took the news of John Brown's impending execution in stride. "No one knew of Brown's intention but Brown himself and his handful of men," she wrote to her sister Annie. "The attempt I must judge insane but the spirit *heroic*. I should be glad to be as sure of heaven as that old man may be, following right in the spirit and footsteps of the old martyrs, girding on his sword for the weak and oppressed. His death will be holy and glorious—the gallows cannot dishonor him—he will hallow it...."[21]

She also wrote a poem in which she imagined a conversation with one of her children about John Brown who lay "upon a prison bed/ With sabre gashes on his head." His only crime had been "To free the wretched slaves."

> "O mother! let us go this day
> To that sad prison, far away;
> The cruel governor we'll pray
>   To unloose the door so stout.
> Some comfort we can bring him, sure:
> And is he locked up so secure,
>   We could not get him out?"
>
> "No, darling: he is closely kept."
> Then nearer to my heart she crept,
> And, hiding there her beauty, wept
>   For human misery.
> Child! it is fit that thou shouldst weep;
> The very babe unborn would leap
>   To rescue such as he.[22]

Julia's sentiments and noble words could do nothing to change the situation. John Brown had already refused to cooperate in any rescue attempts.

Meanwhile, Governor Wise received hundreds of letters asking for a stay of execution. Many Southerners worried that Brown would become a martyr if he were hanged. Northern sympathizers claimed that Brown was insane and should be placed in an asylum rather than on a scaffold. For a time, the governor was persuaded by the latter. He even ordered the superintendent of the lunatic asylum at Staunton, Virginia, to go to Charlestown and examine Brown. But in the end, Wise changed his mind. "I know that [Brown] was sane," he concluded. "He was more sane than his prompters and promoters, and concealed well the secret which made him seem to do an act of mad impulse...."[23]

Brown himself was perfectly content to die. In his cell in Charlestown, the condemned man read in the newspaper a speech given by the abolitionist preacher Henry Ward Beecher: "Let no man pray that Brown be spared.... His soul was noble; his work miserable. But a cord and a gibbet would redeem all that, and round up Brown's failure with a heroic success." Brown wrote in the margin of the paper, "Good."[24]

4

"Blow ye the trumpet, blow!"

On the morning of December 2, 1859, the supposed day of John Brown's execution, startling news arrived from America at the town of St. Peter Port on the island of Guernsey thirty miles west of the French coast. Governor Wise had granted Brown a reprieve until December 16. There were rumors that Brown might even be spared.

The news soon reached Victor Hugo at Hauteville House, a gray, four-story building on a granite bluff south of the town, overlooking Havelet Bay and Castle Cornet. In an attempt to save Brown's life, the French author immediately took up his pen and wrote a long letter to the editor of the *London Star*.

Hugo praised Brown for seeking to deliver slaves from bondage, an act he considered a "sacred duty." But now, the aging abolitionist would pay a price for his interference, as did Spartacus, the leader of a slave revolt in ancient Rome. "Viewed in a political light, the murder of Brown would be an irreparable fault," Hugo warned. "It would penetrate the Union with a gaping fissure which would lead in the end to its entire disruption."[1]

As Hugo set down his pen and posted the letter, the people of Charlestown, Virginia, more than four thousand miles to the west, were waking up to a long anticipated morning. No rumors circulated in Jefferson County about Brown being spared or reprieved. Everyone in the village understood that the leader of the Harper's Ferry insurrection would be executed before noon. As people lined the streets to get a glimpse of the gray-bearded abolitionist, three companies of infantry moved into place around the Charlestown jail. Near eleven o'clock, an open freight wagon carrying a pine box which contained Brown's oak casket pulled up next to the jail.

Victor Hugo's wash drawing of John Brown's hanging. During the Civil War, Hugo arranged for this drawing to be sold for the benefit of the Union Army.

When Brown emerged from the building and discovered the streets brimming with soldiers dressed in blue and gray uniforms, some with red or yellow trim, and carrying rifles with fixed bayonets, he said, "I had no idea that Governor Wise considered my execution so important." Turning, he handed one of his jailers a note: "I John Brown am now quite <u>certain</u> that the crimes of this <u>guilty</u>, <u>land</u>: <u>will</u> never be purged <u>away</u>; but with Blood." Then he mounted the wagon and sat on the pine box. An undertaker also climbed onto the wagon and sat with Brown as the vehicle moved slowly through tree-lined streets past brick houses with white-washed wooden fences.

"You are a game man, Captain," the undertaker told the condemned man.

Brown replied, "Yes, I was so trained—it was one of the lessons of my mother; but it is hard to part from friends, though newly made."

The wagon rolled toward the southeast. In the distance, its occupants could see the purple flanks of the Blue Ridge mountains on the opposite side of the Shenandoah River.

"This is a beautiful country," Brown remarked. "I never had the pleasure of seeing it before."

Soon, the wagon pulled into an open field on the outskirts of the town. In the middle of the field stood a gallows. Nearly a quarter of a mile from the place of execution, militia armed with gleaming bayonets held the crowd back at the edge of the field, in fear that northern sympathizers might yet attempt to free the prisoner. "Why are none but military allowed in the enclosure?" Brown asked. "I am sorry the citizens have been kept out."

He climbed down from the wagon and walked toward the gallows in his loose-fitting carpet slippers. At the foot of the steps, he spotted Andrew Hunter, the man who prosecuted his case for the state. Hunter was standing next to the mayor of Charlestown. "Gentlemen, goodbye," Brown said to them in a clear, unfaltering voice. Then he ascended the steps to the platform, followed by a sheriff and the jailer to whom he had given his last written statement.

Brown shook hands with the two men and thanked them for their kindness. Then he placed a hood over his head and slipped the noose around his neck. The sheriff bound his arms at the elbows, and the jailer asked Brown to step forward onto the trap door which was held in place by hinges on one side and a rope on the other.

"You must lead me," Brown said, "for I cannot see."

Once he was in position over the trap and the noose properly adjusted, a signal was given for the militia units to march into place around the gallows. While they were getting into position, the sheriff asked Brown if he wanted a handkerchief to drop as a signal to cut the rope holding the trap door in place. "No," Brown replied. "I don't care; I don't want you to keep me waiting unnecessarily."

Ten minutes passed as the soldiers took up their positions. At fifteen minutes past eleven, all was ready, and the sheriff cut the rope with a hatchet. The trap swung downward with a bang, and Brown's body fell until the rope around his neck snapped taut. His hands grasped upwards and his muscles twitched for a moment. Then all was quiet as the spectators gaped in horror at the dangling body. Colonel J. T. L. Preston of the Virginia Military Institute broke the silence with the words, "So perish all such enemies of Virginia! All such enemies of the Union! All such foes of the human race!"

But Brown had not yet perished. A doctor examined him and discovered a pulse. That pulse did not cease until his body had been swinging on the gallows for about thirty-five minutes.

Only then was the body cut down and placed in the coffin. It was taken to the train depot where it would be transported by special train to Harper's Ferry. Brown's wife Mary waited at the Ferry. Governor Wise had given her permission to take her husband's body home to North Elba, New York.[2]

All through the northern states, abolitionists, in remembrance of the old man who had made war on slavery, tolled bells for his execution. In Manchester, New Hampshire, the bell ringers met with opposition. The mayor of the town ordered James B. Straw and his associates to stop ringing the city bell. When they refused to desist, the mayor dropped Straw through a scuttle, and threatened to do the same to Straw's companions. They quickly dispersed.[3]

In Arlington, Vermont, Almera Hawley Canfield woke her grandson early in the morning. "Get up, Jim," she told him. "This is the day John Brown is to be hanged. And I want you to go over and toll the bell for him." Jim Canfield quickly rose and dressed, walked across the street, entered the gray St. James Episcopal Church, and climbed up into the belfry. Not daring to disobey his formidable grandmother, Jim tolled the bell very slowly as was the custom for a death. About two hours later, one of his cousins climbed up into the belfry and said, "It's my turn. Aunt Almera said toll." Jim gave one last pull on the bell rope and counted out the time between rings for his cousin so that there would be no break in the tempo. Then he climbed out of the tower and went back across the street to get breakfast.

All that day, Mrs. Canfield arranged for boys from the neighborhood to toll the bell in shifts. People from the outlying districts traveling into town that day kept asking, "Who died?" Villagers referred all inquiries to the small stone house in which Almera Canfield resided. Once there, they found Mrs. Canfield sitting in a straight rocking chair holding a huge Bible in her lap from which she read aloud caustic passages from the Old Testament about God's plans for the evil-doers. Once she had informed the visitors about John Brown's execution, she continued with her ominous reading. Townspeople understood well Mrs. Canfield's outspoken views on the abolition of slavery. Rumors circulated that she had even contributed to Brown's raid on Harper's Ferry, but she never openly revealed any personal connection with the man whose death she mourned that day.

The bell did not cease ringing until nightfall. Ever after that day, Jim Canfield said that he could still hear in the early morning that "heart-shaking, Day-of-Wrath knell, solemnly filling with its deep resonance all our corner of the Vermont valley."[4]

John Wallace Hutchinson of the Hutchinson Family Singers, a musical group well known all over the United States, was giving a series of concerts in Barre, Massachusetts, around the time of John Brown's execution. At their Thursday night concert, Hutchinson had invited the audience to gather with him and his family on the steps of the town hall on Friday morning. The next day, people gathered at the hall on the large common surrounded by white clapboard houses and imposing white churches. John had been unable to persuade any of the conservative ministers of those churches to toll the bells on that day, but he was able to persuade eight boys, including his own son Henry, to sneak into the churches and ring the bells for about five minutes while the crowd was still at the town hall.[5] That night, after their second

The Hutchinson Family Singers were outspoken abolitionists in the period before the Civil War.

concert, the Hutchinsons invited people to speak about Brown and the abolition of slavery.[6]

This was the last time for six years that so many bells would be rung across America for a single death. A majority of these bells were taken down and used to make rifles, bullets, and cannons during the conflict which John Brown had predicted would "purge the land with blood." And after the conflict, those same rifles and cannons would be turned into bells again.

Mary Brown waited at Harper's Ferry along with her escort, Hector Tyndale and J. Miller McKim, for the arrival of the special train carrying her husband's body on the afternoon of December 2, the same day Victor Hugo wrote his letter in an attempt to save her husband's life. She had hoped to take her sons Watson and Oliver home as well, but Watson's body had been donated to the medical college at Winchester, and Oliver's body had been buried in one of a number of boxes containing the bodies of Brown's troops. They had been interred somewhere on the other side of the Shenandoah in the woods, and Mary had not the time nor the stamina to locate her fallen sons.[7] Toward evening, the train finally arrived, and Brown's casket was placed on a train for Philadelphia.

At one o'clock the following day, Mary and the entourage arrived in the "City of Brotherly Love." Black people were gathered at the station along with angry white people who threatened violence. To avoid trouble, the police contrived the expedient of using a large tool box covered with a deer skin as a substitute for Brown's coffin. They placed the box reverently upon a cart which they then led away from the station, the crowd following. Once the station was cleared, the real coffin was removed to another train bound for New York City.[8]

When Mary and the casket arrived in New York, a friend of the family arranged to have John Brown's body transported to the undertakers at McGraw & Taylor at 163 in the Bowery. The friend insisted that Brown was not going to be buried in a southern casket. Here, his body was washed, laid out and wrapped in a linen shroud. Then the undertakers placed him in a walnut coffin and brought him back to the train.[9]

From New York City, the funeral train proceeded north through Albany to Troy and from there crossed over to Vermont and stopped in Rutland where Mary Brown and her party stayed at the Bardwell House.[10] The next day, the party set out by train for Vergennes where they disembarked and crossed Lake Champlain on a ferry to Essex County. The body was taken to Elizabethtown, escorted to the courthouse, and lay in state overnight. It was watched over by an honor guard of six townspeople. One town resident rode to North Elba to alert the family of the impending arrival. On Wednesday, December 7, Mary and her escort made their way through the Adirondacks toward North Elba, arriving at the Brown homestead that evening.[11]

Sometime in the early afternoon of that same day while walking on the street, Joshua Young, minister of the Congregational Unitarian Church in Burlington, Vermont, met young Lucius Bigelow, son of Lawrence G. Bigelow, the most prominent abolitionist in the city. Lucius expressed interest in the fact that John Brown's body was soon to arrive in Vergennes on its way to North Elba, not realizing that the body was already close to its final destination. "I want exceedingly to go to his funeral," the youth said. "Only say you will go with me as my companion and my guest, and we will take the next train."

Young quickly agreed to meet Lucius Bigelow at the station at four o'clock and went home to make preparations.[12] On telling his wife, Mary, where he intended to go, she questioned the wisdom of such a venture. Some prominent Burlington residents were angry with Brown because he owed money to the city's woolen mills, money which they could never collect, since Brown's wool business had gone bankrupt. Others who had business connections with the South were incensed that Brown had tried to free Virginia slaves. But Reverend Young didn't care. Since the controversial minister had fallen out of favor with Lucius's father the previous year, he had been looking for an opportunity to get back in the Bigelow family's good graces. This was his chance.

"It may not be wise," he answered, "but I am going just the same."[13]

Reverend Young had always been a subject of controversy with his parishioners. While living in Boston he had used his house on Unity Street as a station on the underground railroad. When he moved to Burlington in 1852 to take up his ministry at the Congregational Unitarian Church, he continued hiding runaway slaves in the barn behind his house at the corner of Willard and College Streets.[14]

He had angered the more conservative members of his flock in 1854 by going to Boston to see runaway slave Anthony Burns forcibly removed South. On his return, he gave an impassioned sermon in which he maintained that the continuance of slavery would lead to a breech between the North and the South. "Brethren, in the name of Christ, at whose altar we are worshipping to-day," he told the congregation, "I pronounce American Slavery to be a monstrous wrong, a heinous sin before High Heaven, provoking the righteous indignation of God, who will come in terrible judgment upon this nation, if we do not, away with it!" He further stated that Northerners were to blame for the perpetuation of slavery because of their willingness to return runaways to their southern masters. Any people who dared to speak against it were "branded as fanatics, thrown out of office, dismissed from their parishes, politically proscribed, socially ostracised...."[15]

In 1858, Reverend Young infuriated the abolitionists in his congregation as well. He and Lawrence Bigelow, along with many others, planned to hold a "Free Convention" which might be used as a platform to promote anti-slavery sentiment. Their proclamation called for "All Philanthropists and reformers in and out of the State, to meet in Free Convention at Rutland, Vt., on the 25th, 26th, and 27th of June next, to discus[s] the various topics of reform that are now engaging the attention and effort of Progressive minds."[16]

But when Young saw that many of the presenters for the convention were advocates of "free love," spiritualism, and bizarre diets, he became apprehensive and withdrew his support. Lawrence Bigelow and other church members involved in the convention agitated against Young for months afterward, accusing him of being inconsistent and not following through on his obligations.[17]

Reverend Young resigned in an effort "to carry relief to the mind of the Parish,... and promote the cause of Liberal Christianity in this town."[18] On December 11, 1858, Young's resignation was refused by a vote of 40 to 2. Lawrence Bigelow was one of the two who had voted against him. Young was now determined to prove to Lawrence that he could follow through on an obligation.

When Joshua and Lucius arrived in Vergennes, the weather had changed from a drizzle to a downpour, what the locals called a "proper Nor'easter." They were surprised to learn that the funeral procession had crossed the lake the day before and would soon be at its destination. They arranged for a cab to the ferry which docked some six miles from the train station. Having arrived on the shore and located the ferryman, they made known their intentions to cross Lake Champlain to Barber's Point in order to reach John Brown's farm in time for the funeral. The ferryman told them he could not cross the lake so late at night in such foul weather. Besides, he felt that John Brown had deserved to be hanged in Charlestown.

"Why?" one of the men asked. "Do you know any evil of him?"

Reverend Joshua Young of Burlington, Vermont, officiated at John Brown's burial in North Elba, New York (present day Lake Placid). Although this act drove some of his more wealthy parishioners from the Unitarian Church where he presided, he did not immediately lose his position as pastor. He resigned in 1863 for reasons that are still not fully understood.

"No," the ferryman answered, "but a great deal of good. I knew John Brown well. He has crossed this ferry with me a hundred times, and a more honest upright, fair man does not exist. We all like him, but he had no business meddling with other people's niggers."

For two hours, Young and Bigelow pleaded with the ferryman to change his views and help them cross the lake, but the old man was resolute. Suddenly, a brightness from outside lit up the room. Joshua went to the door to see what was happening. The wind had changed direction to the west, and the clouds had broken up. "The stars in their courses fought against Sisera," Reverend Young said. "See, Mr. Ferryman! God's full-orbed moon has thrown a bridge of silver across the lake. He bids us go, and who shall hinder?"[19]

To their great relief, the ferryman finally acceded, agreeing to call his assistant out of bed to see if they could operate the boat. But preparing the ferryman's large scow for service was no easy task. It took some time and effort to thaw and raise the frozen sail. Once raised, the passengers got into the sailboat for the three-mile journey. The boat plowed through the waves, raising a spray of chilly water that dowsed the travelers. Joshua and Lucius arrived safely on Barber's Point, cold and soaking wet.

After climbing up the bank a few yards from the edge of the water, they saw a light at a farmhouse. Soon they were knocking at the door, and asking the fully dressed young man who opened it if he would help them get to North Elba. "I will if father is willing," the man replied. Joshua and Lucius soon found themselves riding in a wagon with all haste to Elizabethtown.

They stopped in Elizabethtown only long enough to change the horses and learn as much as they could about the passage of Brown's funeral procession. It was now two o'clock in the morning. Once the new horses were in place, the party proceeded through the valley of Keene, surrounded by some of the tallest peaks in the Adirondacks. "We had come," Young wrote of their journey, "to what is known as 'Indian Pass,' a ravine or gorge, formed by close and parallel walls of nearly perpendicular cliffs, fully 200 feet in height and almost black in color." The road ran over rocks and stumps which made the wagon sway from side to side like a boat on a stormy sea.

Toward daybreak near the end of their twenty-five-mile journey from Elizabethtown, the road became smoother and more level. The wagon could move faster now, but the bitter-cold wind had nothing to

Wendell Phillips asked Joshua Young to officiate at John Brown's burial.

stop it. They crossed over a bridge and followed a winding, sandy road through the forest to a house in a clearing, the same house that John Brown's sons had helped him build.

"We entered the house stiff in every limb," Joshua recalled, "I might say, half frozen, and glad enough to feel the genial heat of the small stove around which we found ourselves part of a very considerable company of people, mostly friends and neighbors, who had personally known and admired the man who had gone forth from them a simple shepherd and now was brought back dead with a fame gone out into all the world."

Half the people gathered at the farmhouse for the burial services were free blacks residing in the area, including Lyman Epps, a man who claimed African and Native American ancestry. He had come with his wife and children. John Brown's three youngest daughters, Annie, Sarah, and Ellen, were there along with Salmon Brown and his wife, and the widows of Watson, Oliver, and Will Thompson.[20]

Wendell Phillips, a prominent Boston abolitionist and associate of William Lloyd Garrison, came into the room and took Reverend Young aside for a brief discussion. Phillips recognized the great sacrifice Young had made in coming to the farmhouse. He asked Young if he would officiate at the burial service. "It would give Mrs. Brown and the other widows great satisfaction," he explained, "if you would perform the usual service of a clergyman on this occasion." Young agreed.

The funeral began at one o'clock in the farmhouse. The service opened with a hymn which was a particular favorite of John Brown: "Blow Ye the Trumpet, Blow," sung to the tune of Lenox with words by Charles Wesley:

> Blow ye the trumpet, blow!
> The gladly solemn sound.
> Let all the nations know,
> To earth's remotest bound.
> The year of jubilee is come!
> The year of jubilee is come!
> Return, ye ransomed sinners, home.[21]

After the hymn, Young offered an extemporaneous prayer in which he asked God to "cause the oppressed to go free" and to "hasten on the day when no more wrong or injustice shall be done in the earth."[22]

J. Miller McKim who had helped Mrs. Brown bring her husband home for burial said a few words of comfort for the family after Young's

John Brown's body was buried at this site on December 8, 1859.

prayer, and then Wendell Phillips delivered the eulogy. "History will date Virginia Emancipation from Harper's Ferry," Phillips told Brown's friends and family. "True, the slave is still there. So, when the tempest uproots a pine on your hills, it looks green for months,—a year or two. Still, it is timber, not a tree. John Brown has loosened the roots of the slave system; it only breathes,—it does not live,—hereafter." He went on to describe scenes from the raid and asked the listeners to consider why it failed. Only God could proclaim that the "work is done," and that Brown had "proved that a Slave State is only fear in the mask of despotism." Such an achievement could not be a failure. "Insurrection," Phillips continued, "was a harsh, horrid word to millions a month ago. John Brown went a whole generation beyond it, claiming the right for white men to help the slave to freedom by arms."[23]

Another hymn followed, during which the casket was brought outside, placed on a table and opened so that the onlookers could get one last glimpse of the martyr. "It was almost as natural as life," Young wrote in his memoir of the funeral. "There was a flush on the face, resulting probably from the peculiar mode of his death, and nothing of the pallor that is usual when life is extinct."

The casket was closed and carried to the burial site by the huge boulder near the house. As the casket was lowered into the grave and the friends' and family's grief had reached its height, Young quoted from Second Timothy (4:7-8). "I have fought a good fight. I have finished my course. I have kept the faith: Henceforth there is laid up for me a crown of righteousness, which the Lord, the righteous judge, shall give me at that day: and not to me only, but unto all them also that love his appearing." Nothing more was said as the people watered the ground with their tears and slowly departed.

Shortly after his return, at a party given in the Burlington Town Hall, Reverend Young approached a group of women he knew, but they "turned their backs upon him without even a frigid bow."[24] That Sunday, Young discovered his Burlington congregation was a lot smaller than it used to be. Six of the wealthiest families had joined another church. Many others were disaffected. Still, Young had the strong support of the abolition community in Burlington at least up to the time the Civil War came and abolitionists like Lucius Bigelow and his brother George joined the army. The minister would endure the snubs and backbiting of the people of Burlington until March of 1863. Then, he would leave for Massachusetts and a new ministry.[25]

Victor Hugo's letter had not yet reached an American newspaper when the distressing news of Brown's execution reached him at Hauteville House. The gray winter storms that obscure the coast of France had descended on the island of Guernsey as if in sympathy with Hugo's gray mood. He spent the rest of the day doing a wash drawing of a man hanging from a gibbet. At the bottom of the drawing, he wrote the Latin word "Ecce" in remembrance of what Pontius Pilate had said while introducing Jesus to the mob that called for His death. "Ecce homo," Pilate had said. "Behold the man."

Later, his wife would turn the sketch into an engraving which would be used to fund Hugo's favorite charities. In a few years, the same engraving would help provide money for medical supplies for the Union Army during the American Civil War.[26]

J̲ust after Brown's execution, a rumor began circulating in the North about Brown having kissed a slave child before he died. This rumor may have been generated by a letter Brown had written to the wife of George L. Stearns on November 29. "I have asked," he wrote, "to be spared from having any mock; or hypocritical prayers made over me when I am publicly murdered: & that my only religious attendants be poor little, dirty, ragged, bare headed, & barefooted Slave boys; & Girls; led by some old grey headed Slave Mother."[27]

The radical *Vermont Journal*, which had been making political and decidedly abolitionist hay from John Brown's raid, chose to report rumor as fact: "As [John Brown] stepped out of the door [of his jail on December 2] a black woman with her little child in her arms stood near his way. The twain were of the despised race, for whose emancipation and elevation to the dignity of children of God, he was about to lay down his life.... He stopped for a moment in his course, stooped over, and, with the tenderness of one whose love is as broad as the brotherhood of man, kissed it affectionately."[28]

The report of the baby kissing incident, however untrue, did lead the *Vermont Journal* to make an interesting prediction: "That mother [whose child was kissed] will be proud of that distinction for her offspring and someday, when over the ashes of John Brown the temple of Virginia liberty is reared, she may join in the joyful song of praise which on that soil will do justice to his memory."[29]

In this instance, the reporter for the *Journal*, while wrong in every other respect, got two things right. Someday, there would be a song of praise written about Old Osawatomie, and it would be sung in Virginia.

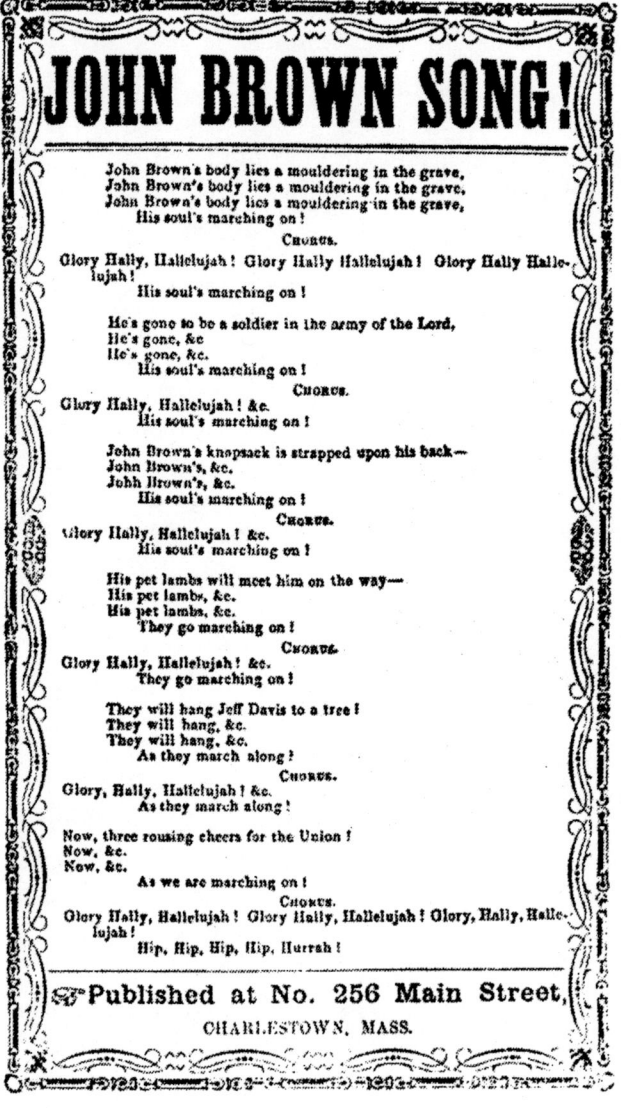

Part II

RAISING THE GHOST

DAGUERD. BY BRADY, N.Y.   ENGD. BY A. H. RITCHIE, N.Y.

POSTMASTER GENERAL.
March 1849 — July 1850.

5

"...all the wild beasts of Ephesus."

In December, 1859, Vermont's Senator Jacob Collamer faced a political crisis. He and his colleagues James Murray Mason of Virginia, Jefferson Davis of Mississippi, James Rood Doolittle of Wisconsin, and Graham Newell Fitch of Indiana were charged with the task of discovering who had secretly supplied arms to John Brown. They also hoped to ease southern tension over the raid. Many northern businessmen had already been forced to leave the South after Brown's attack. Each was seen as a potential abolitionist seeking to free slaves and cause insurrection.

Unfortunately, there was some evidence showing that a northern abolitionist conspiracy had aided Brown's war on southern interests. The English mercenary Hugh Forbes claimed that the weapons used at the Ferry were supplied by Republican Governor Ryland Fletcher of Vermont. Such an accusation reflected negatively on the Republican party as a whole, and would have a devastating impact in the upcoming national elections. Luckily, a letter from Clark Chapman, a secretary for Fletcher, offered some hope of vindicating the Vermont ex-governor and the Republicans.

Chapman admitted that he had witnessed a conversation between John Brown and the governor shortly after the legislature had made an appropriation of $20,000 for the "Suffering poor of Kansas." Neither he nor Fletcher had "the least objections to telling all that old man said to us...." He also offered to help Collamer become president of the United States after "[William] Seward is killed off by showing he was

---

Senator Collamer served on Mason's senate committee investigating the Harper's Ferry incident. In questioning George Luther Stearns, Collamer came closer than any of his fellow senators to uncovering the northern conspiracy.

one of Brown's Lieutenants—in the Harpers Ferry Affair" and "So. Carolina—Georgia—to say nothing of Va—have left the Union...."[1]

The Vermont senator replied to Chapman's letter on Monday, December 19, making it clear to Chapman that he doubted "whether any who have given [Brown] contributions understood he was to apply it in the way he did." The senator most feared that unscrupulous politicians would "make of [the raid] political capital for the Presidential elections."[2]

Chapman wrote to Collamer again five days later, stating in more sober tones that John Brown had only been interested in discussing Kansas affairs with Governor Fletcher, and had said nothing about invading the southern states. He wrote that Brown was "desirous to enlist moral, honest & brave-hearted young men to meet him at Tabor, Iowa, [a gathering place for abolitionists entering Kansas] the next Spring," and he asked for arms for protection against the actions of Missouri border ruffians. But the governor had no authority to give Brown money for arms.[3]

Chapman followed up this letter with one written on January 24, 1860, in which he included an article clipped from the "incendiary" *Vermont Journal*. "It, of course, possesses no value—only to let you know your people and constituents think of you and your colleagues—and are proud of the learning, impartiality-and statesmanship possessed and displayed by the 'Senator from Vermont.'"[4]

Collamer had worked hard all his life to deserve such praise. He had moved with his family from Troy, New York, to Burlington, Vermont, at the age of four. His father, an industrious but poor carpenter, died while Jacob was still very young. The family struggled and managed to send Jacob to the University of Vermont in 1806 when he was 15 years old.[5]

The Collamers were still very poor during Jacob's college days and could not afford proper shoes for Jacob. When Dr. Daniel Clark Sanders, the president of the university, suggested that his students should henceforth come to classes with shoes on, Jacob was placed in a quandary. He told his mother what Sanders had said, and his mother worked diligently to make enough shoe thread for one pair of shoes.

Once he had the shoes, Jacob needed to preserve them. He frequently carried them to class, and rather than carry the shoes back to his home each day, he sometimes hid them in a pine brush fence for the night.

He graduated from the University of Vermont in 1810, studied law in St. Albans and joined the army during the War of 1812. After the war, he practiced law, served in the state legislature, and was elected to the Vermont Supreme Court. Then he became the Vermont representative in the U.S. Congress. In March, 1849, President Zachary Taylor appointed him postmaster general of the United States. Collamer resigned this post in July, 1850, after Taylor's untimely death.[6]

In 1854, Collamer was elected to the U.S. Senate just in time to serve on Stephen A. Douglas's controversial Kansas committee. The Kansas Territory had just been opened for settlement. Douglas intended to make Kansas the first test of "popular sovereignty," allowing the settlers of the territory to decide the issue of slavery for themselves. When the pro-slavery and abolitionist settlers started killing each other, Collamer became increasingly disgusted with Douglas and his Kansas experiment. In 1856, when Douglas suggested that the fighting in Kansas would cease once the territory entered the Union as a slave state, Collamer called "popular sovereignty" a delusion and said that the matter should be settled "by the admission of Kansas as a free State."[7]

The outspoken senator from Vermont soon found favor among his colleagues, including Charles Sumner of Massachusetts who bestowed upon Collamer the title of "Green Mountain Socrates."[8] James Mason of Virginia had also noted Collamer's dogged devotion to the principles embodied in the U.S. Constitution. As chairman of the committee investigating the Harper's Ferry incident, Mason thought the fair-minded Collamer seemed the perfect man to represent northern interests.

Only two weeks after Collamer wrote to Chapman, the Senate committee began examining witnesses. Among the first to appear before the senators were Lewis W. Washington and John H. Allstadt who had been hostages during the raid, and Dr. John D. Starry who had worked diligently to defend the town. Lieutenant Colonel Robert E. Lee testified on January 10, along with Archibald M. Kitzmiller, the acting superintendent of the Harper's Ferry armory. The following day, the committee issued summonses for the appearance of witnesses who might have given Brown money and arms. Among these were three of Brown's secret northern backers: Gerrit Smith, Franklin B. Sanborn, and Dr. Samuel Gridley Howe.[9]

Howe, who had returned to Massachusetts shortly after Brown's execution, still had misgivings about going south to testify about his role in Brown's affairs. His friend, Charles Sumner, however, made it clear to Howe that he would not protect anyone who refused to appear before the committee. In the end, Howe agreed to go so long as he would not be called to Virginia to appear at the trials of Brown's remaining troops. "I think I can take care of myself among bullies & rowdies," he wrote to Sumner, "at least I hope I should have no more fear of violence in Washington than the rest of you; but a Virginia process would be worse to me than a call to fight with all the wild beasts of Ephesus."[10]

The founder of the Perkins School had reason enough to be wary of testifying before the committee. Brown had come to him with maps of the South showing potential areas for strikes against slavery. The old man had intended to base his operations in the mountains where he could not easily be captured. From the high ground, Brown could move on the plantations, freeing slaves, and marching them back to his mountain fortresses. Howe had been intrigued by this plan, having seen the Greeks use similar tactics effectively against the Turks. One of Brown's maps had shown Harper's Ferry as a possible target. If the senate committee learned of this, Howe and his friends might find themselves in jail for conspiracy. He would have to be very careful about how he responded to the senators.

He appeared to testify in his best frock coat and tie on Friday, February 3.[11] When he arrived in the Senate wing of the U.S. Congress, he was directed to the attic room where the investigating committee met. The chamber Howe entered was not designed for luxury, but economy and efficiency. The senators invited him to sit on one of the walnut Gothic revival chairs surrounding a large table also made of walnut. An inexpensive gas chandelier provided light, while a gas fireplace of finished slate heated the space. Drapes covered the windows to keep out the winter cold. On one wall was a bookcase holding back issues of *The Congressional Record*.[12]

Under Chairman Mason's questioning, Howe quickly admitted knowing John Brown.[13] In 1857, Brown had served as the agent for the Massachusetts Kansas Aid Committee of which Howe was a member. Howe also admitted that this committee had given Brown two hundred

Sharps rifles with which to arm free state settlers in the Kansas territory. He made it clear that Brown had a letter from the chairman of the committee allowing him to use the Sharps rifles only for that purpose.

"Who was the chairman who wrote the letter you refer to?" Mason asked.

"I should prefer not to answer the question," Howe replied. George Luther Stearns who had chaired the Kansas committee had been closer to Brown than Howe and might have information that would quickly expose the extent of Brown's backing in the North. Howe intended to do all he could to protect Stearns, but the senators were persistent.

"I see no reason," Mason argued, "why you should not answer the question."

"I am here to answer as to all I have done myself, freely and frankly," Howe explained, "but I would respectfully ask to be excused from answering any question touching the actions of anybody else. I can only answer for my view as one of the committee."

Senator Jefferson Davis became impatient with Howe's equivocation. "The witness confounds his position," Davis told the chairman. "He is not here arraigned to answer for what he did, but to give information as to what everybody did."

"The subject referred to the committee by the Senate," Mason said to Howe, "is to make inquiry into all the facts attending the late incursion at Harper's Ferry, and connected with it in any way."

The doctor finally realized that his position was untenable. "Perhaps I am over sensitive about it, and inasmuch as the gentleman's name is perfectly well known as chairman of the committee, and is in print, I will give it, Mr. George L. Stearns."

The senators also asked about other money contributed to John Brown. Howe admitted having given Brown $50, and that other prominent individuals had contributed to Old Osawatomie for the "promotion of anti-slavery sentiments."

Chairman Mason asked, "Will you state what you mean by that phrase 'contributing' for the promotion of anti-slavery sentiments? What is the meaning of that idea?"

"In the same way that I would promote the Gospel among the heathen. I could not precisely say what. The means are various—lectures, writing, talking, discussing the matter."

"What ends are to be attained by promoting that anti-slavery sentiment? What is the object in view?"

"The promotion of freedom among men; the same object as the fathers in the revolution."

"Was one of its objects the means of attaining the freedom of the African slaves held in this country?"

"That would be the natural and desired result."

"Was that one of the ends to be attained by propagating this anti-slavery sentiment by lecturing and otherwise?"

"It was. I answer these questions out of courtesy to the chairman, but I must think they are rather wide."

Collamer, who took a more practical view of the matter of contributions, asked Howe, "Were not the contributions received by the committees, which were made by the people in Boston and Massachusetts, for and during the Kansas troubles?"

"For that definite purpose," Howe responded.

"Was any money of those contributions ever sent to Brown after 1858?"

"Not that I know of."

Senator Doolittle asked Howe if at any time he had "any intimation of an organized attempt or effort ... to produce an insurrection among the slaves in the slave States of the South."

Howe said, "Never."

Having survived his ordeal before the Senate committee, Howe wrote to Thomas Wentworth Higginson who had been less than pleased with Howe's actions since the doctor had published a "Card" in the newspapers dissociating himself from Brown's raid. Howe's letter was an attempt to get back in Higginson's good graces and to encourage him to go to Washington and testify.

"It is true," Howe wrote, "that if I had known of his purposed attack on the armory, or any other bold stroke at slavery, not involving the taking of property, I might have given him aid and encouragement, such was my confidence in the man; but, it so happened, that I did not know it.

"It is true that I ought to have expected an explosion and onslaught somewhere; but the point is, that I did not expect anything like what happened, or anything more than a stampede.

"As it has turned out, the publication of the Card did no good; but I have the satisfaction of thinking it did no harm except perhaps to me."

Concerning the Senate committee, Howe wrote, "No one is obliged to volunteer any information.... He has only to answer their questions. In my case they were very unskillful and failed to get out of me some information which they might have been glad to have. This will probably be the case with others."[14]

On Friday, February 17, Senator Mason reported to the Committee on the Harper's Ferry Raid that he had given the Senate the names of witnesses who had refused to appear. Warrants had been issued for the arrest of James Redpath, a man who had known Brown in Kansas; John Brown, Jr., one of Old Osawatomie's surviving sons; and Franklin Sanborn, who had served as secretary to the Massachusetts Kansas Aid Society.

The following Friday, George Luther Stearns, the chairman of that same society, appeared as a witness before the senators.[15] He readily admitted to having met John Brown in January, 1857, and read a written statement concerning all the money and arms provided to Brown during the Kansas trouble. Among these arms were 200 Sharps carbines and 200 revolvers costing $1,300 ordered from the Massachusetts Arms Company. The revolvers were a personal gift from Stearns and were not directly in the control of the Massachusetts society. Stearns also gave the Senate committee copies of letters to Brown about how the arms were to be used. In one of these letters written to Brown when he was staying briefly in Chatham, Canada, Stearns warned Brown not to use any of the weapons he had been given for any purpose other than the defense of Kansas. Brown was ordered to hold the arms "subject to [Stearns's] order as chairman of the committee."

Senator Fitch asked Stearns, "Did the order addressed to Brown, at Chatham, ... embrace the pistols as your private property?"

"They did not," Stearns said, "perhaps, technically; but that was my understanding at the time."

To further clarify this point, Collamer asked, "You supposed Brown would understand it so?"

Stearns replied, "I presumed so."

After further questioning, Stearns revealed that John Brown was very secretive about his plans. "The United States government," Brown once told Stearns, "immediately disclose their orders to their military officers. Before the orders leave Washington, they are published all through the papers; well, now, that is not the way; if a man is to do anything, he must keep his plans to himself."

As the testimony continued, Collamer grew more and more curious as to how much Brown might have revealed to Stearns about plans for an invasion of the slave states. The senator got his chance to pursue this just after Mason asked Stearns about Hugh Forbes, a man Stearns had never met or corresponded with.

"Did you at any time before the transaction at Harper's Ferry," Collamer asked, "in any way, directly or indirectly, understand that there was any purpose on the part of Brown to make any inroad upon the subject of slavery in any of the States?"

"No sir; not except that Brown was opposed to slavery, and as he had in Kansas he would work again. I did not suppose that he had any organized plan."

"My idea is, making any forcible entry upon Virginia, or any other State?"

"No, sir."

"Had you ever any intimation of that kind, any idea of it?"

"No, sir. Perhaps I do not understand you. I did suppose he would go into Virginia or some other State and relieve slaves."

"In what way?"

"In any way he could give them liberty."

"Did you understand that he contemplated doing it by force?"

"Yes, sir; by force, if necessary."

"Will you explain in what manner, by force, you understood he contemplated doing it?"

"I cannot explain any manner, because, as I say to you, I never talked with him on the subject."

"Had you any idea that these arms were to be used for any such purpose as making an inroad into any State?"

"I think I do not understand you."

"John Brown has made an inroad into Virginia, with force and arms, to relieve slaves; you understand that?"

"Yes, sir."

"Now, did you ever, before that took place, have any intimation that that was contemplated to be done, intended to be done by him?"

"No, sir; I never supposed that he contemplated anything like what occurred at Harper's Ferry."

Senator Mason, who had now become interested in Collamer's line of questioning, jumped in with one of his own: "What was your general information, then, if you did not know specifically what he intended to do?"

"I supposed," Stearns replied, "that if he had an opportunity, and it came in his way to do what he did in Missouri, where he went in and took several slaves and ran them off, he would do that."

"And, if resisted," Senator Davis asked, "what then?"

Stearns said, "That is not for me to say."

"He would have use for the arms that you furnished," Davis explained, "if he were resisted; that was the idea, I presume. I intended to ask whether that was your idea."

Fitch attempted to clarify the question further. "Was the supposition that Brown would resort to force a supposition of others as well as yourself?"

"From first to last," Stearns replied, "I understood John Brown to be a man who was opposed to slavery, and, as such, that he would take every opportunity to free slaves where he could; I did not know in what way; I only know that from the fact of his having done it in Missouri in the instance referred to...."

At this point, Collamer hit Stearns with one last crucial question. "Then I ask you, did you disapprove of such a transaction as that at Harper's Ferry?"

Stearns mustered his courage and replied, "I should have disapproved of it if I had known of it; but I have since changed my opinion; I believe John Brown to be the representative man of this century, as Washington was of the last— the Harper's Ferry affair, and the capacity shown by the Italians for self-government, the great events of this age. One will free Europe and the other America."

Further questioning led Stearns to reiterate that he and the other members of the society had not given Brown arms for any other purpose than the defense of free state settlers in Kansas. Collamer also established that Stearns's Kansas committee had ceased to function long before Brown invaded Virginia.

Since February 10, Collamer had been asking Mason to call Governor Henry Wise of Virginia to testify before the committee. Now that Stearns had effectively slipped out of the net, the senator from Vermont grew more and more insistent that Wise be called "to furnish to the committee all reliable information within his knowledge as to any citizen of the United States, not present at the invasion at Harper's Ferry, being implicated therein or accessory thereto.... I desire not his suspicions, apprehensions, belief, or opinion," Collamer explained, "or any account or vindication of his course, as Governor of Virginia, on the occasion, but only the facts and information above stated—in short, that knowledge and information in relation to the transaction which he is credibly reported to have said 'rubies could not obtain from him.'"

Chairman Mason refused to honor Collamer's request. "It is not considered competent," he told Collamer, "to any authority of the United States in any manner thus to trench upon, or directly or indirectly to question the separate action of a State administration."[16]

Mason's response may have been prompted by a hope that a conspirator or group of conspirators might still be found among the members of the Massachusetts Kansas Aid Society. But, any possibility of getting further information about the society ended on Tuesday, April 3, when a deputy federal marshal botched an attempt to arrest Franklin Sanborn in Concord, Massachusetts.

The deputy arrived on Sanborn's doorstep that evening with four assistants. Claiming to be soliciting charitable donations to a worthy cause, they gained entry and immediately arrested Sanborn. But his sister ran from the house shouting, "Murder! Murder! Five men arrested my brother." Frank resisted all attempts of the marshal and his assistants to get him in their carriage while his sister whipped up the horses and sent the carriage careening driverless through the streets. A short time later, someone rang the fire bell and the street in front of Sanborn's house was soon filled with angry citizens demanding Sanborn's release, as the prisoner rattled his chains and called on those present to "witness the penalty imposed by slavery on free speech."

A judge hastily prepared a writ of *habeas corpus* and forced the marshal to give up his prisoner. Not satisfied with having Sanborn free, the citizens then chased the marshal and his henchmen from the town throwing rocks and sticks after them. Frank Sanborn spent the rest of that night at the home of George Prescott with a loaded pistol provided by Ephraim Bull, the chairman of the town's committee of selectmen. Henry David Thoreau volunteered to stay in Sanborn's house to protect his sister.[17]

Senator Mason received notice of the failure to arrest Sanborn on Saturday, April 7. On Friday, April 13, Mason ordered that the issue of Sanborn's arrest be submitted to the Committee on the Judiciary for further action, if necessary.

The Senate committee stayed active until mid-June when Chairman Mason closed the investigation and wrote the final report. By then, thirty-two people had testified, including William H. Seward of New York. The senators had sought to uncover a northern conspiracy, but had no evidence there had ever been one. In the report, Mason stated that the raid on Harper's Ferry had been "simply the act of lawless ruffians, under the sanction of no public or political authority—distinguishable only from ordinary felonies by the ulterior ends in contemplation by them, and by the fact that the money to maintain the expedition, and the large armament they brought with them, had been contributed and furnished by the citizens of other States of the Union, under circumstances that must continue to jeopard the safety and peace of the Southern States, and against which Congress has no power to legislate."[18]

Collamer and Doolittle could not tolerate Mason's assertion that the Southern States were still in danger. Refusing to support Mason's conclusions, both senators drafted their own report. "The committee, by its majority," they wrote, "seem to regard it as their duty to inquire whether there are any citizens who, though not 'implicated' in this affair, yet hold such opinions and pursue such courses on the subject of slavery as are dangerous to the national tranquillity, ... although Congress has no power to take any action in relation thereto. This we regard as a departure from the duty and proper power of the committee." They pointed out that witnesses had been examined concerning their opinions and beliefs about the institution of slavery and had even been accused of conspiracy because they had attempted to secure counsel for John Brown so that he could have a fair trial. But the opinions expressed had not exceeded "in severity the terms of reprehension on this subject which were long since indulged by Washington, Madison, Jefferson, [and George] Mason, ... all of Virginia, whose information and opinions ... the people of the free States have not yet learned to disrespect....

"We cannot join in any report tending to promulgate such a view," they concluded, "as we regard it unfounded in fact and ill calculated to promote peace, confidence, or tranquillity, and a departure from the legitimate purpose for which the committee was appointed."[19]

By this time, the national election campaign of 1860 had started. The Republicans, meeting in Chicago, had already nominated Abraham Lincoln, a successful railroad lawyer from Illinois, for the presidency. In this homely, angular man, the delegates saw a compromise candidate. Lincoln openly stated that he was not opposed to slavery where it already existed, but did oppose whole-heartedly its extension into the western territories.

Democrats had not as yet selected a candidate. Their delegates, meeting in Charleston, South Carolina, in late April and early May, had attempted to nominate Stephen Douglas for the presidency. But the Southern Democrats, under the leadership of William Lowndes Yancey, a "fire eating" Alabama secessionist who was thrilled with the way John Brown's raid had pushed the South toward disunion, failed in an attempt to insert a statement into the party platform calling for the protection of the extension of slavery into the western territories. In anger, Yancey and the other southern delegates walked out of the convention, leaving the remaining Democrats in a state of confusion. It was not until June 23 that the Democrats, now meeting in Baltimore, selected Senator Douglas as their candidate. Southern Democrats, who refused to attend this second convention, held a counter-convention of their own in Baltimore, nominating John C. Breckinridge of Kentucky.

To add to the overall confusion, a new political organization calling itself the Constitutional Union party, meeting in early May, selected John Bell of Tennessee to run for president and Edward Everett, the well-known Massachusetts orator, for vice president. Their platform called for a commitment to the Constitution, the Union, and enforcement of the laws. They carefully avoided the topic of slavery.

In this four-way race to the White House, the North with its population of twenty-two million clearly held the advantage. The South had a population of only nine million, and four million of those were slaves. It only remained to see what the larger voting population of the North would do. Would they vote for the anti-slavery Lincoln or the popular southern candidate Breckinridge? Their decision would mean either civil accord or civil war.

Jacob Collamer was selected as one of the two Vermonters to represent the state in Statuary Hall in the U.S. Congress. The other Vermonter selected was Ethan Allen.

6

"Take a lesson from John Brown."

In the winter and early spring of 1860, Henry Wise, recently retired from the governorship of Virginia, purchased property from his brother, John Cropper Wise, in order to set up an estate on the Elizabeth River some six miles outside Norfolk, Virginia, in Princess Anne County. The plantation included slave quarters, out-buildings, and a two-story main house divided into two sections, one for Wise and his family, the other for house servants. With no immediate thought of returning to politics, Wise settled down to the quiet life of a farmer dealing in grains and livestock.

But the 1860 race for president, and its possible consequences if Lincoln were to be elected, brought Wise back into the political arena. That summer, he took to the hustings at Norfolk on behalf of John C. Breckinridge, presidential candidate for the Constitutional Democrats. (Northern Democrats who supported Stephen Douglas now called themselves National Democrats.)

Norfolk residents were particularly interested in the political movement in the North to prevent the formation of slave states in the western territories. Douglas's idea of applying "popular sovereignty" to the settlement of Kansas had resulted in war between the pro-slavery and abolitionist settlers. Pro-slavery forces had lost, and Kansas was expected to enter the Union as a free state before another year passed.

Wise explained that popular sovereignty, which he called "squatter sovereignty," would always result in slavery being excluded from a territory. He demonstrated how two slave owners, one with fifty slaves, one with twenty, would have to live on more than a thousand acres of land and would have only two votes between them. Meanwhile, "five Emigrant Aid Society men go out from Vermont, with flocks and herds,

---

Waitman T. Willey voted against the Virginia Ordinance of Secession and joined western Virginians in fighting against Confederate control of the state.

and settle 40 acres each—200 acres in all," and they would have five votes.

Breckinridge was the only candidate capable of working out a solution to this problem. In the event that Lincoln, who opposed slavery in the western territories, gained the election, Wise intended to wait "until some one sovereign does raise the rightful flag of Revolution."[1]

John Hutchinson left his home at High Rock in Lynn, Massachusetts, that summer to campaign on behalf of Abraham Lincoln. In company with his brothers and his sister Abby, he gave a concert tour of New York state, traveling the line of the Harlem Railroad which stretched 127 miles from Manhattan Island through the rich dairy farmland of Westchester, Putnam, and Dutchess Counties, and the hills and apple orchards of Columbia County, all the way to Chatham, just southeast of Albany. Working himself to exhaustion each day, he took tickets and money at the doors, and then hurried back stage to prepare for the opening number.

In early November, after singing in a string of concerts in New York and Brooklyn, John was too exhausted to continue. After the election, he came down with a severe cold which threatened to turn into pneumonia and quick consumption. He stopped to rest with his sister Abby at her home in Orange, New Jersey. Under her care, he soon regained his health.[2]

The Hutchinson Family Singers' weapon during the campaign was a song entitled "Lincoln and Liberty" with words provided by Jesse Hutchinson to the old Irish tune "Rosin the Beau." Many years earlier, Jesse had written an anti-slavery song, "The Liberty Ball," using the same tune. The new campaign song was no less abolitionist in spirit, comparing Lincoln to the biblical David and calling the "Little Giant" Stephen Douglas "the Slavocrat's giant":

> Our David's good sling is unerring.
> The Slavocrat's giant he slew,
> Then shout for the freedom preferring,
> For Lincoln and Liberty, too.[3]

In the months before his nomination for the presidency, Lincoln had spent about as much time denouncing Douglas as he had attempting to distance the Republican party from John Brown's October raid. Around the time of Brown's execution, Lincoln toured Kansas telling all who would listen that Brown's attack at the Ferry was "a violation of the law" and "futile."[4] In a speech at Leavenworth on December 3, 1859, Lincoln said, "Old John Brown has just been executed for treason against a state. We cannot object, even though he agreed with us in thinking slavery wrong. That cannot excuse violence, bloodshed, and treason." But Lincoln warned his audience that if anyone attempted to destroy the Union after the election, "it will be our duty to deal with you as old John Brown has been dealt with."[5]

Lincoln continued in this same vein in a speech at the Cooper Institute in New York City on February 27, 1860. "You charge that we stir up insurrections among your slaves," he stated. "We deny it; and what is your proof? Harper's Ferry! John Brown!! John Brown was no Republican; and you have failed to implicate a single Republican in his Harper's Ferry enterprise."[6]

Lincoln's clear political stands worked to win him the November election. Although his name had not appeared on the ballots in most slave states, he had a plurality of the popular votes and, more importantly, a majority of the electoral votes.

For the South, this was the last straw. Southern votes no longer controlled the House of Representatives or the Senate. The last two presidents, Franklin Pierce and James Buchanan, had been friendly to southern interests. But Lincoln was openly hostile to the South's most important institution, slavery. Angry Southerners, urged on by secessionists called "fire-eaters," formed conventions of secession.

The first of these in South Carolina passed an ordinance of secession on December 20. Within a month, Mississippi, Florida, Alabama, and Georgia seceded. Louisiana followed Georgia out of the Union on January 26, 1861. Three days later, Kansas was admitted to the Union under a state constitution banning slavery, an act which further enraged Southerners. Texas left the Union on March 2. By then, the Confederate States of America had formed a government, electing Jefferson Davis president, and setting up its offices in Montgomery, Alabama.

In mid-February, the Virginia state government convened its own Convention of Secession sometimes meeting at the Virginia State

Legislature on Capitol Square in Richmond, or sometimes at the Virginia Mechanics Institute located at the corner of Franklin and Ninth Street, just a block and a half away from the State Legislature.

Henry A. Wise represented Princess Anne County. Although Wise had written to the new Confederate president, Jefferson Davis, promising to "stampede the flower of the State to the South,"[7] his fellow delegates had other ideas. Many did not want to leave the Union, especially those who represented counties in the western part of the state. More than a few were willing to support a statement of neutrality in order to save the state from invasion by either Union or Confederate forces. Other representatives pointed out that, either way, Virginia would have to defend itself.

After two months of arguing, the delegates gained a new initiative to take action more quickly. On April 12, Confederate batteries fired on Union occupied Fort Sumter in Charleston Harbor, South Carolina. The next day, Sumter surrendered, and two days later, President Lincoln called for 75,000 troops to suppress combinations too powerful for the ordinary judicial process. The president specifically asked Governor John Letcher of Virginia to provide three regiments of infantry. Letcher replied on April 16 "that the militia of Virginia will not be furnished to the powers at Washington for any such use or purpose as they have in view.... You have chosen to inaugurate civil war, and having done so, we will meet it in a spirit as determined as the Administration has exhibited toward the South."[8]

That same day, George Wythe Randolph, Richmond's own representative to the convention suggested that the Virginians arm themselves, take possession of the Gosport Naval Yard near Norfolk, and tear up the Baltimore & Ohio Railroad track going into and out of Harper's Ferry to halt shipments of weapons to northern cities. "The plan of operation on the other side has to be formed upon your frontier," Randolph warned, "and it is absolutely necessary, without delay, to form your plan of action...."[9]

That evening, an exhausted and despairing Henry Wise emerged from Mechanics Hall and walked around Capitol Square, passing the red-brick Bell Tower and the massive monument to George Washington. Near Tenth St., about two blocks from the Governor's Mansion, Wise chanced to meet John D. Imboden, a captain of artillery in the Virginia militia. The former governor told Imboden about his impatience with his fellow delegates at the convention and the darkness he foresaw if nothing could be done.

"Do you remember, sir, what passed between you and me, when I was governor," Wise asked, "at the moment when you thanked me for the order permitting you to have two brass field-pieces for your company of artillery at Staunton?"

"Yes, I do," Imboden replied. Wise had jokingly said that Imboden would have to obey the ex-governor's call for those guns whenever they were required.

"What was a joke then, is earnest now," Wise told Imboden. "I want those guns with which to aid in the immediate capture of the United States Arsenal at Harper's Ferry; can they be had with all the men you can raise?"

Imboden answered that they could.

Henry Wise then asked about raising troops for the expedition. Imboden named several men then in the city and promised to find more. Wise asked him to gather as many men as he could find and bring them to Henry Wise's room at the Exchange Hotel at 7:00 p.m.[10] The hotel stood on the corner of Fourteenth Street and Franklin, one block east of Capitol Square.

The captain found six prominent men to attend the meeting, including Colonel Turner Ashby and Alfred Barbour, the current superintendent of the arsenal at Harper's Ferry. Superintendent Barbour was representing Jefferson County as a pro-Union delegate at the convention.

Earlier that evening, a relative had sent Wise a telegram stating that a Massachusetts regiment had been ordered to Harper's Ferry to protect U.S. property. The guard at the Ferry consisted of only forty-five or fifty men. If they could take the Ferry before the arrival of fresh troops, all would be well.

In a room lit with brass gaslight fixtures, Wise told the men exactly what was proposed, and asked them to select a committee of three to call on Governor Letcher to get his approval for the scheme. Imboden, Oliver Funsten, and Alfred Barbour accepted the assignment.

The three men arrived at the Governor's mansion after midnight and roused Letcher from his bed. They told him what Wise was planning and asked if he would approve the scheme. The governor stated that he could take no official action until the convention had passed the Ordinance of Secession. The men then asked if Letcher would at least order the movement of troops to the vicinity of the Ferry by telegraph. He promised to send the orders in the morning.

Imboden and the others returned to the Exchange Hotel and reported on their conversation with the governor. They spent the rest of the night sending out telegrams to militia groups and arranging for special trains carrying supplies and ammunition. [11]

While the men prepared for the expedition, Wise received a telegram from William H. Parker stating that the powder magazine at the Gosport Naval Yard near Norfolk, Virginia, could be taken and the ships sunk to block the harbor. "Shall we do it?" Parker asked. Wise immediately telegraphed back a one word reply: "Yes."[12]

The following morning, Wise waited at his hotel to hear some word of the progress of Virginia militia to the Ferry. Once he had word by telegraph that the troops were on the move and that the governor had issued their travel orders, Wise rushed to the convention. The delegates were still arguing the merits of the Ordinance of Secession when Wise arrived.

Wise took the floor and told the assembly, "I know the fact... that there is a probability that blood will be flowing at Harper's Ferry before night. I know the fact that the harbor of Norfolk has been obstructed last night by the sinking of vessels. I know the fact that at this moment a force is on its way to Harper's Ferry to prevent the reinforcement of the Federal troops at that point. I am told it is already being reinforced by 1,000 men from the Black Republican ranks. I know the fact that your Governor has ordered reinforcements there to back our own citizens and to protect our lives and our arms. In the midst of a scene like this, when an attempt is made by our troops to capture the navy yard, and seize the Armory at Harper's Ferry, we are here indulging in foolish debates, the only result of which must be delay, and, perhaps, ruin." He then called for a vote on the Ordinance of Secession.[13]

A debate raged across the floor of Mechanics Hall between John B. Baldwin of Augusta, and Henry Wise. "Sir, the gentleman from Princess Anne [Mr. Wise] says that we are already in the midst of war," Baldwin told the delegates. "The Governor of this State at his instance and the instance of others, has already directed assaults to be made upon Harper's Ferry and Gosport Navy Yard."

"I did not say that," Wise rebutted.

But Baldwin held his ground. "I understood him to say that the Governor, at his instance, had directed steps to be taken with a view of taking Harper's Ferry and Gosport Navy Yard. If that is the case, I feel it to be my duty to tell my people not to march under an order that the Governor had no right to give."

"I will state...," Wise replied, "that it is to protect his people from being cut to pieces by the Wide Awakes—his people, who have marched to Harper's Ferry.... The Augusta troop are acting nobly in this matter, and I only wish my people had the honor of taking that stronghold."

"I have no doubt that my people will be found ready...," Baldwin commented, "to uphold the honor of their country.... But, sir, to me the future looks dark...; and while I trust I shall have a stout heart and strong arm to carry me through this as through any other duty to which my country may call me, while it is yet to be determined upon, my voice is against it."

At this point other delegates joined the argument. Napoleon French of Mercer County stated that he hoped the whole question could be settled "without a resort to arms," but concluded that he would vote for secession. Waitman T. Willey of Monongahela, a western county, said, "When I stand before the bar of my God, I wish to stand with my skirts all clear of the blood and the carnage which this fatal act will bring upon the State, if she shall adopt such a measure." George Baylor of Augusta asked to be excused from voting on the Ordinance of Secession. His request was granted.[14]

The debate on the question of secession continued well into the afternoon of April 17. When the vote was taken, the ordinance had 88 yeas and 55 nays.[15] In order to become official, the ordinance would have to be approved by the voters of the state. The date for this referendum was set for Thursday, May 23, 1861, more than a month later.

Once the ordinance had been passed by the convention, Wise suggested that the members reconvene that evening at 7:30. "I hope we will not adjourn over until tomorrow," Wise explained. "If we do, your secret is out at once." The delegates agreed.[16]

The convention continued its work in the days that followed, preparing a new constitution for the state and taking stock of available supplies for the war effort. But many delegates from the western counties slipped away after passage of the Ordinance of Secession to make plans of their own.

Alfred Barbour arrived by train at Harper's Ferry at 9 a.m. on April 18. The superintendent, in a somewhat disheveled state after his long train ride, told an expectant crowd that the Ordinance of Secession had passed the day before and that he supported it. He also announced that Virginia militia were preparing to take Harper's Ferry by force, and that the townspeople should accept "the new order of things." Someone in the large crowd cried, "Treason," and a fist fight broke out. No sooner had this violence been quelled when it was discovered that John Burk, a secessionist sympathizer, was guarding the telegraph office. Another riot ensued.[17]

Lieutenant Roger Jones, the leader of federal troops charged with guarding the large government complex from any further raids such as the one John Brown had instigated, appealed to the local militia for support. Only fifteen volunteers came forward, among them a giant, Jeremiah Donovan, who offered to stand guard over the armory gate, not fifty feet from the area where Burk watched over the telegraph office. In company with the fifty U.S. Army regulars, the volunteers helped Jones protect the armory and arsenal while preparations were made to detonate 25 pound kegs of gunpowder inside the buildings. Captain A. M. Kingsbury, who oversaw the entire operation, personally arranged for the destruction of the carpenter's shop at the armory.

Near sundown, Jones sent out an advance guard of citizens along the railroad and the turnpike going to Charlestown. The citizens came back at ten o'clock with news that three hundred troops in the Virginia militia were advancing from Halltown three miles to the southwest toward Bolivar Heights. News also came of 3,000 secessionist reinforcements from Winchester who would be arriving soon by train. Jones and Kingsbury consulted briefly and decided the time had come to act. They ordered the fuses lit, and within minutes, the arsenal and armory turned into blazing infernos. With nothing left to protect, Jones and Kingsbury marched the men in their command to Hagerstown, Maryland, more than twenty miles away by road, and from there traveled by omnibus, a vehicle similar to a stagecoach, only much bigger, to Chambersburg, Pennsylvania.[18]

Members of the Virginia militia who first arrived at the Ferry put out the fires. Their efforts were not in vain. Although a large portion of the arms stored in the arsenal had been destroyed, the machines to make them had not. The militia also recovered several thousand rifle barrels and gun locks—enough to prepare for the coming war.[19]

On May 23, 1861, the voters of Virginia in large numbers consented to secession. State officials at Richmond got permission to invite the fledgling Confederate government to make Richmond its capital. Since Montgomery, Alabama, did not have enough room for all the men who wished to serve in the new government, the Confederates graciously accepted the offer.

President Jefferson Davis arrived in Richmond on June 1 and made an impromptu speech from the balcony of his room at the Spotswood Hotel to well-wishers gathered on Main Street before the box-like, brick building. "Upon us is devolved the high and holy responsibility of preserving the Constitutional liberty of a free government," he told the cheering masses. "There is not one true son of the South who is not ready to shoulder his musket, to bleed, to die or to conquer in the cause of liberty here."[20]

Henry Wise also inspired the crowd at the Spotswood with his fiery rhetoric: "The man who dares to pray; the man who dares to wait until some magic arm is put into his hand; the man who will not go unless he have a minié, or percussion musket, who will not be content with flint and steel, or even a gun without a lock, is worse than a coward—he is a renegade. If he can do no better, go to a blacksmith, take a gun along as a sample, and get him to make you one like it. Get a spear—a lance. Take a lesson from John Brown. Manufacture your blades from old iron, even though it be the tires of your cartwheels. Get a bit of carriage spring, and grind and burnish it in the shape of a bowie-knife, and put it to any sort of a handle, so that it be strong— ash, hickory, oak.... Your true-blooded Yankee will never stand still in the face of cold steel."[21]

Wise proposed to take his own advice, having gained a commission as a brigadier general in the Confederate Army. His first assignment would bring him back together with two other men who had been in positions of power during John Brown's raid two years earlier. Robert E. Lee, who had captured Brown, would be his commanding officer; and John B. Floyd, Buchanan's Secretary of War who had sent Lee to Harper's Ferry, would also be serving as a brigade commander. But Floyd and Wise had been long-time political rivals, a fact which would not serve either man very well, as they both led their brigades into the Kanawha Valley on their first military campaign, an attempt to keep the western Virginia counties, which had rebelled against the Richmond government, loyal to the Confederacy.

7

"There is a just God who rides upon the whirlwind...."

Will the people of Western Va, be dragged into this infamous 'Jeff' Davis Government by the traitorous, aristocrat Convention at Richmond, with a drunken mob to help them?" Reverend Gordon Battelle of Clarksburg, Virginia, had written these strong words in a letter to Francis Harrison Pierpont.[1]

The two had been friends since they attended Allegheny College in Meadville, Pennsylvania. Battelle had become a Methodist minister and educator at the Northwestern Virginia Academy in Clarksburg, and Pierpont had become a successful lawyer and entrepreneur in Fairmont, twenty miles to the northeast. Now that Virginia was on the verge of seceding from the Union, both men's lives had been disrupted.

Battelle and other westerners like Waitman T. Willey, who had represented Monongahela County at the Convention of Secession, demanded the formation of a new state separate from the Richmond government. Similar proposals had been unsuccessful in the past, but Virginia's intention to secede from the Union had aggravated the westerners beyond endurance. They wanted to call a meeting to discuss the situation.

Battelle suggested his hometown, Clarksburg, but John S. Carlile, another representative at the Secession Convention, had already organized a gathering at Wheeling, a factory town known for its iron works. Located on the Ohio River in the panhandle of Virginia between Pennsylvania and Ohio, Wheeling was the perfect place to meet in safety. It was certainly safer than Clarksburg, which stood within a day's march

---

Francis Harrison Pierpont served as the governor of Union loyal Virginia during the Civil War.

from Confederate units stationed at Buckhannon, twenty miles to the south.

But how should the western men proceed once their meeting commenced? How were they going to protect themselves from the growing secessionist army and state militia? And how were they going to get recognition from the U.S. government?

In theory, if a state government had the right to secede from the United States, it made sense that part of a state could also secede from a state and form its own government. But the U.S. Constitution allowed for neither event, and Article 4, Section 3a, clearly stipulated that "no new State shall be formed or erected within the jurisdiction of any other State; nor any State be formed by the junction of two or more States, or parts of States, without the consent of the legislatures of the States concerned, as well as of the Congress." The Richmond government, then in rebellion against federal control, was in no mood to allow the westerners to break away and form their own "Union loyal" state. At this point in time, Pierpont could do little but wait for events to unfold.

Francis Pierpont grew up in a portion of Virginia long troubled by lack of proper representation in the state government at Richmond. Since apportionment of representation was determined in part by the number of slaves in each section, and the westerners had little use for slaves, the eastern slaveholders maintained a vice-like grip on control of the Virginia legislature. Only after much agitation from the westerners was a constitutional convention called in 1829. The western Virginians demanded equal manhood suffrage, the reform of the county court system, free public education, and the election of local sheriffs. The slaveholders refused to support any of these measures, and the 1829 state constitution passed without any substantial support from the westerners.[2]

In 1831, when Nat Turner and a band of rebellious slaves attacked and killed white people living in Southampton County, Virginia, the westerners agitated again, this time for an end to slavery. The easterners again prevented the westerners from getting their way, although the western effort nearly succeeded.[3] Agitation continued until a new state constitutional convention was called in 1850. Fearing that the westerners might secede from the convention, easterners finally gave in on the demands for apportionment of representation in the lower house of the legislature while holding onto control of the state senate. The easterners also gave themselves a tax break by decreeing that all property except slaves were to be assessed at full value. Westerners bristled under this new law which allowed a herd of sheep or cattle to be taxed at full value, while a planter who owned slaves worth a thousand dollars a piece would be taxed as though they were each worth three hundred dollars.[4]

Henry A. Wise, an easterner, had sided with the westerners during the 1850 convention. As a result, he handily won the governorship of Virginia in 1855 with the help of western voters. In gratitude, Wise helped westerners get something they had been demanding since 1831, a railroad through the Kanawha Valley. But this new Covington & Ohio Railroad caused some consternation among the westerners who had recently secured the Baltimore & Ohio Railroad running along the Potomac River through Harper's Ferry. Many citizens felt overburdened by taxation to pay for two railroads.[5]

All this agitation had forced Pierpont into the arms of the Whig party which stood in opposition to the Democratic party, a supporter of slavery. But he could not stop at being a Whig only. He was also an abolitionist.

After graduating from Allegheny College in Pennsylvania in 1839, young Frank Pierpont headed south to teach school in Mississippi and visit New Orleans while studying to become a lawyer. The trip gave him a chance to see slavery at close range. In one town, Pierpont pleaded with a slave trader for more humane treatment of a slave who had tried to run away. The slave, named Tom, was handcuffed so tightly that his wrists were bleeding. The trader told the young man to mind his own business and not meddle with other people's slaves.

Pierpont also witnessed a slave auction in New Orleans in which a new horror was on display. A beautiful young girl who did not seem to have any African features at all was lifted to the slave block. Her wavy brown hair reached to her knees. Because she kept her head down, Pierpont could not see her face, but he could see the tears from her eyes splashing at her feet as she was "knocked down" to a young man who demanded that she be delivered immediately to his home.[6]

Francis Pierpont always prided himself on having selected Julia Augusta Pierpont as a wife because she was even more rabid than he was about abolishing slavery.

On December 26, 1854, well after he had established himself as a prominent lawyer and industrialist, Frank Pierpont married Julia Augusta Robertson of New York. Ever afterward, he took pride in having married a woman far more adamant about the abolition of slavery than himself.[7] Being an abolitionist in western Virginia, however, was not easy. Two of his close friends, William Hall and Ira Hart of Clarksburg, had once been arrested for the "crime" of possession of the radical abolitionist *New York Tribune* which they circulated among friends.[8] But after the John Brown raid, Pierpont wrote some incautious words on the subject for a newspaper published in Pruntytown, a village on the Baltimore & Ohio Railroad less than fifteen miles from Pierpont's home in Fairmont.

"Ask thousands of good men in the country why they do not own slaves," he wrote. "They will tell you that they never did own any and they never will. Press the question, and they will tell you, that the system is environed with so many difficulties, that they never were involved with the institution and they never intend to be...." He pointed out that, when Northerners first opposed slavery, southern statesmen openly admitted that the institution was a "social and political evil." But in the 1840's, Senator John C. Calhoun of South Carolina proclaimed slavery "an institution of God's own appointment, for the benefit of both races," while the northern abolitionist was characterized as a "thief, robber, cut-throat and villain."[9]

By the time Lincoln was elected, Pierpont was deeply involved in the nascent Republican party. He also had four children: Samuel Robertson, born in 1855; Anna, born in 1858; and two fraternal twins (Mary Augusta and Francis William) born in September 1860, just two months before the election. With more than a little reluctance, he left his home in early May of 1861 to attend the convention Carlile had organized in Wheeling.

This first convention accomplished little. Virginia had not yet voted on the Ordinance of Secession and there was little anyone could do but wait to see how that polling would turn out. Meanwhile minor flare-ups occurred all over western Virginia between advocates of secession and loyal Union citizens.

Julia Pierpont reported one such incident in a letter to her husband. Two Virginia officers in Fairmont tried to reclaim a musket owned by the state of Virginia. The gun in question was then in the possession of the elderly Charley Scott. Mr. Scott roared out a string of expletives at the two officers who had dared to come to his house, making it clear to them that if they wanted the gun, they would have to send a whole company to collect it. The officers withdrew, but only for the moment.

On returning to Fairmont, they discovered that Charley was whitewashing for Mrs. Pierpont at her home on the corner of Pierpont Avenue and Quincy Street. When they knocked on her door, Julia opened it.

"Good morning, Madame."

"Good morn', gentlemen."

"Is Mr. Scott here?"

"He is."

"We wish to see him."

"You can not see him. Mr. Scott does not wish to see you."

"We have a message for him. Will you ask him to step to the door?"

"No, sir. You cannot see him here. If you wish to see him, you must seek him elsewhere. Of course, you will not intrude upon a lady."

"O no, certainly not. Will you be kind enough to tell Mr. Scott that Captain Thompson's orders are that he must deliver up the musket which he received and holds from the state, and if he does not do so by twelve o'clock today, he will be arrested."

"I understand that matter perfectly well, and young gentlemen, we don't care anything about it. We are not to be intimidated."[10]

The two officers bowed and Julia curtseyed before closing the door. As the officers walked away "looking very small by degrees & their nodding plum[e]s beautifully less," Julia took the opportunity to give the retreating Virginia Confederates one last broadside. Going into the front room, she threw open the windows and sang a vigorous rendition of "Hail Columbia."[11]

The next day, Francis Pierpont was back in Fairmont waiting for the vote. Meanwhile, Confederate sympathizers plotted to kidnap him and spirit him away to Richmond. Three or four of these men followed Pierpont around the steep hills of the town as he walked with his law partner, James Otis Watson. Finally, Pierpont headed for the train station where he jumped aboard a passing caboose. "You will look after my business, I know, Otis," he yelled back to his partner, "and don't forget Julia and the babies." Watson had to assure the assembled pro-Confederates that Pierpont had simply gone up the road and would be back shortly. In fact, Frank Pierpont was fleeing back to Wheeling. He cast no vote.[12]

Despite family considerations, Francis Harrison Pierpont sent his wife and children north while he took on the dangerous tasks of keeping Virginia out of the Confederacy and forming the state of West Virginia.

On May 23, the ordinance passed, but thanks to the actions of young General George Brinton McClellan, much of western Virginia was free of Confederate troops. McClellan had taken advantage of the strong Union sentiment in that section to recruit troops for the U.S. Army. He then used these soldiers on June 3 to drive Confederate forces out of Philippi, thirty miles south of Fairmont. The Confederates retreated south to Rich Mountain, near the town of Buckhannon. This made it possible for Union loyal politicians to meet in relative safety at the second convention held in the Virginia panhandle starting on June 11.

The western Virginians, meeting at Washington Hall, a three-story, yellow-gray stone building at the corner of 12th and Market Streets in Wheeling, still had no idea how to proceed, but Pierpont and others had a surprising suggestion. "The proper course...for us to pursue," he told the delegates on Monday, June 17, "is to institute a government for the whole State of Virginia." He reminded them that ex-governor Wise was now commanding forces bent on invading western Virginia, and that the U.S. Constitution guaranteed every state a republican form of government and Washington had to protect such states from invasion.[13] "The Government of the State," Pierpont continued, "is in rebellion against the United States—against the laws and the loyal people of Virginia. We, representing the loyal people of Virginia, are bound to take immediate action to protect their lives and their property." He pointed out that the Supreme Court had already ruled that, in the case where two governments existed for one state, the president of the United States would decide which is the true government. "Congress has only to see that the government so recognized is republican in form. I am sure and satisfied that the president and Congress must and will recognize us as the rightful government of the State; and will not only recognize us, but will applaud us for the course we have taken, and see that we are sustained in carrying it out."[14]

Before the end of the day, the representatives passed "A Declaration of Rights of the People of Virginia," which nullified the acts and ordinances of the Virginia Convention of Secession, declared the offices of the state vacated, and supported the formation of what would be called the "Restored Government of Virginia."[15] On Thursday, June 20, the assembly unanimously chose Francis Harrison Pierpont to serve as governor under the new Union loyal state government. Waitman T. Willey and John S. Carlile had been elected to represent Virginia in the U.S. Senate. Gordon Battelle was elected to serve on the committee

Here at Washington Hall in Wheeling, delegates met during the Civil War to form the state of West Virginia.

that would be writing the constitution for the proposed state of West Virginia.

But would President Lincoln recognize the legality of what they had done? The day after his election, Pierpont wrote Lincoln a brief and very carefully worded letter proclaiming himself the governor of Virginia and stating that "large numbers of evil-minded persons" were "now making war on the loyal people of the State." Citizens were being forced against their will into the Confederate Army, and Confederate officials were "seizing and appropriating" property.

"I have not at my command sufficient military force to suppress this rebellion and violence," he wrote. He asked Lincoln to "furnish a military force to aid in suppressing the rebellion...."[16]

Secretary of War Simon Cameron responded to Pierpont's letter on June 25, promising that a "large additional force will soon be sent to your relief" and that the troops raised by Lincoln in Virginia (Governor Letcher having refused to organize them) would now be under Pierpont's direction, and all officers for the newly formed Virginia regiments would have their commissions confirmed by Pierpont.[17]

With the strength of the federal government behind him, Governor Pierpont called the "Restored Government" into session on July 2. He apologized for not letting the men go home to their families for the summer, and explained that they were engaged in a struggle to protect their own freedom. "But ... we must not despair, or fold our hands," he said. "There is a just God who 'rides upon the whirlwind and directs the storm.' Let us look to him with abiding confidence."[18]

While they had launched themselves well on the way to independence, the western men faced a long, uphill battle for recognition and support. What they had done, forming a government which represented only a small minority of the actual population of Virginia, was barely legal, and might be successfully challenged in the courts. And if the national government should ever officially recognize the Richmond government for even an instant, their house of cards could fall to ruin.

For the moment, Pierpont and the westerners applied themselves to the operations of the government and the formation of the state of West Virginia, and prayed that somehow their efforts would bear fruit.

173 Say, Brothers, Will You Meet Us.

From "Lee Avenue Casket." By permission.   Arr. by Franklin H. Lummus.

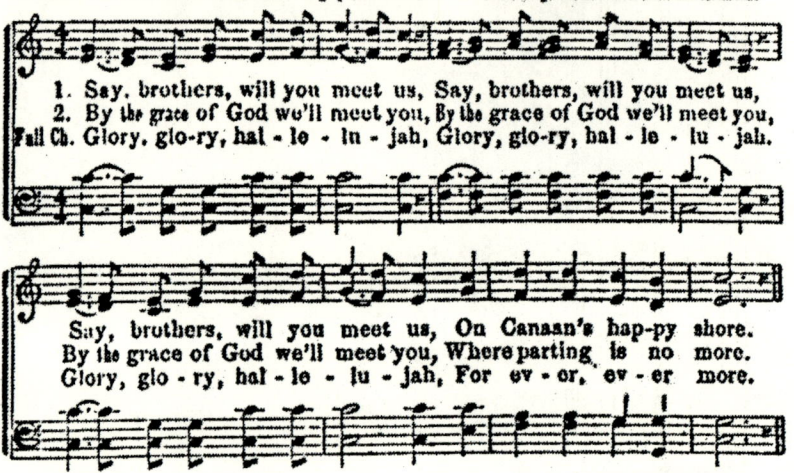

1. Say, brothers, will you meet us, Say, brothers, will you meet us,
2. By the grace of God we'll meet you, By the grace of God we'll meet you,

Full Ch. Glory, glo-ry, hal - le - lu - jah, Glory, glo-ry, hal - le - lu - jah.

Say, brothers, will you meet us, On Canaan's hap-py shore.
By the grace of God we'll meet you, Where parting is no more.
Glory, glo - ry, hal - le - lu - jah, For ev - er, ev - er more.

Jesus lives and reigns for ever,
Jesus lives and reigns for ever,
Jesus lives and reigns for ever,
On Canaan's happy shore.

CHO. — Glory, glory, hallelujah,
Glory, glory, hallelujah,
Glory, glory, hallelujah,
For ever, evermore.

8

"John Brown's body lies a moulderin' in the grave...."

ohn Albion Andrew, recently elected governor of Massachusetts, received a letter dated April 13, 1861, from his friend, Dr. Samuel Gridley Howe. Andrew had served as Howe's legal counsel in 1859, when Howe feared extradition to the South to testify at Brown's trial. The doctor was elated about the bombardment of Fort Sumter which marked the start of a war between North and South. He asked that the political leaders "see to it that war shall not cease until emancipation is secure," and offered his services to the governor "in any capacity (save that of spy.)" The governor put his friend to work as a medical inspector in an organization which soon developed into the U.S. Sanitary Commission.[1]

Governor Andrew had many other preparations to make at the beginning of the war. Lincoln's call for 75,000 volunteers on April 15 demanded a quick response. Regiments had to be raised. Clothing, equipment, guns, and ammunition had to be provided for the volunteers. Andrew was soon making recommendations to the War Department concerning the production of guns at armories, the development of experimental weapons, and ways of protecting Harper's Ferry which, it was rumored, was about to be attacked by the Virginia militia.[2]

Most of all, Governor Andrew wanted to garrison the forts in Boston Harbor, an expanse of ocean water east of the city filled with treacherous shoals, uncertain currents, and tiny islands. It was especially important to place troops at Lovell's Island, and at the nearly completed Fort Warren on George's Island.

This hymn first appeared in print in 1858. The "Tiger" battalion made up new words for it partly to honor the abolitionist John Brown, and partly to spoof the activities of a certain Sergeant John Brown.

Fort Warren and Lovell's Island overlooked the deepest navigable sea channel coming into the inner part of Boston Harbor. If the Confederates were able to put together a navy of any size and they sent those ships to Boston Harbor to shell the state capitol, the vessels would first have to pass under the guns at these two forts. Warren, in particular, was a state-of-the-art, star-shaped fortification.

Enemy forces attacking this fort from the sea would face a formidable line of obstacles. Landing on the northern sea wall, they would first have to charge up a grassy, sloped outer wall called a coverface, while taking fire from the upper walls of the fort's interior ramparts. Assuming they made it to the top of the coverface, the troops would then have to descend about fifteen feet into a dry moat. They would then be facing fire from musket loop holes cut in the side of the interior wall, and from a demilune, a semicircular structure at the bottom of the dry moat from which soldiers could fire along the full length of the moat.[3]

Andrew applied to Major General John E. Wool, inspector general for the War Department, for permission to garrison the harbor forts. Wool gladly granted Andrew's request, but by the time permission came, the governor had already sent the Second Battalion, Boston Light Infantry, commanded by Major Ralph W. Newton, to Fort Warren.[4] In doing so, he had set in motion a chain of events which would bring John Brown back from the dead.

When the Second Battalion, also called the "Tiger" Battalion, arrived on the damp, wind-swept island on April 29, 1861, the buildings and fortifications were completed, but the workmen had left piles of rubble all over Fort Warren's parade ground. The "Tigers" were given the task of cleaning up the mess.[5] While they worked, the musical members of the "Tigers" sang hymns, national airs, and popular songs to pass the time.

Henry J. Hallgreen of the "Tigers" heard two homesick recruits from Maine singing a mournful hymn called "Say, Brothers, will you meet us?" The melody had a nice lilt to it, and its chorus of "Glory, Glory, Hallelujah" was irresistible to Hallgreen's ear. The fact that the song consisted of one verse repeated three times with a simple tag-line for the fourth verse made its verses easy to remember. Hallgreen quickly learned it and taught it to members of the Second Battalion who then sang it as they worked, and eventually invented new verses for it.[6]

During the Civil War, Fort Warren served to guard the seaways into Boston Harbor and as a prison for captured Confederates.

The most popular of these new verses may have been suggested by one version of the song published by Charles Dunbar in 1858. Dunbar had added a verse to the song which goes as follows:

> Must my body lie slumbering in the ground,
> While the spirit rests with God.[7]

This verse, if known to the battalion, would have been very significant, because in their ranks, they had a living, breathing corpse in the person of Sergeant John Brown.

The fact that Sergeant Brown, of Scottish ancestry, shared his name with the fiery abolitionist who had been hanged at Charlestown, Virginia, led to many jokes and comments from his companions. Whenever the sergeant showed up a few minutes late for assembly, someone would remark that Brown would have to arrive on time in future if he wanted to free the slaves.[8]

On another occasion, soldiers returning from Boston were greeted with the question "What news from the city?" One of Brown's companions on the boat noticed the sergeant sitting near the guardhouse and shouted, "Oh, nothing special, except John Brown's dead." Brown, who normally took this gentle ribbing without comment, fretted and fumed. Another member of the battalion remarked, "He's a pretty lively corpse, any way, and moves around considerably."[9]

Brown was part of a singing group which included Henry Hallgreen, and James E. Greenleaf, an organist for the Harvard Church in Charlestown, Massachusetts. In the process of teasing Sergeant Brown, Hallgreen invented the verse, "John Brown's body lies a moulderin' in the grave," and Greenleaf came up with the tag-line, "His soul is marching on."[10]

Once this first verse was completed, more followed which commented on the antics and adventures of Sergeant Brown. "He's gone to be soldier in the Army of the Lord," commemorates the fact that the sergeant, along with many other members of the "Tiger" battalion which was not large enough to be mustered into the U.S. Army, joined Colonel Fletcher Webster's new regiment, the Twelfth Massachusetts Volunteers, also stationed at Fort Warren. "John Brown's knapsack is strapped upon his back," was inspired by the trouble Sergeant Brown had adjusting his knapsack and bedroll. Another line which followed up this verse, "It is filled with leaden bullets and moldy hardtack," was cut from the song.[11]

The "Tigers" wanted to include a verse in the song about what they would do to Jefferson Davis, the president of the Confederacy, if they caught him. Since Davis had been accused of stealing apples (i.e., states) from the national orchard, their first thought was "We'll feed him on sour apples till he has the di-ar-rhee!" Eventually they decided to replace this verse with the simpler and less subtle, "They will hang

ROBBERY OF THE NATIONAL APPLE ORCHARD.

PRESIDENT LINCOLN. "I say, Jeff, this thing has been going on long enough. Suppose you drop those apples now and come down."

JEFF DAVIS. "Please don't shoot, Mr. Lincoln, ALL I WANT IS TO BE LET ALONE!" *

This cartoon from Harper's Weekly *may have led to the creation of the verse in the John Brown song: "We'll hang Jeff Davis to a sour apple tree."*

Jeff Davis to a tree." This verse evolved over the course of the war to become the more familiar, "We'll hang Jeff Davis to a sour apple tree."[12]

With only a few verses written down, this new song was first performed at Fort Warren on May 12, 1861, with the assistance of William J. Martland's Brockton Band. The occasion was a flag raising, followed by an address given with patriotic fervor by Chaplain George Hepworth. At the close of Hepworth's remarks, the band began to play the song and the men joined in singing the unpolished lyrics. Patrick Sarsfield Gilmore's band, which frequently alternated at the fort with the Brockton Band, also picked up the song and started spreading it through the army.[13]

None of this appealed to Major Newton of the "Tigers." Although the song reported some of the doings of Sergeant Brown, the ultimate intention of the song was to honor that murdering abolitionist, Old Osawatomie Brown. The major warned his men that if they wanted to continue "howl[ing] that John Brown tune," they should write verses for it about some other fallen hero and avoid being "tainted with the stigma of abolitionism."[14] It was not until May 24, nearly two weeks after the song's official premiere, that a suitable hero was found, one that threatened John Brown's newly acquired position as the conscience of the nation.

His name was Colonel Elmer Ephraim Ellsworth, flamboyant leader of the dashing Eleventh New York Fire Zouaves. His untimely death, worthy of the hero in a Wagnerian opera, stunned the nation, and gave the American people a new kind of patriot to sing about.

Born in 1837 in Mechanicville, Saratoga County, New York, Ellsworth grew up on a steady diet of poetry, particularly that of Tennyson, and embraced the ideals of knighthood and chivalry. In later years, he took lessons in fencing from a French master who introduced him to the techniques of combat prescribed by the colorfully uniformed Zouave troops of French Algeria. Ellsworth spent hours mastering the French language so that he could read more about the Zouaves and their methods.[15]

While working as an office clerk in Chicago in the late 1850's, Ellsworth took charge of a depressed group of amateur soldiers. Drilling the men with an iron hand four or five hours a day, three days a week, he soon helped them master some five hundred complex drill maneuvers. Once this was accomplished, he dressed his troops in Zouave style: crimson kepis, gold-embroidered light blue shirts, short dark-blue "monkey jackets," red baggy trousers, and drab gaiters. His Chicago Zouave Cadets, armed with muskets, bayonets, and foot-long bowie knives, were now prepared for national competitions.

Colonel Ellsworth, leader of the New York Fire Zouaves, helped form colorful Zouave units all over the United States.

In 1859, the cadets won the national championship in a drill contest in Chicago. They then toured extensively in the East and South spreading the knowledge that a new kind of soldier had arrived in America. The idea of Zouave troops caught on everywhere, and soon many towns and states had their own Zouave cadet corps.[16]

By the time of the presidential election of 1860, Ellsworth was working in the law office of Lincoln and Herndon in Springfield. The energetic young man gladly campaigned for Lincoln in Illinois, and after the election, accompanied Lincoln to Washington as an unofficial bodyguard. In gratitude for all of Ellsworth's help, President Lincoln secured a commission for him as a lieutenant in the First Dragoons. But Ellsworth had more ambition than could be realized as a horse-soldier. Resigning his commission, he left for New York City where he recruited the city's firemen for a regiment of Zouave troops, the Eleventh New York.[17]

Dressed in the usual Zouave style with gaiters, gray baggy pants, and gray monkey jackets with maroon trim, Ellsworth's Fire Zouaves were mustered into the U.S. Army on May 7, 1861. They caused a major sensation in Washington as part of the growing Army of the Potomac. For the sheer fun of it, the firemen climbed all over the walls of the

Here on the parade ground at Fort Warren, soldiers in the "Tiger" Battalion made up a song called "John Brown's Body."

unfinished capitol building. Some of the men borrowed a fire engine from the Franklin engine house and drove all over the city ringing the bell.[18]

On May 23, after the people of Virginia gave their approval to secession from the Union, the Fire Zouaves attended to more serious business. On that day, the Union Army prepared to make a massive incursion into northern Virginia to set up a buffer zone between Washington and the Confederacy. Ellsworth's regiment was scheduled to move across the Potomac River into Alexandria, Virginia, in the early morning hours of May 24.

The boyish colonel prepared for the coming combat in the manner of men who have never been in battle. First he wrote letters to his parents in Mechanicville and his fiancée, eighteen-year-old Carrie Spafford of Rockford, Illinois. The two letters begin with a statement that he is about to see action for the first time and that he might be injured or worse. To his parents, he wrote, "I am perfectly content to accept whatever my fortune may be, confident that he who knoweth even the fall of a sparrow will have some purpose even in the fate of one like me."[19] In Carrie's letter, he continued this theme of his own mortality: "If anything should happen—Darling just accept this assurance, the only thing I can leave you—the highest happiness I looked for on earth was a union with you."[20]

This done, he dressed in his best uniform: red kepi, blue jacket with gold trim, red baggy trousers, and gaiters. At the time, he mentioned to one of his captains that he was selecting the clothes in which he would die.[21]

Near dawn, the Eleventh New York boarded the U.S.S. *Pawnee* for the journey to Alexandria.[22] The crossing proved less hazardous than Ellsworth had originally imagined; only five hundred Confederate soldiers guarded the town. A few Confederate sentinels, who had been warned under flag of truce some hours earlier to vacate the village, fired their guns into the air and fled as the *Pawnee* approached. The Fire Zouaves were on shore and forming into companies by 5 a.m.

Colonel Ellsworth ordered Company E to tear up the railroad tracks going to Richmond. Leaving Lieutenant Colonel Noah P. Farnham in charge of the remaining men, Ellsworth left with a small party to take the telegraph office. With him were four corporals, including Corporal Francis E. Brownell; Edward House, correspondent for the radical *New York Tribune*; H. J. Winser, the regimental secretary; and Chaplain E. W. Dodge.

While marching the detachment through the streets, Ellsworth caught sight of a Confederate Stars and Bars flying from the roof of the Marshall House, a three-story hotel. For the past month, President Lincoln had complained to Ellsworth that this flag was visible from the White House. With some hesitation, Colonel Ellsworth decided to forego taking the telegraph office until he could bring down that offensive flag.

The colonel drew his sword and charged into the hotel with seven men behind him. He discovered a barefooted man dressed in a shirt and trousers pulling up his suspenders.

"Who put that flag up?" Ellsworth demanded.

"I don't know," the man answered bluntly. "I am a boarder here."

Ellsworth posted one corporal on the door, one at the foot of the stairs, and one on the first floor. Corporal Brownell, House, Winser,

Colonel Ellsworth was killed while removing a Confederate flag from the Marshall House in Alexandria, Virginia (pictured above). He nearly replaced John Brown in popularity as a national hero and martyr to the cause of freedom.

and Dodge followed their impetuous leader up the stairs. In the attic, Ellsworth and Winser climbed onto the roof and used a conveniently placed ladder to reach the flag staff. The colonel handed his gun to Winser and borrowed Winser's knife to cut the halyards and bring down the flag.

This done, the two men climbed back through the attic window, and tramped with the rest of the party down the stairs. Corporal Brownell, carrying a rifle with a long saber bayonet attached, went first. Ellsworth followed while folding the large flag. House was to the rear of Ellsworth with his hand on his shoulder. Winser followed House. (It is not known where Chaplain Dodge was at this time.)

On the first landing, Corporal Brownell confronted a civilian carrying a double-barreled shotgun, the same man who had told them he was just a boarder. He was, in fact, James W. Jackson, the proprietor of the Marshall House. Using his rifle, Brownell parried Jackson's shotgun, but not before Jackson pulled the trigger. The corporal aimed and fired his weapon point-blank into Jackson's face and jabbed him with his bayonet. Only then did he dare reload his weapon.

Someone shouted, "My God." Winser asked loudly, "Who is hit?" Colonel Ellsworth's body lay on the stairs, his blood flowing from a chest wound onto the rebel flag. It was later discovered that an ornamental gold button had been driven into his chest by the shotgun blast. The button carried the legend in Latin: "Non Solum Nobis sed Pro Patria," which means, "Not for ourselves alone, but for country."

The officers carried Ellsworth's body to a room and laid it on a bed with the bloody flag over his feet. Before they were finished, Jackson's wife arrived in the smoke-filled corridor. She ran to her husband's lifeless form and screamed in a frenzy of grief and rage which lasted for some minutes, the soldiers being unable to console her.

House, the reporter for the *Tribune*, remembered that Colonel Ellsworth was supposed to take the telegraph office. He borrowed a revolver from Winser and left to organize a detachment to finish the job. Meanwhile, Brownell and the other corporals stationed themselves on each floor, threatening to shoot any residents who tried to leave their rooms.

Ellsworth's body was moved to the Navy Yard where, that afternoon, President and Mrs. Lincoln tearfully gazed at the body. "My boy! my boy! was it necessary this sacrifice should be made!" the president said in broken tones. Later, the colonel's remains were placed in the East Room of the White House where a funeral service was held. After that, his body was shipped home by rail to Mechanicville, causing as much of a stir as John Brown's rail journey had caused in December of 1859.

By the time word of Ellsworth's death reached Fort Warren, many members of the "Tigers" singing group, including Sergeant Brown, were serving in the Twelfth Massachusetts. Their colonel was Fletcher Webster, a son of Daniel Webster who had been a major critic of slavery. Colonel Webster had no objection to the men in his command singing anti-slavery songs. But the songsters believed they had a better subject in the spirited and gallant Ellsworth than they did in the bearded abolitionist from New England who had killed unarmed civilians in the name of freedom. They resolved to transform their air into a tribute to Colonel Ellsworth.

With every verse they created, John Brown's marching spirit moved closer to oblivion. Old Osawatomie might certainly have been forgotten forever were it not for the fact that the new verses were clumsy and not very appealing: "We lament the death of Colonel Ellsworth;" "Ellsworth's death we will avenge;" and "When Ellsworth died he died like a brave." The "Tigers" soon got bored with the Zouave colonel and returned to John Brown's mouldering body, but they did keep one verse from the Ellsworth version: "His pet lambs will meet him on the way." (Ellsworth sometimes referred to the soldiers in his command as "pet lambs.")[23]

To put the entire song in proper shape for its first printing, James Greenleaf went to his friend C. S. Hall of Charlestown, Massachusetts. Hall was given the task of selecting the final verses for the song from the many that had been created since May. He chose five and added a sixth of his own: "Now three rousing cheers for the Union."[24] These verses without music were first printed on a sheet of paper called a broadside, and later, with the help of C. B. Marsh, on a second broadside using music.

The men of the Twelfth Massachusetts had the opportunity to sing the new song in Boston on July 18, the day they received their battle flags, commonly called "colors." Usually there were two flags in the set: one based on the "Stars and Stripes" and one based on the state flag where the regiment was recruited. Both banners bore the name of the regiment. If the soldiers ever saw combat, their flags would be painted to include the names of the engagements in which they fought.

Around 4 p.m., the regiment marched in review three times on Boston Common while Governor John Andrew and other members of the state government looked on. After the review, the commissioned officers and color guard were ordered to the front. Edward Everett, the well-known orator, presented the flags on behalf of the ladies of Boston. Commenting on the federal flag, Everett said, "It bears upon its field as a motto, ...the soul-stirring words, 'Not a stripe erased or polluted, not a single star obscured.'" He explained that similar flags had been "borne by the armies of the United States...from the shores of Canada to the burning plains of Mexico.... They are now displayed in defence of the Union itself, in this most unrighteous and fratricidal war."[25]

Colonel Webster, in accepting the colors for the regiment, promised Everett, "When next, sir, you shall see this banner, it may offer a strong contrast to its present radiant appearance. You may see its brilliancy gone, its gay colors dimmed with smoke, and its silken folds battered by shot, but it shall never bear a stain of dishonor."[26]

By 6 p.m., the festivities ended, and the regiment marched down State Street toward the harbor singing "John Brown's Body."

This first performance in Boston caused enough of a sensation to stir some of the city's loyal citizens to invent new verses for the song. One individual, Johnny Rounders, inspired by an excess of rum, sang a loud and impromptu, "John Brown's bones hang dangling in the air," to his disgruntled neighbors. A passing police officer immediately arrested him for causing a disturbance.[27]

On Tuesday, July 23, the Twelfth Massachusetts prepared to leave Fort Warren for the front. The soldiers dressed for the occasion in white havelocks, and carried their greatcoats on top of their knapsacks folded in such a way as to display the red inner lining. Once in Boston, the 1,040 men, most armed with Enfield rifled muskets, marched up State Street toward Old Colony Depot while singing "John Brown's Body."

In the crowds of spectators that day was Franklin Sanborn, one of the six northern backers of John Brown's raid. On hearing the song, Sanborn turned to a college friend from Baltimore and asked, "What are they singing?" The friend told Sanborn that a boy on the sidewalk was selling broadsides of the song. "I approached [the boy]," Franklin later reported, "and bought a handbill which, without the music, contained the rude words of the John Brown song, which I then heard for the first time, but listened to a thousand times afterward during the progress of the emancipating Civil War."[28]

By the next evening, the Twelfth Massachusetts was marching down Broadway in New York City singing the John Brown song again. The song, which was published a few days later in the *New York Tribune*, gained some attention among the city's fastidious music critics, professional and amateur. The acerbic Richard Grant White who wrote music columns for several New York newspapers called the song a "nonsensical farrago," but admitted that "the alternate jig and swing of the air caused it to stick in the uneducated ear as burrs stick to a blackberry girl." White's friend, George Templeton Strong, a New York lawyer, called the soldier's effort a "queer, rude song," but compared John Brown to the fourteenth century English scholar and philosopher John Wycliffe, who had openly opposed the Pope of Rome. Strong expected that Brown would some day be considered the "Wycliffe of the anti-slavery Reformation."[29]

Although Ellsworth's name would still be associated with some versions of this song, the "Tigers'" musical effort would henceforth be closely associated with the man who had dared to free slaves by attacking Harper's Ferry. The song even provided a special name for the Twelfth Massachusetts which had adopted it as its official song. Soon people all over Massachusetts and New England would be praising the exploits of Colonel Fletcher Webster's "Hallelujah" regiment.

As the song spread through the Union Army, so did a new concept of John Brown as a hero of legendary proportions. And as the Union Army marched through the South, giving soldiers their first glimpse of slavery, many who had opposed Brown before came to the conclusion that the old man had been right to wage war on enforced servitude.

Part III

THE GHOST GOES MARCHING ON!

9

"Mine eyes have seen the glory..."

I n late May, Julia Ward Howe noticed an interesting advertisement in the newspaper. Some gentlemen in New York City had formed a committee to come up with a national anthem for the country. The group included two former U.S. senators and a variety of public officials, historians, and news columnists.[1]

Perhaps the most important person on the committee was the aging professional soldier and politician, John A. Dix. On January 11, 1861, during the period that secession sympathizers were abandoning their government posts in the Buchanan administration, the staunch unionist Dix had replaced Philip F. Thomas of Maryland as secretary of the treasury. Two weeks later, Dix received a note from a nervous revenue officer in New Orleans who was concerned that rebels might take down the United States flag from the U.S. Revenue Cutter *Robert McClelland*. Secretary Dix telegraphed back, "If any one attempts to haul down the American flag, shoot him on the spot." The *McClelland* was taken anyway, but Dix achieved everlasting fame from his telegram.

At the commencement of the Civil War, there were already three contenders for the top honor of national song, although the New York committee felt each was totally unsuitable for the purpose:

"Yankee Doodle" dated back to the time of the French and Indian Wars. In 1758, Dr. Richard Shuckburg, a British army doctor serving in America, wrote the song intending to make fun of the English colonists and their ways. His joke backfired. The colonists loved the song so much that they wrote their own verses for it.

"Hail Columbia" or "The President's March" was originally an instrumental piece written in 1789 by Philadelphia violinist Philip

---

Although Julia Ward Howe felt she could make no contribution to the war effort, she did write patriotic poems, including the "Battle Hymn of the Republic."

Phylo for President George Washington's inauguration in New York City. Although the complex melody was never meant to be sung, Joseph Hopkinson wrote words for the tune in 1798.

"The Star Spangled Banner," written by Francis Scott Key to commemorate the unsuccessful British attack on Fort McHenry near Baltimore on September 13-14, 1814, was the strongest contender, but for the tune Key had chosen "To Anachreon in Heaven," a British drinking song which is barely singable even when one is inebriated.

Writing for the committee, Richard Grant White commented that "people stood mute" while "The Star Spangled Banner" was sung by one person. He dismissed "Yankee Doodle" as a "mere childish burlesque," and considered "Hail Columbia" "common-place, vulgar, and pretentious."[2] The committee offered a reward of $500 for anyone who could come up with a song that was "purely patriotic" but "not a war song." It had to have between 16 and 40 lines, and the melody should be appealing but simple enough that it could be "readily sung by ordinary voices."[3]

Mrs. Howe, who complained that she "could not leave [her] nursery to follow the march of our armies," and that she lacked the "practical deftness which the preparing and packing of sanitary stores demanded,"[4] had enough skill as a poet to make a modest submission to the New York committee. Her poem, entitled "Our Country," invoked images of the pilgrims who had settled Massachusetts:

> O Exile of the wrath of Kings!
> O Pilgrim Ark of Liberty!
> The refuge of divinest things,
> Their record must abide in thee.[5]

Unfortunately, the national anthems submitted to the committee were found unsuitable. Most of them had bland, unimaginative titles such as "National Hymn," "A National Hymn," "The Nation's Hymn," or "Hymn of Our Union." The committee members also rejected some entries which were too fanciful for popular taste. Charles Farnham wrote an eerie poem called "Our Fathers' Graves," which modern readers might think more appropriate for Memorial Day than the Fourth of July:

> That land is ours—that beauteous land
>   Where Marion and Sumpter rest;
> And Jackson's tomb—Oh, let it stand
>   To guard the gateway of the West!
> Preserve the grave of Washington—
>   His land—his name—his home, is ours!
> To Vernon's mount, march on, march on,
>   And strew your Father's grave with flowers.[6]

The New England poet John Pierpont chose to write verses to the tune of "To Anachreon in Heaven" which had already been declared unsingable. His effort, called "E Pluribus Unum," describes the harmony of states in the Union in very erudite ways. In the verse that follows, Pierpont compares that harmony to the motions of the planets:

> The science that measures and numbers the spheres,
>   And has done so since first the Chaldean began it,
> Now and then, as she counts them, and measures their years,
>   Brings into our system and names a new planet.
>   Yet the old and new stars,
>   Venus, Neptune, and Mars,
>   As they drive round the sun their invisible cars,
> Whether faster or slower their races are run,
> Are "E Pluribus Unum"— of many made one.[7]

The committee's work ended abruptly in August 1861 after the members had received some 1200 songs and poems from all over the globe. No winner was named, but those submissions thought to contain some merit (and Mrs. Howe's was not one of those) were published in a book, the proceeds from its sale going to a patriotic fund. All the other entries were burned.[8]

Out of force of habit, Mrs. Howe continued to write verses inspired by the war and hoped that one or another of them would gain national attention. She had already devoted her literary energies to a poem commemorating the death of four soldiers in the Sixth Massachusetts killed in the streets of Baltimore on Friday, April 19, 1861. The regiment had been marching through the city on its way to a Washington train when they encountered armed citizens. The civilians fired into their ranks, and the soldiers discharged their muskets into the hostile crowd. Julia chose the title "Our Orders" for her gloomy verses:

Weave no more silks, ye Lyons looms,
   To deck our girls for gay delights!
The crimson flower of battle blooms,
   And solemn marches fill the nights.[9]

More verses followed as inspiration moved her to write, but it was not until November 1861 that, as she later wrote, "a word was given me to say, which did strengthen the hearts of those who fought in the field and of those who languished in the prison."[10]

At that time, Julia traveled with Dr. Howe, Reverend James Freeman Clarke (her minister), and Governor Andrew to Washington, D.C. Samuel Gridley Howe's work for the Sanitary Commission and his concern for ending slavery as quickly as possible brought him to Washington frequently. While traveling by train through Maryland, Julia noticed soldiers posted along the railroads and gathered around campfires. Her husband explained that the soldiers guarded the railroad. In fact, the whole of Washington was surrounded on all sides by the great Army of the Potomac to protect the capital from attack.

The travelers saw troops everywhere around the area: companies of artillery with their cannons and pyramids of case, canister, or solid shot beside each gun; rows of marching men, rifles fixed with bayonets; even within the city limits, army officers galloped through the streets, and ambulances drawn by four-horse teams ran to and fro. Once the party reached the Willard's Hotel, Julia was appalled that, from the window of her room, she could see a grisly advertisement for an agency devoted to the embalming and transport home of soldiers who died either in battle or of the fevers that swept with deadly efficiency through the camps.[11]

In the days that followed, Mrs. Howe visited army bivouacs and hospitals in company with Reverend Clarke and William Henry Channing, nephew of the Boston Unitarian minister and author William Ellery Channing. But the memory she cherished most was of a visit arranged by Governor Andrew to the White House to see President Lincoln. Seated before Gilbert Stuart's famous portrait of Washington, Julia listened in on a long conversation between the president and the Massachusetts governor. "I remember well," she wrote afterward, "the sad expression of Mr. Lincoln's deep blue eyes, the only feature of his face which could be called other than plain."

In 1861, Massachusetts poet John Pierpont submitted a poem "E Pluribus Unum" to a contest to come up with a national anthem. Although he did not win, his poem still survives.

Mrs. Andrew asked Lincoln when it would be possible to meet his wife. The president gave the day of the next White House reception and continued his conversation with Governor Andrew, saying, "I once heerd George Sumner tell a story." The backwoods pronunciation stuck in Julia's mind. Once the interview ended and the president had gone off to attend to other duties, Reverend Clarke gave his impression of

Lincoln. "We have seen it in his face," he said in exasperation. "Hopeless honesty; that is all."[12]

On Monday, November 18, Mrs. Howe was invited to attend one of General George McClellan's troop reviews at Munson's Hill, Virginia, in Union occupied territory. She rode out to the review in a carriage with James Freeman Clarke and Mr. and Mrs. Edwin P. Whipple. In the middle of the display, Confederates pulled a surprise raid in the area, causing the review to be canceled. The spectators returned to their carriages and attempted to get back to Washington on roads jammed with soldiers.

To pass the time, Julia and her party sang popular army songs, including "John Brown's Body." Soldiers marching past the carriage said, "Good for you," and joined in the chorus. Reverend Clarke asked, "Mrs. Howe, why do you not write some good words for that stirring tune?" She commented that she had often wanted to do so, but had not yet found any verses for it.[13]

Julia described what happened next in her *Reminiscences*:

I went to bed that night as usual, and slept, according to my wont, quite soundly. I awoke in the gray of the morning twilight; and as I lay waiting for the dawn, the long lines of the desired poem began to twine themselves in my mind. Having thought out all the stanzas, I said to myself, "I must get up and write these verses down, lest I fall asleep again and forget them." So, with a sudden effort, I sprang out of bed, and found in the dimness an old stump of a pen which I remembered to have used the day before. I scrawled the verses almost without looking at the paper. I had learned to do this when, on previous occasions, attacks of versification had visited me in the night, and I feared to have recourse to a light lest I should wake the baby, who slept near me. I was always obliged to decipher my scrawl before another night should intervene, as it was only legible while the matter was fresh in my mind. At this time, having completed my writing, I returned to bed and fell asleep, saying to myself, "I like this better than most things that I have written."[14]

The six verses she wrote combined passages from the Bible with the sights and sounds of wartime Washington. Artillery shot was transformed into "grapes of wrath." The campfires for the Army of the Potomac became "the watchfires of a hundred circling camps" which

Rev. James Freeman Clarke asked Julia Ward Howe to write new words to the song "John Brown's Body."

THE

ATLANTIC MONTHLY.

A MAGAZINE OF LITERATURE, ART, AND POLITICS.

VOL. IX.—FEBRUARY, 1862.—NO. LII.

BATTLE HYMN OF THE REPUBLIC.

MINE eyes have seen the glory of the coming of the Lord :
He is trampling out the vintage where the grapes of wrath are stored ;
He hath loosed the fateful lightning of His terrible swift sword :
    His truth is marching on.

I have seen Him in the watch-fires of a hundred circling camps ;
They have builded Him an altar in the evening dews and damps ;
I can read His righteous sentence by the dim and flaring lamps :
    His day is marching on.

I have read a fiery gospel writ in burnished rows of steel :
" As ye deal with my contemners, so with you my grace shall deal ;
Let the Hero, born of woman, crush the serpent with his heel,
    Since God is marching on."

He has sounded forth the trumpet that shall never call retreat ;
He is sifting out the hearts of men before His judgment-seat :
Oh, be swift, my soul, to answer Him ! be jubilant, my feet !
    Our God is marching on.

In the beauty of the lilies Christ was born across the sea,
With a glory in his bosom that transfigures you and me :
As he died to make men holy, let us die to make men free,
    While God is marching on.

Entered according to Act of Congress, in the year 1862, by TICKNOR AND FIELDS, in the Clerk's Office
of the District Court of the District of Massachusetts.

were so bright that she could read God's "righteous sentence" by their "dim and flaring lamps." A bugle blast suggested "the trumpet that shall never call retreat." It may also be true that John Brown, the man who had died to end slavery "even as Christ had willingly offered his life for the salvation of mankind," was not very far from her thoughts that night. Wouldn't it be a sacred honor for men to die in this terrible war not just to preserve the Union, but also to "make men free."[15]

In the weeks that followed, Mrs. Howe polished every part of this new poem. For example, "He is trampling out the wine press" was changed to "He is trampling out the vintage," and "He has waked the earth's dull bosom with a high ecstatic beat" in the fourth verse was transformed into "He is sifting out the hearts of men before his judgment seat." A problem also arose because the tag-line for the third to sixth verses was always "Our God is marching on." To compensate, she varied the first word of the line. The sixth verse also caused problems:

> He is coming like the glory of the morning on the wave;
> He is wisdom to the mighty, he is honor to the brave;
> So the world shall be his footstool, and the soul of wrong
>   his slave.
> Our God is marching on.

It was a very fine set of lines, but it detracted from the drama of the fifth verse about Jesus, who had "died to make men holy." She eliminated it from the final version.

By early December, the poem was ready for submission. She sent it to James T. Fields, editor of the *Atlantic Monthly* with a curious note: "Fields! Do you want this, and do you like it, and have you any room for it in January number? I am sad and spleeny, and begin to have fears that I may not be after all, the greatest woman alive." Fields gave her five dollars for it and provided it with a suitable title: "Battle Hymn of the Republic." It appeared in the February 1862 issue of the magazine.[16]

Julia Ward Howe's "Battle Hymn of the Republic" as it first appeared in the Atlantic Monthly.

In early January of 1862, one month before the debut of Mrs. Howe's new poem, John Hutchinson, the itinerant musician who had arranged for the bells in Barre, Massachusetts, to toll the death of John Brown, was in Washington seeking permission to give concerts for the Army of the Potomac.[17] He traveled in company with his daughter Viola, a contralto, and son Henry, a tenor. A close friend, Frank Martin, sang the bass parts. John's wife, Fanny who often traveled with the group, was stuck discontentedly at their home in High Rock, Lynn, Massachusetts. She was expecting yet another child.

On Tuesday, January 7, just after doing a concert in Georgetown, the Hutchinsons attended a reception at the White House. President and Mrs. Lincoln recognized John Hutchinson at once and asked the group to sing. They performed "The War-drums Are Beating—Up, Soldiers, and Fight." President Lincoln then requested "Ship on Fire," a piece he had heard the Hutchinsons do in Springfield, Illinois, some years ago. The music, one of the more dramatic concoctions of the nineteenth century, required special effects for a thunderstorm on the ocean, and the terrified screams of trapped voyagers. A keyboard instrument of some kind was required, but no one had the key to the White House piano. After some searching, the key was found, but the piano proved to be horribly out of tune. John sent for his melodeon, and the White House visitors soon got the thrill of hearing the singers' bold rendition of the song:

> The cheeks of the sailors grew pale at the sight—
> And their eyes glistened wild in the gleam of the light—
> And the smoke in thick wreaths mounted higher and higher—
> Oh God it is fearful to perish by fire![18]

About a week later, Hutchinson saw his long-time friend, Salmon P. Chase, secretary of the treasury. Chase sent him to Simon Cameron, the secretary of war, to get the needed papers for crossing into Union-occupied Virginia. Cameron gladly provided them with a letter allowing them "to pass over bridges and ferries, and within the main lines of the Army of the Potomac" which would remain in effect until February 1st.

As he handed John the document, Cameron playfully said, "But mind you don't sing secesh!"

156

In January 1862, John Hutchinson and his son and daughter performed for Lincoln at the White House.

John wasted no time in getting himself and his troupe into Virginia. They took up quarters with Surgeon Edward L. Welling and Chaplain Robert B. Yard, the chaplain acting as their official patron. On their behalf, Yard secured a large hall in nearby Fairfax Episcopal Seminary. The room was large enough to seat an entire regiment. Each regiment in turn would be invited to the hall and charged a fee of ten cents admission. A problem arose when their first appearance, an afternoon recital, was canceled. That evening, the First New Jersey would hear them sing, but soldiers in another regiment, also of New Jersey, who had been scheduled to hear them in the afternoon insisted on attending the evening concert. Spectators jammed the hall, many sitting in the pews, others on the floor. Many more stood in the back of the hall or along the walls.

The large crowd responded enthusiastically to the first part of the program. But then, the singers performed a song using the text of a poem by John Greenleaf Whittier: "We Wait Beneath the Furnace Blast," a nine verse hymn done to Martin Luther's "Ein' Feste Burg." Nothing happened until the third verse:

> What gives the wheat fields blades of steel?
> What points the Rebel cannon?

What sets the roaring rabble's heel
  On the old star-spangled pennon?
    What breaks the oath
    Of the men of the South?
    What whets the knife
    For the Union's life?—
Hark to the answer: SLAVERY![19]

As this verse was completed, someone in the back of the room hissed. Major David Hatfield, commander of the First New Jersey, threatened to throw out anyone disturbing the concert. Dr. Lewis W. Oakley, Surgeon in Chief of the First New Jersey Brigade, yelled, "If there is to be any putting out, you had better begin with me." Hatfield replied, "I can put you out—and if I cannot, I have a regiment that will!"

Angry cries of "Put him out!" filled the hall. The Hutchinsons, much used to dealing with rowdies at their concerts, sang the conciliatory hymn "No Tear in Heaven":

No tear shall be in heaven; no gathering gloom
Shall o'er that glorious landscape ever come;
No tear shall fall in sadness o'er those flowers
That breathe their fragrance thro' celestial bowers.

The next day, Surgeon Oakley registered an official complaint against the Hutchinson family's choice of songs, and Brigadier General Philip Kearny of the First New Jersey Brigade confiscated Chaplain Yard's keys to the Fairfax Seminary. Later, Kearny demanded to see the chaplain and the offending singers. He forbade the Hutchinsons to give any more concerts. "General, I have a permit from the Secretary of War to sing," John protested. "We are no strangers to the soldiers, many thousands of whom know and have heard us—whatever the officers may think and feel on the subject." Kearny replied in haste, "I rule supreme here. You are abolitionists. I think as much of a rebel as I do of an abolitionist."

As news of the incident at the seminary proceeded up the chain of command, the Hutchinsons' situation became more serious. Brigadier General W. B. Franklin demanded to see texts of all the songs the Hutchinsons used. On seeing the text of Whittier's poem, he pronounced it "incendiary" and upheld General Kearny's decision.

John Wallace Hutchinson and his son Henry and daughter Viola entertained Union forces in northern Virginia in 1862. Their performance of Whittier's "We Wait Beneath the Furnace Blast" nearly caused a riot.

Major General McClellan, who wished to have nothing to do with freeing slaves, ordered that the Hutchinsons' pass be canceled. John immediately applied to General Franklin for permission to remain in Virginia until Monday morning, and this was granted.

On Sunday, January 19, Chaplain Yard asked Kearny for permission to hold a church service and if a choir could sing during the service. Kearny readily consented, not realizing that the "choir" would be the Hutchinson family. That evening, Chaplain Merwin held forth on the subject of temperance. Yard lent him the "choir" to sing temperance songs.

On Monday morning Henry Hutchinson and Frank Martin returned to Washington. John intended to follow with his daughter Viola, but fog prevented the boats from getting across the Potomac. He proceeded to Alexandria and eventually got back to Washington before McClellan could arrest him for being in Virginia without a proper pass. Once back in the nation's capital, John sought out Secretary Chase and told him what had happened. Chase asked for a copy of the offending song, promising to read it at the next cabinet meeting. Simon Cameron, who had issued John's original pass had resigned from his position, but Chase was not worried. "Stanton is Secretary of War," Chase told Hutchinson, "and he thinks just as I do."

The next morning, an anxious John Hutchinson went to the Treasury Department. He found Secretary Chase on the stairs. Chase grasped John's hand and smiled. "I want to tell you that the poem was read at the Cabinet meeting and they were all in your favor. Mr. Lincoln remarked that it was one of just the kind of songs he wanted the soldiers to hear. He also said you should have the right to go among any of the soldiers where you were invited to sing."

The singers returned to Alexandria, Virginia, this time under the patronage of Colonel John Franklin Farnsworth of the Eighth Illinois Cavalry. The colonel, who was an outspoken abolitionist, found them quarters in a large Southern Methodist church virtually abandoned by its parishioners, most having joined the Confederate cause. That night, at their first concert in the church, a large crowd demanded to hear the song that had caused the singers so much trouble. The Hutchinsons obliged by singing Whittier's poem and other radical songs, including "John Brown's Body."

Some years later, Lincoln met with John Greenleaf Whittier and told the Quaker poet how he had come to hear 'We Wait Beneath the Furnace Blast" at a cabinet meeting. The president admitted that the poem inspired him in his search for a method of emancipating the slaves.

In the same month that saw the publication of Mrs. Howe's new war poem, the Twelfth Massachusetts went on a tour of duty in the area where John Brown had made his last stand against slavery.[20] They arrived by train at Sandy Hook, just across the Potomac River from Harper's Ferry on Thursday, February 27. From there, the men marched across a pontoon bridge into the town. (Confederates had destroyed the railroad and highway bridge.) They spent the night in an old flour mill, one of the few buildings left standing.

The lower part of the Ferry around the former armory and arsenal was a huge mass of charred rubble, thanks to the efforts of Major Hector Tyndale of the Twenty-eighth Pennsylvania. Colonel John W. Geary ordered Tyndale to destroy the town on February 7, after Confederates at the Ferry had shot and killed a Union scout trying to cross the Potomac. Geary knew that Tyndale would carry out his orders with enthusiasm, because the major was an abolitionist who had not only admired John Brown, he had also been a member of the party traveling with Mary Brown and her husband's body on the rail journey to North Elba, New York.

Tyndale burned and wrecked the crude wood and brick buildings in the lower town. When the soldiers in the Twelfth toured the Ferry the day after their arrival, all they found were the scorched remains, with one notable exception. Tyndale had drawn the line at destroying the Fire Engine House where Brown and his men had been captured.[21]

On March 1, at noon, the Twelfth Massachusetts continued their tour of the area, marching up the steep road over Bolivar Heights to Charlestown. Once there, they marched past the red-brick Jefferson County Court House where John Brown was tried and the weathered gallows where he was executed. The scaffold still stood in the open field where Brown had gazed on the Blue Ridge Mountains.

In both places, they sang "John Brown's Body" accompanied by the band with the regimental colors flying in full splendor. Other Union regiments repeated this scene so often that residents of the town must have wondered whether soldiers in the Union Army knew any other songs.[22] But such was the devotion of the men of the Twelfth Massachusetts to Old Osawatomie Brown that one soldier later admitted that he and some of his mess mates "visited the Court House and sat in the very seat occupied by the would-be liberator when he received his sentence."[23]

Both the Union and Confederate armies wrecked Harper's Ferry during the war. The Confederates destroyed the Potomac River bridge while federal forces burned much of the lower town.

By this time, the regiment's inherited song had picked up a few new verses. In early April 1861, soldiers of the Fourth Massachusetts stationed at Fort Monroe just across from Norfolk, Virginia, had invented a John Brown song based on "The Grave of Uncle True," a sentimental pot-boiler reminiscent of Stowe's *Uncle Tom's Cabin*. One of the soldiers' verses, "May Heaven's rays look kindly down, Upon the grave of Old John Brown!" had been transformed for use in "John Brown's Body": "The stars of heaven are looking kindly down, On the grave of Old John Brown!"[24] The verse about hanging "Jeff Davis to a sour apple tree" had also been given its final form.[25]

The Scots sergeant who had served as the original inspiration was all but forgotten, probably much to his own relief. Sergeant Brown kept "marching on" with the Twelfth until June 6, 1862. On that day, he was traveling on the North Fork of the Shenandoah in a boat also occupied by two men in a regiment of Maine cavalry. The boat capsized, and all three men drowned.[26]

The regiment suffered an even greater loss on August 30, 1862, during the Second Battle of Bull Run (Manassas). Their colonel, Fletcher Webster, was killed after being separated from his men for a moment in the confusion of the fight.[27]

In all, more than two hundred and fifty men serving in the Twelfth would die, either in combat, from wounds sustained in the fighting, by accident, or from disease during its term of service. Better than three hundred additional men would be discharged due to disabilities. Although the men of this regiment probably felt they were suffering and dying, as Mrs. Howe had put it, "to make men free;" in the summer of 1862, Union soldiers were primarily fighting to preserve the Union. Secondarily, they were fighting to protect the many slaves who had fled into Union lines asserting that they were "contraband of war."

The "contraband" issue first surfaced on May 23, 1861, when Union General Benjamin Butler received three slaves into his lines at Fort Monroe. Confederate Colonel Charles K. Mallory owned the slaves and sent Major John B. Cary into the fort under a flag of truce to demand their return. Butler, on discovering the slaves in question were being used to construct Confederate fortifications, refused to return them unless Mallory took an oath swearing allegiance to the United States. Mallory refused and Cary left without Mallory's property.

On May 30, Simon Cameron, then secretary of war, approved Butler's action. Soon a trickle of slaves was passing into Union lines as "contraband."[28] It was not until August 6 that same year that the U.S. Congress passed the first of a series of Confiscation Acts making General Butler's action legal. The act did not make the slaves free. That would have to be decided later.

Union Major General John Charles Frémont out in Missouri was so pleased by this legislation that he freely misinterpreted it, openly declaring slaves belonging to rebels in that state liberated. President Lincoln responded to Frémont's unilateral action by rescinding the general's order and soon thereafter relieving him of command.

The contraband legislation inspired songwriter Henry Clay Work, the son of an abolitionist family from Middletown, Connecticut, to write "Kingdom Coming." The text of the song, written in dialect, depicts a situation where a master has run away from his plantation in anticipation of the arrival of the "Linkum gunboats." The slaves lock the overseer in the smoke house cellar, throw the key to the cellar down a well, and then move into the master's house where they drink his wine and cider and speculate about how long it will be before they are all "cornfiscated." The second verse describes the fleeing master:

> He six foot one way, two foot tudder,
> An' he weigh three hundred pound,
> His coat so big, he couldn't pay de tailor,
> An' it won't go half way round.
> He drill so much dey call him Cap'an,
> An' he get so drefful tann'd,
> I spec he try an' fool dem Yankees
> For to tink he's contraband.[29]

10

"'Prophets and kings' have waited for this day..."

Five months after the start of the war, Dr. Howe met with other abolitionists to form a group with the purpose of putting pressure on President Lincoln and other politicians to free the slaves. In late January 1862, about a week after Lincoln had given John Hutchinson permission to sing anti-slavery songs to the Army of the Potomac, this new organization, known afterwards as the Boston Emancipation League, came into official existence. Samuel Sewall, the namesake and descendant of a man who in 1700 called slave trading a crime worthy of the death penalty, became its president. Howe served as one of its vice presidents, and George Luther Stearns, who had testified before a senate committee about his involvement with John Brown, was named treasurer.

In early March, Howe received word from political allies in Washington that Lincoln had prepared a "message to Congress, which, if sent, will prove to be a bombshell." the president intended to ask Congress to prepare a plan for gradual manumission of slaves. While this news was heartening, Howe feared the nation's chief executive would remain irresolute on the subject of slavery. He complained that Lincoln had already been procrastinating for too long like a man who "stands shivering with his hand on the string of the shower-bath."[1]

But the president did not disappoint Howe this time. A few days later, Howe read in the newspapers that Lincoln had called for a joint resolution "to co-operate with any state which may adopt gradual abolishment of slavery." Lincoln conceded "that the adoption of the

---

George Luther Stearns commissioned this bust of John Brown to commemorate President Lincoln's Emancipation Proclamation. Courtesy of Boston Athenæum.

proposed resolution would be merely initiatory," but that it might "lead to important practical results."[2]

The idea met with little response or support from the border state representatives. Just before Congress adjourned for the summer, Lincoln called those representatives to his office to make a direct appeal. The president emphasized that his emancipation scheme would be gradual. He also made it clear that he intended to colonize the freed slaves on a voluntary basis either in Liberia, where a colony of freed American slaves already existed, or in Chiriqui, a district of New Granada near the Isthmus of Darien, one of the proposed locations for a canal linking the Atlantic and Pacific Oceans.

"Our common country is in great peril," the president told them, "demanding the loftiest views, and boldest action to bring it speedy relief." Once slavery was ended, the future of the United States government would be assured. "To you, more than any others, the privilege is given, to assure that happiness, and swell that grandeur, and to link your own names therewith forever."[4]

Congress voted down the proposal the next day. Lincoln did get minor support for the idea from Senator Waitman T. Willey of western Virginia. On Thursday, August 14, the president met with a delegation of freedmen to see if they would support his position. He again mentioned the possibility of colonization either in Liberia or Chiriqui, and insisted that "without the institution of Slavery and the colored race as a basis, the war could not have an existence. It is better for us both, therefore, to be separated."[5]

Lincoln put special emphasis on the advantages of voluntary colonization in Chiriqui. Government inspectors had discovered coal fields in the area near the proposed route for a canal across Central America. Black colonists would be able to make a lot of money selling coal to the ships passing through the canal.

E. M. Thomas, the chairman of the African American delegation told the president they would consult on the issues he had raised and give him a response. "Take your full time," Lincoln said. "No hurry at all."

The weeks that followed produced not a single volunteer for the black colony of Chiriqui. Instead, the state department received bad news about the venture. First, they learned that New Granada was in contention with Costa Rica for control of Chiriqui. Second, Professor Joseph Henry of the Smithsonian Institute examined coal samples from

Chiriqui and pronounced them unsafe. Instead of coal, the samples proved to be coal dirt high in lignite and sulphuret of iron. Henry wrote that the coal would be dangerous carried on ships at sea because of its tendency to "spontaneously take fire."[6]

But bigger things were already in the works. On July 22, Lincoln read to his cabinet a draft for an emancipation proclamation which would free all slaves then held in the rebellious states. Lincoln told the cabinet that he felt they would have to "change [their] tactics or lose the game." Secretary of State Seward objected to the timing of the proclamation, because three weeks earlier, General George B. McClellan had withdrawn the Army of the Potomac from the approaches to Richmond, Virginia, retreating to Harrison's Landing on the James River. "Now, while I approve the measure," Seward said, "I suggest, sir, that you postpone its issue, until you can give it to the country supported by military success...."[7]

On September 17, 1862, Lincoln got his victory when General McClellan defeated Robert E. Lee in the war's bloodiest one-day battle, fought along Antietam Creek near Sharpsburg, Maryland. The day after the battle, Lee's army retreated back across the Potomac River. The following week, on Monday, September 22, the president announced that he would give the Confederate states one hundred days to return to the Union. If they would not, on January 1, 1863, he would proclaim that "all persons held as slaves" within Confederate territory "shall be then, thenceforward, and forever free...."[8]

Governor John A. Andrew of Massachusetts, who was staying in Philadelphia in preparation for a governor's conference at Altoona, Pennsylvania, was ecstatic when he learned of the president's preliminary proclamation. "It is a poor *document*, but a mighty *act*," he wrote to a friend; "slow, somewhat halting, wrong in its delay till January, but grand and sublime after all. 'Prophets and kings' have waited for this day, but died without the sight."[9]

Two days later at Altoona, Andrew introduced a statement of support for Lincoln's action and urged his fellow governors to sign the document. The statement said, in part, that the president's decision "to strike at the root of the rebellion will lend new vigor to the efforts and new life and hope to the hearts of the people."[10] Many of the state governors present signed, including Francis Harrison Pierpont of the "Restored Government of Virginia," but the governors of the border states and the governor of New Jersey refused to sign because of Andrew's inclusion of a statement supporting emancipation.[11]

On returning to Boston, Governor Andrew asked to see a friend, Edward Kinsley, in a council chamber at the State House. Kinsley had been keeping the governor informed of events in Washington. Together, the two sang "Coronation" and "Praise God from whom all blessings flow." Then Kinsley sang "John Brown's body lies a moulderin' in the grave," while the governor marched around the room and joined in singing the chorus.[12]

While enthusiasm for emancipation grew steadily in the North, Lincoln was inspired to propose a gradual emancipation scheme for the nation during his annual address to Congress on December 1, 1862. As was then the custom, the president did not deliver the address himself. Instead one of his secretaries, John Hay, was chosen for the task.

In this speech, the president suggested an amendment to the Constitution providing for compensated emancipation of all slaves to be completed by January 1, 1900. He wanted the slaveholders to be reimbursed for their loss because he felt the whole country, North and South had contributed to the problem. Many northern ports had grown rich on the slave trade. The South had a perfect right to ask the northern states to contribute their fair share to discontinue chattel slavery.[13]

In December, a few weeks before Lincoln's proclamation would be enacted, emancipation leagues all around the country increased the pressure on the president and the Congress to make sure Lincoln would issue the final Emancipation Proclamation. Senator Charles Sumner of Massachusetts, a friend of Dr. Howe, received hundreds of letters on the subject. On December 28, Sumner wrote Howe that the president "is firm. He says that he would not stop the proclamation if he could, and he could not if he would."[14]

While the rest of the nation waited to see whether Lincoln would act to emancipate the slaves of the Confederacy, the loyal people of western Virginia waited for Lincoln to sign the bill that would create the state of West Virginia. Congress had already passed the bill on December 10, and Lincoln had to sign it into law before midnight of December 31. The president, however, ignored the bill, and it sat on his desk through Christmas and into the week following without any action being taken.

Having already spoken to Lincoln about the bill and followed up with a letter and two telegrams urging its passage, Governor Pierpont felt that he could do no more, but when three of his constituents visited his office on December 31, just hours before the bill would die in

When Governor John Andrew of Massachusetts learned of Lincoln's Emancipation Proclamation, he sang "John Brown's Body" in a chamber of the state house in Boston.

Lincoln's pocket, the governor decided to send one last telegram begging the president to sign the bill. He stated that the loyal troops

171

and people of Virginia "have their hearts set on it; and if the bill fails, God only knows the result."[15]

The telegram was delivered to Lincoln that night, and the president signed the bill. "We can scarcely dispense with the aid of West-Virginia in this struggle," Lincoln wrote in support of his action. "Her brave and good men ... have been true to the Union under very severe trials. We have so acted as to justify their hopes."[16]

On the morning of January 1, 1863, politicians in black frock coats, military officers in Union blue coats decorated with gold braid, and women wearing crinoline gowns in every color of the rainbow arrived at the White House for the yearly president's reception. For three hours, Lincoln stood in the Blue Room shaking hands with officers, legislators, and their wives. Around noon, Secretary of State William Seward and his son Frederick brought the Emancipation Proclamation to the White House. They found the president in his office.

Just before signing the document, Lincoln hesitated and said, "I never, in my life, felt more certain that I was doing right, than I do in signing this paper. But I have been receiving calls and shaking hands since nine o'clock this morning, till my arm is stiff and numb." He worried that his hand might tremble while signing the document and that this would be misinterpreted by future historians. "But anyway, it is going to be done," he concluded. Taking some care with his writing, he signed his name to the proclamation.[17]

In Boston on New Year's Day, abolitionists gathered at Boston's Music Hall for a "Jubilee Concert" in celebration of Lincoln's proclamation. Ralph Waldo Emerson read a poem he had prepared for the occasion called the "Boston Hymn." Toward the end of the poem, Emerson included some lines inspired by Lincoln's recent demands for compensated emancipation that brought the excited listeners, including many former slaves, to their feet:

> Pay ransom to the owner
> And fill the bag to the brim.
> Who is the owner? The slave is the owner,
> And ever was. Pay him.

That evening, Emerson repeated the poem at a celebration at the home of George Luther Stearns in Medford. Julia Ward Howe was also on hand to read the "Battle Hymn of the Republic." The centerpiece of the evening was the unveiling of a bust of John Brown. Stearns had commissioned sculptor Edwin A. Brackett to create the piece.[18]

That same day on Port Royal Island, South Carolina, Union soldiers and civilians gathered at Camp Saxton to celebrate Lincoln's proclamation in a special way. They were about to witness the muster of the First South Carolina Volunteers consisting of African Americans serving under white officers. Their enlistment in the army had been made possible by a provision in Lincoln's Emancipation Proclamation calling for the formation of colored regiments. The colonel for the First South Carolina, Thomas Wentworth Higginson, had openly supported John Brown's raid on Harper's Ferry. Like Brown before him, Higginson was now prepared to lead black troops into combat.

Charlotte Forten, a black teacher who had come to the islands to help set up schools for freed slaves, arrived on the island aboard the steamboat *Flora*. Lines of black soldiers wearing dark blue infantry uniforms greeted the passengers. Charlotte thought they "made a splendid appearance" among the magnolia trees lining the path that led up to a decaying house next to a church. Beyond the church, white cotton tents stood in neat rows. An officer told Charlotte that the men of the new regiment were very honest. "In many other camps," he said, "the Colonel and the rest of us would find it necessary to place a guard before our tents. We never do it here. Our tents are left entirely unguarded, but nothing has ever been touched."[19]

The ceremony was held in a grove of oaks beside the camp. Black women with multicolored handkerchiefs on their heads and black men dressed in their Sunday best gathered around a raised wooden platform to hear a prayer delivered by the regimental chaplain. After an ode written for the occasion was sung, Dr. W. H. Brisbane, a South Carolinian plantation owner who had freed his slaves, read Lincoln's proclamation. Then Reverend J. French presented two flags to Colonel Higginson on behalf of the Church of the Puritans in New York City. As Higginson took the flags, some of the men in his regiment began to sing:

> My Country, 'tis of thee,
> Sweet land of liberty,
> Of thee I sing!

"It was a touching and beautiful incident," Forten wrote afterwards, "and sent a thrill through all our hearts." Higginson, who had intended to make a little speech after the colors were presented, wrote in his diary: "I never saw anything so electric; it made all other words cheap; it seemed the choked voice of a race at last unloosed."[20] After a number of other brief speeches, the ceremony was brought to a close when the new inductees sang "John Brown's Body."[21]

Governor John Albion Andrew of Massachusetts had his own plans for a black regiment, but his plans were not in place in time for the celebration of the president's proclamation. In early February, 1863, a month after the proclamation took effect, Andrew commissioned Colonel Robert Gould Shaw of a prominent abolitionist family in Boston to lead the 54th Massachusetts, a regiment of black tradesmen, sailors and farmers.

When Andrew asked Samuel Gridley Howe about the formation of "colored" regiments, the doctor strenuously objected. "I want to sink the differences of race," he wrote to Andrew; "& treat the blacks exactly as I would whites in their condition." Howe did not believe that the races should be separated. Instead, he sought a "free and unobstructed course to that natural law by which the weaker & poorer race is to be absorbed & by the stronger & better one to the improvement of humanity, & the glory of God."[22]

After Lincoln signed the Emancipation Proclamation, Howe started lobbying for the creation of a committee to look into the problems of freeing the slaves. The government obliged Howe by creating the American Freedmen's Inquiry Commission (precursor of the later Freedmen's Bureau) on March 16, 1863, and appointing Howe to serve on it.

With the approach of summer, members of the commission separated to continue research on their own. Dr. Howe visited settlements of runaway slaves in Ontario. While there, he witnessed the dedication of a newly completed Methodist church in a black community. After a prayer and a hymn, the pastor asked the members of the congregation to speak, encouraging each participant with exhortations like "That's right, brother!" and "Hallelujah!" The ceremony ended with the pastor leading his flock in an enthusiastic rendition of "John Brown's Body." "The concrete christianity shown in the old hero's self-sacrifice," Howe commented later, "was comprehensible to their religious sense."[23]

On returning to Massachusetts, Howe realized he should consult someone considered an expert in the science of race. He chose to approach the Swiss taxonomist Louis Agassiz, a defender of "polygenesis," the theory that all races of men are separate species.

Until coming to America, Agassiz had believed that all people were members of one species. But in Philadelphia, he had come in close contact with a black waiter at a hotel restaurant. "It is impossible for me to repress the feeling that they are not of the same blood as us," he wrote to his mother of the incident. The dark skin, livid palms, and woolly hair of his attendants frightened him. "I wished I were able to depart in order to eat a piece of bread elsewhere, rather than dine with such service."[24]

Encouraged by Howe's interest, Agassiz described blacks as "indolent, playful, sensuous, imitative, subservient, good natured, versatile, unsteady in their purpose, devoted, affectionate, in everything unlike other races, they may but be compared to children, grown in the stature of adults while retaining a childlike mind." Although, in his opinion, African Americans should be granted legal equality, they were "incapable of living on a footing of social equality with the whites, in one and the same community, without being an element of social disorder."[25] To make matters worse, Agassiz maintained that mulattos had a "sickly physique and ... impaired fecundity" making it difficult if not impossible for them to have children.[26]

Howe rejected much of what Agassiz told him. Although he reported that he believed that African Americans would be "docile and easily governed" and that mulattos had "inferior fertility," he also stated that he thought black people would be "industrious and thrifty." Where Agassiz insisted on blacks being separated from whites, Howe said it would not be "desirable to have them live in communities by themselves." He concluded that "The negro does best when let alone, and...we must beware of all attempts to prolong his servitude, even under pretext of taking care of him."[27]

WWhile Dr. Howe was considering the practical and social aspects of emancipation, the people of western Virginia were suddenly forced to consider the legal issues of manumission. After Lincoln had signed the House bill on the last day of December, the bill had been sent to the Senate for consideration. But the senators refused to grant statehood for West Virginia unless they changed their proposed state constitution to provide for gradual emancipation. The Virginians had pushed through an ordinance preventing the importation of slaves, but had not dared to consider manumission, fearing that western residents who owned slaves would take offense and side with the Confederacy.

Members of the West Virginia Constitutional Convention reassembled in mid-February to deliberate the issue. They soon had a moderate statute granting freedom to the children of slaves born after July 4, 1863. Slave children under the age of ten on that day would be free when they became twenty-one, and older slave children would be free when they reached twenty-five years of age.

Convention members then called for a popular referendum on the altered constitution to be held on March 26. Western Virginia voters approved the document overwhelmingly. President Lincoln then issued a final proclamation, dated April 20, 1863, declaring that West Virginia would become a state in sixty days on June 20.[28] This would allow time for the organization of elections and other matters relating to the installation of the new state government.

While these preparations were underway, Confederate Cavalry Brigadier General John D. Imboden, the same man who had assisted Henry Wise in taking Harper's Ferry in 1861, planned a raid through western Virginia. Although the mission was Imboden's idea, the senior officer on the raid would be Brigadier General William E. "Grumble" Jones. The two men would lead their troops through separate parts of the state. Jones would destroy the Baltimore and Ohio Railroad in the northern part of the state while Imboden hoped to defeat and capture federal troops stationed farther south at Beverly, Philippi, and Buckhannon. They also planned to enlist Confederate sympathizers and disrupt the West Virginia state elections.

On April 20, the same day that Lincoln issued his proclamation for the formation of the State of West Virginia, Imboden started on the raid. Jones rode with his men the following day, moving through federally held territory west of Harper's Ferry. After terrorizing Preston County and Rowlesburg, Jones, encountering heavy Union resistance, withdrew to Evansville near Sandy Creek, less than twenty miles southeast of Governor Pierpont's home in Fairmont. The resistance collapsed, and by April 27, Jones was in Morgantown. Two days later, he and his men rode into Fairmont.

Jones's raiders discovered the location of Pierpont's law office and broke into the building. Gathering up armsful of the absent governor's law books, the Confederates brought them outside to the town square, put them in a pile, and set fire to them. Lieutenant Edward Zane of Wheeling led a group of gray and butternut clad soldiers to Pierpont's house where they located the Pierpont family's private library stored in a small building beside the house which served as Pierpont's private office. The soldiers smashed their way in and carried these books to the bonfire in the town square. Zane, who had found the Pierpont family Bible, tied the book behind his horse and dragged it through the streets. When he reached the square, Zane threw the Bible on the burning pile. A neighbor rescued it and sent it by post to Mrs. Pierpont, then living in relative safety with her sister in Washington, Pennsylvania, about fifty miles to the north.[29]

Jones and Imboden rode through the state wreaking as much havoc as they could before withdrawing from the state on May 21. Although one of their objectives had been to recruit men for the Confederate Army, this part of the mission proved a failure. Both generals lost more men from desertion than they had recruited. They had also failed to disrupt the state elections which were held seven days after the raid ended.

On June 20, West Virginia became a state, and Pierpont made plans to move his Virginia state government to Union held territory near the nation's capital. He settled on Alexandria, Virginia, so close to Washington that he might be in daily contact with Lincoln. In August, he took up residence in "pleasant quarters" in the city hotel. "The bedroom and parlour [of the residence]," the governor wrote to his wife, "form part of a hall which tradition says was [George] Washington's Ballroom. The old orchestra where the musicians sat is still preserved in another room. The church is here and pew preserved in which they say he used to worship."[30]

Once ensconced in Alexandria, Pierpont came under a new threat from Lieutenant Colonel John Singleton Mosby, the "Gray Ghost" of the Confederacy. In late August, Mosby, who thought of Pierpont as the "bogus" governor of Virginia,[31] sent him a note: "You did not see the farmer who rode by your hotel on a hay wagon yesterday, did you

Governor? My driver pointed out your window, and I marked it plain. It's just over the bay, and I'll get you some night, mighty easy."[32]

Toward the end of September, 1863, Mosby, hoping to quash rumors of his death, led four of his men into Fairfax County with the intention of capturing Pierpont. But the governor was staying in Washington that night, so Mosby had to settle for the capture of Pierpont's military aide, Colonel Daniel H. Dulany.[33] Although Governor Pierpont laughed off any such threats or actions, he had enough fear of his situation not to allow his wife and children to live with him in Alexandria. They remained in Pennsylvania. Meanwhile, Pierpont's government in Alexandria took up the task of rewriting Virginia's state constitution. Inspired by Lincoln's example, the lawmakers intended to end slavery in Virginia forever.

Lincoln's proclamation also inspired poets and songwriters across the nation. Abolitionist songwriter Henry Clay Work wrote "Song of a Thousand Years" to commemorate the president's war measure. The lyrics rather naively support the notion that, once freed, all African Americans' problems would suddenly cease:

> Lift up your eyes, desponding freemen!
> Fling to the winds your needless fears!
> He who unfurl'd your beauteous banner,
> Says it shall wave a thousand years![34]

Edna Dean Proctor chose to honor Lincoln's action with a set of lyrics called "The President's Proclamation," to be sung to the same tune as "John Brown's Body." The seven verses, however, mention John Brown nine times, while the president is only alluded to once in the second verse:

> John Brown sowed and his harvesters are we;
> Honor to him who has made the bondmen free;
> Loved evermore shall our noble Ruler be—
> Freedom reigns today![35]

All these rivals of Howe's "Battle Hymn," although popular in their time, were soon to be eclipsed. In the middle of 1863, a champion arose from among the soldiers and officers in the Union Army who would make Julia's "Battle Hymn" nationally famous. But in the early morning hours of June 15, 1863, just outside Stevenson's Depot, Virginia, about thirty miles southwest of Harper's Ferry, that champion, Chaplain Charles Cardwell McCabe of the 122nd Ohio Volunteers, was hiding behind a tree.

11

"I seem doomed to raise money."

In the early morning hours of June 15, 1863, just a few miles north of Winchester, Virginia, and about thirty miles south of Harper's Ferry, Chaplain McCabe and surgeon William M. Houston of the 122nd Ohio took cover behind a tree while minié balls whistled all around them in the night air. With them was Willie Morgan, a boy of fifteen whose mother had allowed him to follow the Ohio regiment so long as he stayed near Surgeon Houston or Chaplain McCabe. The three intended to stay behind to take care of the wounded, as was expected of most non-combatants during the war.[1]

At daybreak, a Confederate provost-marshal found the chaplain and his party. The marshal escorted the men to the headquarters tent of Brigadier General John B. Gordon. The general graciously promised them fifty soldiers and all the ambulances they needed to take care of the wounded.

When this work was done, all the Union non-combatants were brought before Major General Jubal A. Early. Although Early had been a delegate to the Convention of Secession in Richmond and had voted against passage of the Ordinance of Secession on April 17, 1861, he had still decided to fight for the Confederacy.

Chaplain McCabe, who had been chosen to speak for the group, asked Early if the men could now be sent back to their regiments. "You are a preacher, are you?" Early asked. McCabe said he was. "Well," Early said, "you preachers have done more to bring on this war than anybody and I'm going to send you to Richmond."

Chaplain McCabe was captured after the battle of Stevenson's Depot and spent time in Libby Prison. While there, he sang the "Battle Hymn of the Republic" in celebration of the Union victory at Gettysburg.

The chaplain protested that they would rather go to Harper's Ferry which was much closer. Early exploded. "They tell me you have been shouting, 'On to Richmond' for a long time, and to Richmond you shall go."[2]

Before the war, Chaplain McCabe had aspired to become a Methodist minister. In his youth, the Methodist Church had split into two separate bodies, a southern branch which supported slavery and a northern branch which openly condemned the institution. McCabe, who lived in Athens, Ohio, wanted to be a minister in the northern branch. He entered Ohio Wesleyan University where he developed his abilities as a public speaker and his rich baritone singing voice.[3]

He soon became exhausted from doing revival meetings and left school in ill health. For two years, he served as a principal and teacher of mathematics at a high school in Ironton, Ohio, where he met Rebecca

In 1862, Charles Cardwell McCabe left his wife Rebecca at home to join the 122nd Ohio Volunteers.

182

Peters. The two were married July 6, 1860. Their first and only child, John P. McCabe, was born in 1861 just after Christmas.

In February 1862, McCabe discovered a poem called the "Battle Hymn of the Republic" in the *Atlantic Monthly*. The poem moved him so deeply that he committed it to memory on the spot. Later, at a war rally in Zanesville, Ohio, he heard it sung to the tune of "John Brown's Body."

McCabe used his talents at speaking and singing to help recruit soldiers for the 122nd Ohio Volunteers. He wanted to be the 122nd's chaplain, but he lacked the proper credentials to administer the sacraments and perform the other functions of an ordained minister. But the ambitious and dedicated young man soon came to the attention of someone who could help him achieve his goal, Bishop Thomas A. Morris. The bishop waived the requirements and ordained McCabe as an elder in the Methodist Church at Zanesville on September 7, 1862. McCabe received his commission as regimental chaplain on October 8.[4]

Once in the U.S. Army, Chaplain McCabe used every opportunity to hold revival meetings so that he could preach and sing his favorite hymns. One of the most popular was Howe's "Battle Hymn of the Republic." Little did he suspect, at the time of his capture, that fate was about to give him an opportunity to make the "Battle Hymn" world famous.

As McCabe and his friends marched under guard down through Richmond toward the James River, they saw a three-story brick building stretching one hundred and forty feet along the James River Kanahwa Canal. On one end of the structure, a flag staff carried a Confederate battle flag. They had arrived at Libby Prison, a former ship chandlery and grocery.[5] The Union soldiers were startled to see men dressed in dark blue jackets guarding the building. The chaplain later discovered that the inmates of the prison had exchanged their superior wool garments for Confederate gray and butternut in order to get a little extra food.[6]

Once inside, the Confederates demanded that the prisoners surrender their valuables. They promised to return them when they were exchanged. Chaplain McCabe had been carrying eighty dollars in greenbacks which he was holding for soldiers who had asked him to send the money home to a wife or mother. On being relieved of the eighty dollars, the chaplain protested that the money was not his. "I know it," the Confederate officer responded. "It is mine now."[7]

Afterward, the guards led the prisoners upstairs to a crowded room on the second floor. McCabe fully expected to see half-dead men lying about on the floor looking dejected and sullen. Instead, the inmates greeted the new arrivals with cheery cries of "Fresh fish! Fresh fish!" One soldier shook McCabe's hand, and asked how he was and why he hadn't come sooner. To add to the fun, the man then turned to an imaginary porter and said, "Here, Jim, take the gentleman's baggage and show him to room thirty-six, and see that he does not want for anything while he is with us."

Although this four story warehouse was originally intended for storing tobacco, it became a prison for Union officers and non-combatants during the Civil War.

There were no beds in the cramped, low-ceilinged room. McCabe, Surgeon Houston, and Willie were told to lie up against a door and not to move left or right, as space was at a premium. Just as the chaplain was dozing off, he heard someone cry out, "Right wheel!" All the prisoners rolled to their right. The chaplain asked one of the older residents about this application of tactical maneuvers. "When your bones get sore on one side," the man replied, "don't roll over without giving the word of command, or things will get into confusion here." A little while later, another voice called out "Left wheel!" McCabe dutifully rolled to the left.

In the morning, a man came around to count all the prisoners. Chaplain McCabe grew curious about the need for such counts. A man asked if McCabe had ten dollars. This money could be used to bribe the guards and escape. The only problem was that, once escaped, those same guards tracked down the fugitive with bloodhounds.

Some time later, McCabe asked an elderly African American who assisted at the prison how runaway slaves dealt with the problem of bloodhounds. The man smiled and offered to bring the chaplain a packet of cayenne pepper, promising in his colorful dialect that once a hound sniffed a little of the red-hot powder "he's gwine to fergit all about dis war."[8]

Not willing to remain idle in captivity, McCabe sought out fellow prisoners with good singing voices and formed a quartet. One night, another imprisoned chaplain, L. N. Beaudry, heard the quartet singing "Old Hundredth":

> Praise God from whom all blessings flow;
> Praise Him all creatures here below;
> Praise Him above, ye heavenly host,
> Praise Father, Son, and Holy Ghost.

Beaudry asked the commandant of the prison who was standing nearby, if he permitted the prisoners to hold religious services and sing. "Oh yes," the commandant replied with a sneer; "you Yankees seem disposed to sing anywhere, and we have to endure it even here."

Not long after that, Beaudry discovered that the magnificent baritone voice he had heard singing in the quartet belonged to Chaplain McCabe. Commenting on the incident years later, Beaudry said, "There is a certain something in Chaplain McCabe's voice, a deep and tender pathos, which once heard is forever remembered.... At times not a few of the rebel guards and passers-by grouped themselves on Cary Street to hear us."[9]

The singers had many opportunities to use their voices, one such occasion being the Fourth of July. The Union prisoners longed to have a flag for the celebration, but the only stars and stripes on the premises were in the commandant's office ingloriously hanging upside-down. The men, however, did manage to locate a red shirt, a blue shirt, and after some trouble, a yellow shirt that had once been white. These were given to a tailor who made a passable flag from the garments.

On the Fourth, a captain placed the flag in the rafters, and a colonel opened the festivities with a brief speech asking the men not to make too much noise and disturb their jailers. Shortly after that a Confederate officer came up and ordered the prisoners to stop the "fuss."

"Fuss!" the colonel said in disbelief. "Do you call this a fuss? Do I understand you to mean that we can't celebrate the Fourth of July here?"

"Yes sir, you can," the officer protested, "but—" and then he spotted the flag in the rafters.

After looking at it a while, the Confederate ordered that it be taken down. From the back of the room, a trembling voice said, "Let any Union boy here touch that flag that dares!" With some effort, the rebel officer climbed into the rafters himself and removed the flag. The prisoners never saw their home-made flag again, but their celebration proceeded without any further interruptions.[10]

Two days later, Confederate Major General John H. Winder, in charge of all Confederate prisons, ordered that the seventy-three captains then in the prison be sent downstairs along with two chaplains. McCabe and an eighty-year-old chaplain went down. The officers stood in a hollow square while a rebel officer addressed them: "Gentlemen, I have an unpleasant duty to perform. I am ordered to select two of you for execution; and as the fairest way to do this I have written your names on slips of paper and put them in this hat. One of the chaplains will take out two names and the other captains can go back upstairs." The executions had been ordered in retaliation for two Confederate officers executed by order of Major General Ambrose E. Burnside for recruiting for the Confederacy inside Union lines.

The octogenarian chaplain made the selection. Henry Washington Sawyer of the First New Jersey Cavalry and John M. Flinn of the 51st

Indiana Volunteers were selected. The execution was scheduled for July 14. Sawyer asked for the opportunity to write to his wife, thinking that if she could get word to the government about his situation, he and Flinn might be saved. The guards allowed him to do so on condition that they read the letter before it was sent. Afterwards, Sawyer and Flinn were placed in a room in the basement and fed on corn bread and water.[11]

War news came to the prison, dispensed by an elderly black man affectionately called "Old Ben." Each morning, Ben would clomp up the prison stairs to sell his copies of the Richmond newspapers. If the news was favorable to the Union war effort, he would call out, "Great news in de papers," a cry which would bring the depressed inmates to their feet in an instant. One of the prisoners would light a candle and hold it aloft while another read the paper out loud.

As early as the morning of July 6, the day that Sawyer and Flinn were selected for execution, Old Ben brought news of a great battle in the southern Pennsylvania town of Gettysburg. The paper stated that some northern newspapers claimed that the battle was a Union victory while the southern reporters maintained that there was no proof that Lee had lost the battle.[12]

During this time, Chaplain McCabe got some bad news relating to the battle at Gettysburg when a distant relative, Reverend John Collins McCabe of the Episcopal Church of Richmond, came for a visit. The minister had sought out his Union loyal relative in an attempt to help mitigate the hardships of prison life as much as possible. Reverend McCabe also told his chaplain cousin that rumors were circulating around Richmond that General Lee had won a great battle in the North and 40,000 Union prisoners were on their way to Richmond.

"I was astounded," Chaplain McCabe said later of the meeting. "In dumb amazement I listened to the rebel officers speculating where the new prisoners should be stowed away and how they were to be fed. I went up stairs and told the news. Despondency settled down into every heart."[13]

That night the prisoners assembled for prayers and sang "Old Hundredth" with added fervor. McCabe got no sleep that night, passing the time by listening for the cries of "All's well" from the sentries outside.

But the next day, the newspapers reported that Lee had lost over 28,000 men during the battle and had only captured 4,000 prisoners, not 40,000. His battered army crossed back over the Potomac River into Virginia on July 14, the day when Sawyer and Flinn were supposed to be executed. (By this time, the execution of the two captains had been postponed.) More good news poured into the prison in the days that followed: Major General U. S. Grant had captured the Mississippi River town of Vicksburg on the Fourth of July; and Port Hudson, also on the Mississippi River south of Vicksburg, had surrendered two days later to Union forces.[14]

With each report of a Union victory, the prisoners began singing every patriotic song in their repertoire from "Yankee Doodle" to "Old Hundredth." McCabe personally led the men in singing his favorite, Howe's "Battle Hymn of the Republic." The chorus of "Glory, Glory, Hallelujah" sounded so loudly through the prison that Sawyer and Flinn down in the basement could hear it. Eventually, the prison guards would make them stop, but they could not dampen the prisoners' revitalized spirits.

Thanks to Sawyer's wife, news of the impending execution of the two Union captains reached the attention of President Abraham Lincoln. The Union Army had already captured Brigadier General Fitzhugh Lee and a son of Confederate Major General Winder. Both men were placed in the hands of Major General Benjamin F. Butler, who communicated to the Confederate government that if he heard so much as a rumor that Sawyer and Flinn had been executed, he would immediately execute General Lee and Winder's son. The Confederates had no choice but to abandon their ploy, and the two captains were released from their basement prison twenty-one days after they first entered it.[15]

One day, Chaplain McCabe met Captain Warner, the quartermaster for the prison, and discovered that Warner was from Ohio and had gone to school under the tutelage of McCabe's mother, Sarah. The captain offered to provide McCabe with goods for Union greenbacks. Luckily, an enterprising colonel managed to sneak seven hundred dollars into the prison.[16] McCabe used the money to purchase three bathtubs and college textbooks from Warner.[17] At the end of July, the chaplain wrote to his wife that he was studying "French and Butler's Analogy."[18]

By the end of August, McCabe was writing that the prisoners had transformed the former tobacco warehouse into a college. "The hitherto idle prisoners are *students* now," he wrote her. "Classes are formed in various useful sciences. I have bought, through the kindness of the

Chaplain Charles Cardwell McCabe of the 122nd Ohio was incarcerated here in the summer of 1863.

authorities, a large number of books, and all is changed. The men do not seem to feel their captivity as they did before."[19]

Captain I. N. Johnston of the Fourth Kentucky Volunteer Infantry later wrote that his fellow prisoners studied "languages ancient and modern..., mathematics..., morals and religion..., dancing, vocal music, and sword exercise...." Johnston claimed that "few colleges in the land could boast of a faculty so large in number or varied in accomplishments, and none, certainly, could compare in the number of pupils."[20]

McCabe also wrote his wife that he was still healthy. But in a place where the drinking water came from the same place used as a latrine, it was inevitable that large numbers of prisoners would be exposed to cholera and typhoid.

On September 25, McCabe wrote, "I have been threatened with my old enemy, *the ague* [a chill accompanied by fever], but I feel confident I shall escape it now."[21] The Confederate surgeon for the prison, was not so certain. He realized that McCabe had typhoid fever, and immediately ordered that the chaplain be taken to a hospital.

As the guards carried McCabe out, they could hear footsteps running down the stairs. Chaplain McCabe looked up to see who was coming after them. It was Willie Morgan.[22]

Chaplain McCabe stared at the youth. "Where are you going, Willie?"

"I'm going with you sir."

The chaplain suggested that Willie had better go back with Surgeon Houston.

"No," Willie said defiantly. "I'm going to take care of you."

Willie prepared a bed of straw for McCabe in the prison hospital. With his hands, the youth brushed away the hoard of insects that made their homes in McCabe's garments and hair. He also folded up McCabe's overcoat to make a pillow. The chaplain lapsed in and out of consciousness. One time, he awoke to hear one of the doctors telling Willie to administer medicine every hour. Their long faces told McCabe that they didn't expect him to live much longer.[23]

Fellow prisoner Colonel William H. Powell soon joined them in the prison hospital. Powell was recovering from a wound but was mobile enough to assist Willie with the chaplain. In appreciation of Powell's efforts, McCabe later wrote of him, "He found me covered with vermin from head to foot and supposed to be dying with the fever. He sat down by my side and took out his little pocket scissors, which he carried with him, and cut my long hair, which hung down to my shoulders. Then he cut my long beard. He then secured from the physician of the prison an insect exterminator and soon relieved me from the suffering I was enduring on this account. He gave me a bath with his own hands, then went down to the prison kitchen and tried his hand at cooking for me, and brought me some nourishing food."[24]

Once McCabe was more comfortable, Powell asked him if he would like to hear a letter sent him from Dr. Isaac Crook, a member of the Ohio Methodist Conference. Crook's letter mentioned a recent session of the conference, and that people there had asked about the chaplain.

When they learned McCabe was in Libby Prison, the presiding bishop suggested that the assembled preachers might pray for the prisoner's release just as Paul and Barnabbas had been prayed out of prison. The two hundred and fifty ministers readily agreed and went down on their knees.

"I was used to suffering," McCabe commented later; "I could endure loneliness without tears, but I was not used to tenderness, and that tender letter broke me down. The tears rolled down my cheeks like rain. As soon as I could control myself, I began to sing. I broke out into a profuse perspiration and the tide was turned." That evening, a doctor came by and found McCabe much improved. He rolled a blue mass pill, part chalk and part mercury, and gave it to the chaplain with a glass of water. "I got well all the same!" Chaplain McCabe said afterward.[25]

Twelve days later, Willie Morgan excitedly announced that the two of them were to be exchanged as prisoners of war and would be going home. The youth bathed McCabe and got the chaplain, who now weighed less than one hundred pounds, dressed and onto the waiting ambulance.

They traveled south to Petersburg by boat and from there took a train to City Point at the confluence of the Appomatox and James Rivers. While on the train, a man identifying himself as Captain Hatch came directly up to McCabe and gave him some bread and fried chicken. When the chaplain asked how this stranger knew who he was, the man answered mysteriously, "Ask your father when you get home."

Chaplain McCabe later learned that his father, on hearing his son was imprisoned in Richmond, had traveled all the way to Fort Monroe. When he could not get any further, he used his influence as a Mason to "send word along the line."

"I never knew how Captain Hatch happened to know me," the chaplain commented on the incident; "but some how I have always associated Masonry and fried chicken; and if any one asks me what Masonry is, I answer, 'It is a thing that gives a fellow fried chicken when he is hungry.'"

Once on the James, McCabe and Morgan were transferred to a Union vessel. The chaplain laid down on the deck directly under the United States flag. Some time later, a Union soldier brought him a piece of beefsteak and a baked potato on a tin plate. That meal plus some hot coffee so revived the chaplain that he was able to walk around the deck with Willie's help in half an hour.

McCabe discovered that, of the four hundred exchanged Union soldiers on the deck, two were dying. One of the two begged the doctor for something that could strengthen him so that he could get home. But there was nothing the army physician could do. Both men died and were placed in simply constructed coffins to be shipped home.[26]

McCabe and Morgan finally reached Washington. The chaplain lost no time in finding a telegraph office to send a note home to his wife: "I am coming home, but slowly. Health improving."[27]

A few weeks later, McCabe was well enough to take action to free his friend, William Houston, who was still in Libby Prison. The chaplain traveled to Ohio to see Governor David Tod and later left for Johnson's Island in Sandusky Bay, Lake Erie, bearing a letter from the governor allowing him to negotiate "with some rebel prisoner for the exchange of Dr. Houston."[28]

While McCabe was on Johnson's Island, the Ohio governor pursued a mission of his own, traveling to Gettysburg, Pennsylvania, to attend the dedication of a national cemetery for the Union dead on November 19, 1863. During the dedication ceremony, he and other loyal governors would hear the oration of Edward Everett, the great Boston orator who had spoken on the day the Twelfth Massachusetts had received their battle flags. He would also listen to President Lincoln's brief address. It was exactly two years since the day Julia Ward Howe had penned the line, "As he died to make men holy, let us die to make men free." And now Lincoln told his listeners that the soldiers who died at Gettysburg "shall not have died in vain—that this nation, under God, shall have a new birth of freedom—and that government of the people, by the people, and for the people, shall not perish from the earth."

On January 8, 1864, Chaplain McCabe reluctantly resigned his commission in the 122nd Ohio due to continued medical problems resulting from the typhoid fever he had suffered in Libby Prison. Now he took on a new task as a fund-raiser for the U.S. Christian Commission. The work did not appeal to him as much as the missionary work he had done while serving as a chaplain.

Chaplain McCabe went to this Union prison on Johnson's Island to find a Confederate surgeon willing to be exchanged for McCabe's friend, surgeon William Houston.

"I seem doomed to raise money," he wrote despairingly in his journal. "And I hope I am not grieving the Lord when I do it."[29]

His activities brought him to the second anniversary celebration of the Christian Commission held in the hall of the House of Representatives in Washington, D. C., on Tuesday night, February 2, 1864. A military band in the reporters' gallery played patriotic airs as army officers and soldiers, cabinet officers, and clergymen crowded into the hall to hear the words of Lincoln's vice president Hannibal Hamlin and a host of other church and political figures. Lincoln arrived in the middle of a speech delivered by G. H. Stuart, the president of the commission.

Chaplain McCabe spoke last. Standing beside Colonel Powell, McCabe told the story of his days in Libby Prison and of singing Howe's

"Battle Hymn" on learning of General Meade's victory at Gettysburg. Then he and Powell performed the hymn, the band accompanying them.

Everyone in the hall rose, one of the first to do so being President Lincoln. McCabe did his best to conduct the band and lead the audience in a rendition of the chorus. The hall sounded loudly with cheers from the audience once the piece was finished.

Above the uproar, President Lincoln could be heard, saying, "Sing it again!" McCabe obliged, but first told the story of a man imprisoned in Libby who was slowly starving to death. That man had told the chaplain to tell Lincoln "not to back down an inch" concerning the war effort and its possible effects on prisoners. "I deliver my message to you, Mr. President," the chaplain concluded, "in the name of the martyrs of Liberty."[30]

On February 20, McCabe was invited to attend a White House reception. President Lincoln recognized McCabe as the man who had sung the "Battle Hymn of the Republic." "Take it all in all," Lincoln told McCabe, "the song and the singing, that was the best I ever heard."[31]

"A War-time Aurora Borealis."

T he war had not been kind to Confederate Brigadier General Henry A. Wise. While other commanders gained important victories against Union forces, the sickly and contentious Wise had accomplished nothing. In 1861, while serving under Lee in the Kanahwa Valley in western Virginia, Wise had fought with his political rival, Brigadier General John B. Floyd who outranked him. The Confederate Secretary of War had removed Wise from this command and placed him in charge of troops defending Roanoke Island, a guardian of the North Carolina sounds and the back door to Norfolk. In early February 1862, Wise was sick in bed while Union forces battled for control of the island. With ease, they rolled back Wise's two thousand Confederates. One of the casualties that day was Wise's eldest son, O. Jennings.

The ex-governor served next at Chaffin's Farm in Virginia where he spent his time directing troops in building fortifications. There, on July 16, 1862, Wise learned by mail that federal troops had taken control of his farm Rolleston in Virginia's Princess Anne County, just six miles outside of Norfolk. Early the next morning, Wise penned a letter to his wife.

"I expect we are stripped of every thing," he wrote, "but I am resigned to submit to the will of God in this wretched war." He complained that he had been awakened "by a dream that my negroes had my house and effects and showed signs of insulting dear Mary," but was resigned to the knowledge that "Time & trial will prove the probation of all these events."[1]

General William Tecumseh Sherman before the famous "March to the Sea."

Rolleston had been taken shortly after Norfolk and Portsmouth, located just south of Fort Monroe at the mouth of the James River, fell under Union control during General McClellan's Peninsula Campaign in the spring of 1862. Almost immediately, missionary organizations invaded the two towns, setting up schools for slaves. One of these was the American Missionary Association established September 3, 1846, from the remnants of the *Amistad* Committee.

That committee formed soon after the capture of the *Amistad*, a Spanish coastal slave ship, on August 26, 1839. Lieutenant Thomas R. Gedney, in command of the brig *Washington*, discovered the vessel off the east coast of Long Island. He found that a group of slaves, led by the African Mendi tribesman Cinque, had risen up against their captors, killed the captain and a cook, the other members of the crew having escaped in a life boat. The slaves were attempting to sail home to Africa. Gedney brought them to New Haven, Connecticut, to be tried for crimes on the high seas.

The Spanish government applied to U.S. Secretary of State John Forsyth for the return of the Africans, but by then, American

Wise's estate, Rolleston, was occupied by the Union Army in 1862 and converted into a freedmen's school by the American Missionary Association in 1863.

198

abolitionists were suing for the release of the prisoners. S. S. Jocelyn, Joshua Leavitt, and Lewis Tappan had organized the *Amistad* Committee for the purpose of funding a defense for Cinque and his companions. The defense team included Connecticut lawyer Roger S. Baldwin and former U.S. President John Quincy Adams.

Their efforts were not wasted. On March 9, 1841, the Supreme Court ruled that the *Amistad* slaves had been illegally taken from Africa and were therefore justified in killing their captors. The Africans were released, and the members of the *Amistad* Committee generously provided them with a ship and three Christian missionaries for their return voyage. This venture proved so successful that Jocelyn and the others reformed their committee as the American Missionary Association in 1846 to carry on missionary work in developing countries.[2]

The temptation of doing in the South what they had done so well overseas proved too much for association members. By early 1863, they had schools operating in Norfolk and Portsmouth, and were looking to expand the effort nearby. But Confederate sympathizers managed to set fire to some of the buildings used to teach slaves. One association correspondent complained that there were "a good many incendiary fires" in both cities, and that, "as soon as the fire engines begin to work some one always manages to cut the hose."[3]

The missionary organizations began using buildings belonging to Confederate officers or the homes of prominent people which had been abandoned, believing that Confederates would not dare touch the home of a prominent Confederate general or politician. Historic buildings also served as safe houses for schools. The American Missionary Association started one school in the home of former U.S. President John Tyler and another at Henry Wise's home on the banks of the Elizabeth River.

Among the new missionary teachers at Rolleston in the summer of 1863 were Sarah and Lucy Chase, Quaker spinsters from Worcester, Massachusetts. Both of them were thrilled to be in the home of the murderer of John Brown. They milked one of Wise's cows, rode around in his carriage, and made an inventory of his household goods while wondering "if [Wise's] blood-stained fingers gave the rosy hue to his finger-bowls." Sarah was asked to name a baby born among Wise's former slaves. Standing on the threshold of Rolleston, she called the male infant "John Brown Wise." Lucy later reported, "While we were at the Wise farm a woman and two children found an asylum there—

an asylum in the human stable, now washed and made clean by the blood of John Brown!"[4]

Some time between the summer and winter of 1863, many of Wise's possessions at Rolleston were moved to Fort Monroe, after the association left the farm during the harvest season. This caused some problems for association member Reverend William S. Bell, who had come to the Wise farm as superintendent of the new freedmen's school in November. He immediately requested furnishings for the house, including eight to ten yards of toweling, eighteen yards of bed ticking, half a dozen teaspoons and tablespoons, and a carving knife.[5]

Within a few weeks of his arrival, he had a "negro" school going in the dining room. "Here, where treason was talked over, and toasts drank to the success of the traitors," Reverend Bell wrote to *American Missionary* magazine, "we every day hear sung the famous John Brown song."

In mid-December, the school attracted a distinguished visitor: John Brown's daughter, Annie, who had served as look-out at the Kennedy Farm on Maryland Heights during the summer and early autumn before the raid on Harper's Ferry. "The scholars sang for her," Bell wrote of the event, "a song tributary to her late honored father, and both herself and the scholars seemed greatly interested."

In one of his letters to the association, Bell requested a portrait of Brown, stating that "the young folks want very much to see the likeness of the old hero."[6] African American journalist Willis Augustus Hodges honored the request during his visit to the farm in September 1864. Years earlier, when Hodges had printed an anti-slavery paper called *The Ram's Horn*, he agreed to publish an article Brown had written called "Sambo's Mistakes." Now Hodges gladly provided Bell with Brown's likeness, and placed the picture "upon the Nail [where] his Murderer's looking glass once hung."[7]

The Confederate Army granted General Wise a furlough in January 1864. At that time, he was helping General P. G. T. Beauregard defend the city of Charleston, South Carolina. Since Wise had lost his property in Princess Anne County, he didn't have a place to go on his furlough. Luckily, his family came to his rescue, arranging for him to

Ellen Wise had to face down a Union cavalry officer who was searching for her father, Henry. The officer called her father "the man who murdered John Brown."

stay at "Eastwood," a tobacco plantation in the area near Goochland west of Richmond. Toward the end of February, Henry's wife Mary traveled to Eastwood while their nineteen-year-old daughter Ellen remained in Richmond awaiting her father's arrival by train.[8]

Henry arrived on or about February 29. He and Ellen made plans to travel to Goochland County by way of the James River Kanawha Canal. Lily pads fringed the canal's banks, and graceful weeping willows decorated its shores. Their transport was a barge called *The Packet*, which was pulled through the murky waters by three broken-down horses. A slave compelled the tired nags to move forward, and blew on a tin horn whenever the boat stopped to let passengers off.

The Packet, which Ellen thought bore a strong resemblance to Noah's Ark, was comprised of four main compartments. The passenger section in front could be divided into two separate areas to provide sleeping quarters for men and women. Just behind it was the kitchen. A gangway separated the kitchen from the passenger compartment. This gangway had the barge's only toilet facilities, a comb, brush, and tin basin, all attached to the wall by chains to prevent them from falling overboard. Behind the kitchen was a compartment for servants, and at the stern was the captain's cabin. The deck above was loaded with trunks, bags, and barrels.

The barge left Richmond at 5 p.m., traveling at a top speed of a little more than three and a half miles per hour. Given the pleasant weather and the stuffiness of the passenger section, many of the young people and soldiers on the boat chose to ride on the deck sitting on the bags and trunks. It was a somewhat risky venture, because of the many low bridges crossing the canal. One very elderly servant named Dinah failed to hear the helmsman's cry of "Low breeege!" and fell into the water feet first. Her hoop skirts retained air, holding her upright as she floated to shore screaming, but otherwise unhurt.

As night came on, many of the passengers prepared for bed. The crew hung up hammocks in the passenger section and dragged out bedding to place in the hammocks and on the tables.

Henry and his daughter would have to wait for their rest, as they were getting off at Dover Mills, just twenty miles up the canal. They arrived at their destination about 10:30. A carriage from Eastwood waited for them in front of the country store at the landing. Light from the store caused the sides of the carriage and the horses' tack to glitter as they pranced and fretted restlessly in the cold night air. Plumer Hobson, owner of Eastwood, greeted Henry and his daughter. Once Hobson had picked up the mail delivered by the barge, he and his guests boarded the carriage. Then he signaled the driver Ephraim to proceed.

The carriage soon moved past the tobacco barns at Eastwood, and Ellen could see the lights of the main house shining in a grove of oaks about a half mile away. She also saw what she thought was an Aurora Borealis in the night sky, but she paid little attention to it.

Once they arrived, Henry and Ellen were treated to a feast of biscuits, real coffee, sugar, sorghum, and cream. Then they went upstairs to beds luxuriously made up with fluffy white pillows, lavender-scented linen sheets, and warm blankets.

The sleep of the household was disturbed toward dawn by pounding on the oak doors downstairs. A soldier in Henry Wise's brigade on furlough and on route to his home in Goochland County had run into Union Colonel Ulric Dahlgren's cavalry. Having failed to get across the flooded James River to support General Judson Kilpatrick's raid on Richmond, Dahlgren's men were roaming the countryside setting fire to the Dover mills and the outbuildings of local plantations. This accounted for the unusual lights Ellen had seen in the night sky.

A troop of these soldiers had discovered that Henry Wise, the man who had "murdered" John Brown, was staying at Eastwood, and were now galloping toward the plantation to gain the honor of capturing him. Hobson arranged for two horses, Pulaski and Lucy Washington, to be saddled, as he and Wise hurriedly dressed. At dawn, they galloped toward the woods just as Ellen saw Union cavalry coming toward Eastwood from the plundered Seddon plantation, Sabot Hall.

A cavalry man riding a gray, worn-out horse with a McClellan saddle halted his steed at the steps of the front porch. He glared at Ellen with flashing eyes and demanded to know the whereabouts of the man who had hanged John Brown.

Out of the corner of her eye, Ellen saw Hobson and her father disappear into the woods just as she gave the soldier a withering glare. Clutching the child beside her, she declared with a straight face that her father was currently in Charleston, South Carolina. The soldier told her she was a liar and that he intended to capture her father even if he had to chase him all the way to hell. "Take your damned white head into the house," he shouted. With relief, Ellen went back inside.

From the windows on the second floor, she could see the barns at Dover plantation and Sabot Hill burning. She watched helplessly as the soldiers invaded the Eastwood barn, exchanging their worn-out horses for fresh ones. They did not set fire to Eastwood, but they carried away some of the plantation's slaves to freedom whether they wanted to be free or not, including the carriage driver, Ephraim.

Hobson and Wise rode back to Eastwood two days later. They had arrived in Richmond just in time to warn Confederate authorities about the Kilpatrick-Dahlgren cavalry raid. Richmond military units quickly organized and marched to reinforce the fortifications three miles north of the city. When Kilpatrick arrived, he discovered the forts were too well manned and ordered his men to ride back toward Union lines.

General Wise faced Union troops again in June 1864 when he was ordered to help with the defense of Petersburg, Virginia. Arriving in the town on June 15, Wise hastily placed his 2200 men in the batteries and trenches guarding the eastern approaches to the city while his commanding officer, Major General Pierre G. T. Beauregard tried to persuade General Robert E. Lee that the Union army's objective was not to attack Richmond, as Lee believed, but the Petersburg railroads. Wise met the initial assault of 16,000 Union soldiers under the command of Major General William "Baldy" Smith. Union General Ulysses S. Grant had ordered Smith to take Petersburg if possible and cut off the rail line stretching twenty-five miles north to Richmond.

The attack came toward nightfall, and Wise's men were badly mauled. Confederate forces were pushed out of Batteries Five through Eleven and the connecting trenches. But Smith failed to press the attack, Wise having convinced him by subterfuge that his forces were much larger than they actually were. Early on the 16th, Beauregard sent all the reinforcements he could to the Petersburg defenses, as Union soldiers, heavily reinforced, continued their attacks. In two days, the Union army seized Batteries Four, and Twelve through Fourteen, but in that time, Lee received information that Grant's army was south of the James River and moving on Petersburg, forcing him to send the main part of his army to the beleaguered city. On June 18, Lee's army stood tall and stalled from a new line Grant's sledgehammer attacks, and the nine month Petersburg siege ensued. Wise's initial efforts had kept the Union army from overrunning the rail lines. For the first time in the war, his fellow officers saw Wise as a hero.

To relieve some of the pressure that Grant was applying to the Confederate Army, Lee had ordered Jubal Early to take his Corps and move on Washington. The Corps had left on the mission on June 13, just before Grant's army stole a march on Lee and crossed the James River to assail Petersburg. Early fought his way up the Shenandoah Valley to Harper's Ferry, and into Maryland. In mid July, he stood within sight of the Capitol dome at Washington.

Thanks to Jubal Early's raid, Annie Pierpont, daughter of the governor of Union loyal Virginia, got her first and last look at the Civil War.[9] Her father had allowed his wife and children to move to Laurel, Maryland, on the rail line between Baltimore and the nation's capital, believing that they would remain safe north of Washington.

One morning, the Pierpont children discovered a set of mysterious tiny footprints, in all likelihood animal tracks, under the currant bushes in the garden behind their home. Annie speculated that they must be fairy footprints, but another child insisted they were made by angels. Annie's mother Julia was in the house with visiting Aunt Gordon. They were making plans for a fair, the proceeds of which would benefit the U.S. Sanitary Commission.

Suddenly, the distant booming of artillery disturbed the air. Mrs. Pierpont dismissed it at first as thunder. But when it continued, and frightened townsfolk outside the house started shouting, "The rebels are coming!" Mrs. Pierpont acted.

She and Aunt Gordon carried Governor Pierpont's important papers and the family silver next door to the cellar of the Masonic Lodge, believing that rebels would not dare burn such a place. Annie watched at the lodge's door, ready to give the alarm if anyone came, while the two women frantically pried up floorboards to hide the papers and silver.

The women returned to the house and took the children to the nursery where they swiftly bundled each child up in two layers of clothes, hid sandwiches in their garments, and looped identification tags around their necks. Mrs. Pierpont told the children to stay on the front lawn, and if they saw the rebels coming, they were each to grab the hand of an adult.

The children watched through the slats on the front gate as disheveled soldiers ran by the house and the booming grew louder. Annie's older brother Sammie suggested that they could gather rocks and use them to drive the rebels off. Annie thought it a good idea, and soon all the Pierpont children were armed and ready.

The Eastwood tobacco plantation near Dover Mills, Virginia.

The rebels never came. Jubal Early had found the road to the nation's capital every bit as hard to travel as the Union soldiers had found the road to Richmond. The children went back into the house and took off their extra clothes with sad expressions.

"We had been defrauded of seeing the Rebels run when Sammie's stones went flying after them," Annie wrote later of the experience. "We had missed the joy of sleeping out of doors that night when the town was burned, as we had ardently hoped, and had been led to expect it would be; and we had been extremely uncomfortable in our heavy clothes, all for nothing.... Truly, the grownups had given us a very disappointing day." At least the sandwiches had not contributed to their discomfort. After having been told not to eat them, the children, in their excitement during the battle, had forgotten the instruction and nibbled them into oblivion.

In October of 1864, Chaplain McCabe returned to the Army of the Potomac now besieging Petersburg. He traveled from Washington down to City Point, Virginia, and visited the soldiers in the trenches and works, holding revival meetings and singing at every available opportunity.

He also lost some of his old prejudices. Up to this point, McCabe had believed that black men lacked the courage and discipline to fight and be good soldiers. But black soldiers held a long section of the federal line. The chaplain beckoned to one of the older black men in a unit manning the line. His uniform showed the wear of a soldier who had seen hard fighting.

"How is it that General Grant trusts you with these lines?" McCabe asked the man. "Suppose the enemy should break through here."

The old soldier's eyes widened with anger and he bared his teeth. "General Grant trusts us with these lines, *because we took them.*"

"They will be true," McCabe wrote of the black soldiers later that day in his journal. "They are fighting in no common way. If captured, their death is well-nigh certain.... They still enlist, and God grant that they may fight their way to liberty and social position."[10]

With Grant's army bogged down in front of Petersburg, and his other generals making very slow progress subduing the Confederate armies in the field, Lincoln faced a difficult re-election campaign. He was running for a second term against Democratic nominee George Brinton McClellan. But thanks to Clement Vallandigham, a man who had always chosen to defend southern interests, especially after John Brown's raid, the Democratic party had a "peace plank" calling for the end of hostilities "at the earliest practicable moment ... on the basis of the Federal Union of the States."[11]

Vallandigham, who had been arrested and deported as a traitor, but had sneaked back into his native Ohio just in time to be named a delegate to the Democratic Convention, defended his peace plank with surprising vehemence. "Whoever charges," he told the crowd, "that I want to stop this war in order that there may be Southern independence charges that which is false, and lies in his teeth, and lies in his throat!"

Sherman put in effect John Brown's plan to march through the South freeing slaves as he went. The general, however, proved to be a very reluctant liberator.

To confuse matters, McClellan told the Democratic delegates who had eagerly nominated him that he could not support their peace plank. "I could not look in the face of my gallant comrades of the army and navy who have survived so many bloody battles," he explained, "and tell them that their labors and the sacrifices of so many of our slain and wounded brethren have been in vain...."[12]

Before going north to help with Lincoln's re-election bid, Governor Pierpont met with a very depressed president. Speaking of the Democratic depiction of the war effort, Lincoln said, "They have declared the war a failure, and by false representations they are not only doing great mischief in the country, but they are creating dissatisfaction among the soldiers in the Army." The president concluded, "We must have military success, if we [are to] succeed this fall in the elections.... All looks to me like uncertainty without military success."[13]

By the time of the Democratic Convention, Admiral David Farragut had already entered Mobile Bay in Alabama and defeated a rebel fleet, while the Union army captured the forts guarding the bay's entrance. And more good news reached the War Office over the telegraph wires. On September 2, Major General William Tecumseh Sherman took Atlanta, Georgia, and in September and October, General Philip Sheridan and his troops defeated Confederate General Early in a series of battles in the Shenandoah Valley, including the Battle of Cedar Creek fought on October 19. With these three victories, Lincoln easily beat McClellan in the November election, getting 212 electoral votes to McClellan's 21, and gaining more than 52% of the popular vote.

Now that the election was over, President Lincoln considered allowing General Sherman to carry out a new, bold venture: a march through Georgia without access to telegraph lines or supply lines. Ever since Atlanta had been emptied of civilians, Sherman had been pressing Ulysses S. Grant, Henry Halleck at the War Department, and President Lincoln for permission to do this. "I can make the march and make Georgia howl," Sherman boasted in a telegram to Grant.[14] He argued further that, by raiding Georgia's interior, he could prevent supplies of food and reinforcements from reaching Lee's men in Petersburg.

At first Grant and Lincoln were reluctant to allow Sherman to conduct the massive raid. Confederate General John Bell Hood, who had fought to keep Sherman out of Atlanta, still commanded a sizable army. Sherman sent part of his army to serve under Major General George Thomas in Tennessee. Thomas promised to engage Hood and keep him out of Georgia. Only then did Grant give permission for Sherman's march to the sea.

General Sherman gave the order for his men to leave the city on November 15, 1864. As the troops marched out, other troops, under orders, set fire to the city's factories and warehouses. Many homes burned as well when the conflagration spread. The following day, the Union troops were gone and Atlanta lay in ruins.

On the morning of November 16, 1864, General Sherman rode his horse to Bald Hill. From this position, he could see the Fourteenth Corps leaving the city. "Behind us lay Atlanta, smouldering and in ruins," he wrote in his *Memoirs*, "the black smoke rising high in air, and hanging like a pall over the ruined city...." A band played "John Brown's Body." Soldiers sang the song in time with the band as they marched along. Sherman commented that "never before or since have

As members of the Fourteenth Corps marched out of the burning city of Atlanta, they sang "John Brown's Body."

I heard the chorus of 'Glory, glory, hallelujah!' done with more spirit, or in better harmony of time and place."[15]

At the beginning of the war, while superintendent at a military academy in Louisiana, Sherman had denied having any abolitionist sentiments, although he did argue that slaves should be allowed to learn to read and write, thereby increasing their value, and that families sold at auction should not be separated.[16] Now Grant and the president pressured him to fulfill John Brown's abolitionist dream of an army liberating slaves as it marched through the Deep South. General Grant had, in fact, asked Sherman to arm all the slaves and draft them into the army. Fearing that they might needlessly attack and kill their masters, Sherman preferred to accept slaves only as volunteers, and did not arm those who did not want to be soldiers.

He also feared that slaves following his soldiers would put too great a burden on the supplies set aside for his army. "You must stay where you are and not load us up with useless mouths," Sherman advised one black man. "We can take along a few of the young, strong men— but if you swarm after us, old and young, feeble and helpless, you'll just cripple us."[17]

But large numbers of slaves did swarm after the Union soldiers. The newly freed men and women cheered the troops as liberators and provided them with information about the movements of rebel units.

210

One Illinois artilleryman wrote: "They thought it was freedom now or never, and would follow whether or no... Some in buggies, costly and glittering; some on horseback, the horses old and blind, and others on foot; all following up in right jolly mood, bound for ease and freedom."[18]

At night, the slaves gathered in the encampments to entertain the troops with singing, dancing, and juggling. They also gave demonstrations of African languages. The girls frequently slept with Union soldiers to gain privileges. David Conyngham of the *New York Herald* wrote: "It would be vexatious to the Grand Turk or Brigham Young if they could only see how many of the dark houris were in the employment of officers' servants and teamsters."[19]

Sherman's troops were never short on supplies. He had given orders to his men to forage the countryside for whatever food was available. The troops found such an abundance of sweet potatoes, pigs, chickens, turkeys, and other foods that the supply wagons were seldom or never used. The soldiers burned whatever they couldn't carry, sometimes burning down houses and barns that had been abandoned.

Slave quarters were also robbed. A black girl in the town of Covington was incensed when she discovered that Union soldiers had stolen all her clothing. When she saw a black man wearing one of her new hats, she rushed up to him and yelled in his face, "Oh! If I had the power like I've got the will, I'd tear you to pieces."[20]

One of Sherman's officers, General Jefferson C. Davis, was annoyed by the large numbers of freedmen following the army. Davis was a pro-slavery man from Indiana who had remained in the United States Army strictly to preserve the Union. On Friday, December 2, 1864, he discovered the perfect place to rid himself of the freedmen. His corps had reached Ebenezer Creek, a turgid flow of muddy water a hundred feet wide that ran down to the Savannah River. The creek lay east of the town of Springfield, some thirty-five miles from Savannah. In hopes of slowing the Union advance, Confederates had destroyed a bridge over the creek. The general ordered his men to hold back the freedmen while soldiers in an Indiana regiment assembled a pontoon bridge, working through the night to complete it. The next morning, Davis's corps crossed over to the other side. Then the remaining soldiers jumped onto the bridge, cut the ropes, and pulled the pontoon bridge up behind them.

The freedmen cried out in anguish. Many plunged into the icy waters to escape from Major General Joseph Wheeler's approaching rebel cavalry. Union soldiers aware of the desparate situation threw pieces of timber to the struggling people who quickly constructed a crude raft. Freedmen tied blankets together to make a towline for the makeshift conveyance. Only six people at a time could cross using the raft, but it proved to be very unstable, frequently dumping its occupants into the deep water.

Some soldiers jumped into the water to rescue the drowning swimmers. Other troops chopped down trees and threw them in the stream. Some of the freedmen grabbed the branches of the trees and pulled themselves to safety. Others drowned, and Wheeler captured those few who could not face the waters.

Davis's men were outraged by their corps commander's callous behavior. One refered to Davis as a "military tyrant, without one spark of humanity in his makeup." Another called him "inhuman and fiendish." Major James Connolly summed up this resentment when he labelled the incident "an inhuman barbarous proceeding."[21] Sherman ignored these reports and refused to condemn or condone Davis's action.

Once Sherman had taken Savannah, negative reports of the Ebenezer Creek incident and Sherman's reluctance to deal with Davis reached Washington. On December 30, 1864, Chief-of-Staff Henry Halleck at the War Department in Washington wrote to Sherman that many federal officials were accusing Sherman of having, "manifested an almost criminal dislike to the negro." He also expressed disappointment that Sherman's army had not brought more runaway slaves to Savannah, "thus stripping Georgia of that number of laborers and opening a road by which as many more could have escaped from their masters." The letter concluded with a plan to use Sherman's course to Savannah as a route for slaves escaping from the plantations. "I believe that a manifestation on your part of a desire to bring the slaves within our lines will do much to silence your opponents."[22]

Sherman made no reply to Halleck's letter, there being many other duties for him to perform as the pressure mounted. The War Department wanted Sherman to take the former slaves into the army and use them to guard the city of Savannah, but Sherman refused to use the black troops. On New Year's Eve, he gave his recommendations for the troops needed to guard the city. "Five thousand men will be plenty, and white troops will be best, as the people are dreadfully alarmed lest we garrison the place with negroes."[23]

That day, Halleck wrote to Major General John G. Foster, commanding the Department of the South headquartered at Port Royal, South Carolina, asking him to recruit blacks into the army. "It would be well to circulate a notice," Halleck wrote, "that you will receive, pay, clothe, and arm all able-bodied negroes who will join you."[24]

Early in January, army recruiting agents from a number of northern states arrived in Savannah. These agents locked up former slaves who were eligible for army service and refused to let them go until they agreed to become soldiers. The agents intended to fill the assigned army quotas of men from their own states with liberated slaves from Georgia so that white men from their states would not be drafted. Sherman was infuriated by this practice and released all men held by the recruiting agents.

The situation became so serious that Secretary of War Edwin M. Stanton traveled down to Savannah on January 11 in order to meet with Sherman and learn first hand what was happening. The next day, he and General Sherman met with twenty black preachers living in Savannah.The men ranged in age from forty to seventy-two. Three of these men had been liberated by the wills of their masters or mistresses, four were free born, and four were able to purchase their freedom. But the largest number, nine, had only become free when Sherman's army marched into Savannah.

Sixty-seven-year-old Garrison Frazier was selected as spokesman for the group. He had been a slave until 1857 when he was able to purchase his and his wife's freedom for $1,000 in gold and silver. He had also served as a minister in the Baptist Church for thirty-five years but was then in poor health and no longer had a congregation.

Under Stanton's questioning, Frazier exhibited a detailed knowledge of the war effort and Lincoln's plans to free the slaves held in Confederate territory. He disapproved of the state recruiting agents who were simply trying to prevent white people from doing their duty. The minister suggested that Stanton set a quota for recruitment in the state of Georgia, and he and the other ministers would act as agents to fill that quota. Sherman could direct them in this effort.

Stanton then dismissed Sherman from the room, and asked Frazier how the black people felt about the general. "We looked upon General Sherman," Frazier replied, "as a man, in the providence of God, specially set apart to accomplish this work, and we unanimously felt inexpressible gratitude to him, looking upon him as a man that should be honored for the faithful performance of his duty."[25]

Bolstered by Frazier's favorable opinion, Sherman replied to Halleck's accusations. "I know enough of 'the people'" he told the general, "to feel that a single mistake made by some of my subordinates will tumble down my fame into infamy. But the nigger? Why, in God's name, can't sensible men let him alone?"

Sherman defended General Davis's actions at Ebenezer Creek, claiming that Davis did not want to leave the freedmen behind. He only wanted his pontoon bridge. As for any accusations that he disliked blacks, Sherman announced, "I profess to be the best kind of a friend to Sambo, and think that on such a question Sambo should be consulted."

He also openly denounced the recruiting agents while bolstering his own image: "It is hard to tell in what sense I am most appreciated by Sambo—in saving him from his master, or the new master [the State Recruiters] that threatens him with a new species of slavery."[26]

Although Frazier had made some good suggestions, this did not speed up the process of recruiting young black men. By early February, Major General Foster, who as commander of the Department of the South was in charge at Savannah, was frustrated with the slowness of the recruitment of freed slaves. In a letter to Halleck, he wrote, "These men, just freed from long servitude, are, of necessity, ignorant and improvident.... Needing their services as soldiers, I respectfully ask that the Department will fix a quota for the States of South Carolina and Georgia, and allow me to fill it by conscripting the able-bodied young colored men...."[27]

By that time, General Sherman was in South Carolina moving his army along a route marked by destruction. Rumor had it that the Union soldiers on the march had purchased $5,000 worth of matches to set the Carolinas ablaze.

In April of 1864, the Senate passed a bill by a two-thirds vote calling for a new amendment to the Constitution which would end slavery forever. In January 1865, with Grant still holding Lee's army along a line that stretched fifty miles from Petersburg to Richmond, and Sherman planning to torch the Carolinas, the bill went to the House of Representatives under very favorable conditions. Still, there was substantial resistance to overcome before the measure would pass the House.

All through that month, Lincoln and Republican representatives carried on secret negotiations to pass the bill. The Washington rumor mill maintained that the negotiations involved political patronage, the release of prisoners of war related to Democratic representatives, and favors granted to a New Jersey railroad monopoly. The bill finally came up for a vote on January 31. When Speaker of the House Schuyler Colfax announced that the measure had passed by a vote of 119 to 56, there was cheering in the galleries where women waved their handkerchiefs, and on the floor of the House where Republicans danced and waved their hats and canes.

Representative Thaddeus Stevens of Pennsylvania regretted that "The greatest measure of the nineteenth century was passed by corruption, aided and abetted by the purest man in America." President Lincoln, however, felt that the effort was worth while, calling it "a great moral victory" and "a King's cure for all the evils" the country had endured.

The amendment now had to be approved by three-fourths of the states. Maryland and Missouri had already ended slavery by state law, as well as the newly reconstructed state governments of Louisiana and Arkansas. Governor Pierpont's new constitution for Virginia also banned slavery.

Everyone in the North had reason to hope that the long nightmare of war caused by slavery and secession would soon be ended by force of arms and rule of law, and that everyone living in America would be heir to the benefits of freedom. Representative George Julian of Indiana said, "It seemed to me I had been born into a new life, and that the world was overflowing with beauty and joy."[28]

Two months later, on April 3, the country rejoiced again, as news reached Washington that Lee's defensive lines had collapsed the day before, and Richmond had been occupied. The remainder of Lee's army fled westward toward Danville hoping to reach essential supplies, and Grant's army followed in hopes of capturing Lee and his men.

The following day, President Lincoln visited Richmond, now a burned city. He made his way to the house Confederate President Davis had used. While there, he met with John A. Campbell, a former U.S. Supreme Court justice and Assistant Secretary of War for the Confederacy. Campbell proposed that Lincoln allow the Virginia state legislature to make arrangements for the surrender of Lee's army. The president made no promises but said that he would discuss the matter with Campbell the following day.

At 10 a.m. on April 5, Lincoln met with Campbell again aboard the U.S.S. *Malvern*, then at anchor in the James River just off the Rockett's navy yard in Richmond. He gave Campbell a list of the conditions of surrender and told him that he would decide tomorrow whether the Virginia legislature could meet. The next day, Lincoln wrote an order for Union Major General Godfrey Weitzel, then in charge of Richmond, to allow the Confederate legislature to assemble "and take measures to withdraw the Virginia troops and other support from resistance to the general government." If the assembly refused to order a surrender, Weitzel was to break up the meeting. Lincoln confessed to Grant that he didn't think anything would come of this. In any case, the president promised that this action would not "hinder, or interfere with you in your work."[29]

Lincoln's plan would interfere with the work of Governor Francis H. Pierpont. All through the war, Lincoln had always acknowledged Pierpont as the legitimate governor of Virginia, but the president's recognition of the Richmond government and its right to operate under federal sanction, might undo the work of Pierpont's restored Virginia government. All Pierpont could do for the moment was pray that Grant's army would capture Lee before the Richmond politicians negotiated a surrender.

13

"Fair assassin, murder white...."

On Friday morning, April 7, 1865, General Robert E. Lee found Major General Bushrod R. Johnson whose division had borne much of the brunt of the federal attack the day before at Sayler's Creek. The exhausted Johnson reported that his division had ceased to exist. In the middle of his discussion with Johnson, Lee spotted men in tattered gray uniforms marching toward him in proper formation. It was General Wise's brigade from Johnson's division. Somehow, they had escaped annihilation the day before. Wise led the men on foot, wearing a gray blanket and an odd hat tilted at an angle. His face and hair were covered with red mud from the puddle he had tried to use as a wash basin.

Lee approached Wise and asked about the condition of his men. Wise answered smartly, "Ready for dress-parade." The ex-governor then demanded rations for his men who were tired and hungry, insisting that "they shall not move another step until *somebody* gives them something to eat!"

"They deserve something to eat, and shall have it," Lee promised; "and meanwhile you shall share my breakfast."

As the two men sat down to their sparse rations, Wise denounced General Johnson's conduct during the Battle of Sayler's Creek. Lee jokingly pointed out that Wise could be court-martialed and shot for showing disrespect to his superior officer. "Shot!" Wise exclaimed. "I wish you would shoot me. If you don't, some Yankee probably will within the next twenty-four hours."

Lee, switching to a more serious tone, asked Wise what he thought of the army's situation. "Situation?" Wise said in disbelief. "There is no situation! Nothing remains, General Lee, but to put your poor men

---

After his defeat at Appomattox in 1865, General Lee became president of Washington College.

on your poor mules and send them home in time for spring ploughing....
I say to you, sir, emphatically, that to prolong the struggle is murder,
and the blood of every man who is killed from this time forth is on
your head...."

General Lee asked Wise not to engage in such wild talk. "What
would the country think of me, if I did what you suggest?"

"Country be damned!" Wise replied. "There is no country. There
has been no country, General, for a year or more. You are the country
to these men. They have fought for you. They have shivered through a
long winter for you. Without pay or clothes, or care of any sort, their
devotion to you and faith in you have been the only things which have
held this army together."

For the time being, Lee chose to keep the army moving westward,
in hopes of reaching supplies at Appomattox Station or beyond. Wise
was placed in charge of all stragglers regardless of rank, including his
disgruntled division commander, Bushrod Johnson, who was told to
go home.[1]

That same evening at Farmville, Virginia, General Ulysses S. Grant
sat on the piazza of the Prince Edward Hotel watching soldiers in the
Sixth Corps march by in pursuit of Lee's fleeing army. As night fell,
bonfires were lit at the sides of the road to aid the soldiers in the dark.
Some were inspired to use burning pieces of wood as torches. Marching
past Grant, they began to sing, "John Brown's body lies a-moulderin'
in the grave." Soon, an entire corps was singing the chorus, while Grant
sat on the porch smoking a cigar and reviewing his troops.[2]

On Palm Sunday, at Appomattox Court House, Henry Wise
received the order to cease hostilities. As his men stacked their arms,
Wise walked down a road to reconnoiter the situation. While walking
back to his command, a Union cavalry officer with long yellow hair
charged up the road at a gallop, yelling, "Surrender! Surrender!" When
the officer overtook him, Henry looked up at him, arms akimbo and
rocking back and forth on his feet while chewing a quid of tobacco.
"Ain't you a *little late*?" Wise asked the officer. "I surrendered about an
hour ago." The officer identified himself as Major General George
Armstrong Custer.[3]

That evening, a telegram from Secretary of War Stanton arrived
at Governor Pierpont's hotel room in Alexandria, Virginia. Lee had
surrendered his army to General Grant.[4] The news could not have come
at a better time for the governor of Restored Virginia. Although Lincoln

had rescinded the order allowing the Richmond government to assemble, the chances of the order being reissued were good so long as Lee's army remained in the field. But with Lee's army dissolved, Pierpont's administration could now act as the legitimate government of Virginia.

The day after Pierpont received the telegram, Lincoln asked him to come to the White House. The president explained at some length that he had always intended Pierpont's government to be installed in Richmond. "If I had known that General Lee would surrender so soon," Lincoln continued, "I would not have issued the proclamation."[5]

By April 10, news of Lee's surrender reached Boston and Julia Ward Howe wrote in her diary: "Today, we have the news of Lee's surrender, with the whole remnant of his army. The City is alive with people. All flags hung out—shop windows decorated—processions in the streets. All friends meet & shake hands. In the newspaper Bulletins with placards as 'Gloria in Excelsis Deo.' 'Thanks be to God.' We all call it the greatest day of our lives."[6]

On Tuesday, April 11, Confederate soldiers were stacking their arms at Appomattox. General Henry Wise, who had now exchanged his gray blanket for a more comfortable blue great coat decorated with gold braid, marched his men up to the 118th Pennsylvania, giving commands in a high pitched, raspy voice which irritated his soldiers. One Confederate called out, "Look at him! He is brave enough now, but he never was so near the Yankees before in his life." The Pennsylvanians were curious about the soldier's remarks and asked who his commander was.

When they learned their general was Henry Wise, the man who had been governor of Virginia when John Brown was executed, the Union soldiers joined in the taunting. One asked, "Who killed John Brown?" Another asked Wise, "Where did you steal your coat?" Others shouted, "Hang him to a sour apple tree!" and "Shoot him!"[7]

Brigadier General Joshua Lawrence Chamberlain of Maine rode down the line to determine the cause of the commotion. When he saw the red-faced Wise with tobacco juice trickling from the side of his mouth shouting at a group of Confederate soldiers and Union volunteers, Chamberlain told Wise to be quiet and proceed with the surrender in an orderly fashion. "This promises well for our coming good-will," Chamberlain explained; "brave men may become good friends."

Wise turned and glared at Chamberlain. "You are mistaken, sir," he yelled. "You may forgive us but we won't be forgiven. There is a rancor in our hearts which you little dream of. We hate you, sir."

"Oh, we don't mind much about dreams," Chamberlain retorted, "nor about hates either. Those two lines of business are closed."

Wise gazed sadly at Chamberlain's coat which had two ragged bullet holes in the breast. "Those were ugly shots, General," he said. "Where did you get them?" Chamberlain said he had been shot during an action at Lewis' Farm on the Quaker Road. "I suppose you think you did great things there," Wise interrupted; "I was ordered to attack you and check your advance; and I did it too with a vim, till I found I was fighting three army corps, when I thought it prudent to retire." Chamberlain explained that only three Union regiments were involved in that battle. "I know better," Wise said; "I saw the flags myself."

Their talk turned to other matters concerning the end of the war and what would happen next. Chamberlain, in an attempt to reassure Wise, said, "Don't worry about the end of the war. We are going home pretty soon, but not till we see you home."

"Home!" Wise said. "We haven't any. You have destroyed them. You have invaded Virginia, and ruined her. Her curse is on you."

"You shouldn't have invited us down here, then," Chamberlain said. "We expected somebody was going to get hurt when we took up your challenge. Didn't you? People who don't want to get hurt, General, had better not force a fight on unwilling Yankees."[8]

By evening of the 11th, the nation's capital was in a festive mood. A huge crowd armed with banners and shouting "Hurrah!" filled the east White House lawn, while bands played patriotic airs. Lincoln appeared on the balcony above them carrying a candle in his left hand, and a sheaf of foolscap in his right. At first, the president tried to hold the candle while juggling the papers of his speech, but this proved to be too much for him. His old friend Noah Brooks volunteered to hold the candle while Lincoln read the sheets and dropped them into the eager hands of his son Tad.[9]

Lincoln stated that plans had been approved for the readmittance of Louisiana to the Union, but that there was disagreement about certain details. "It is ... unsatisfactory to some," the president explained, "that the elective franchise is not given to the colored man. I would myself prefer that it were now conferred on the very intelligent, and on those who serve our cause as soldiers."[10] He made no mention of colonizing freed slaves. All those plans had been abandoned the previous year. Lincoln had been so thrilled with the performance of the black regiments in battle, that he no longer would consider exile for African Americans. Instead, he offered them the right to vote.

Among the throng of onlookers that night, one man, John Wilkes Booth, a famous actor, bristled at the implications of the president's pronouncements. Just before the presidential election of 1864, Booth had written to his sister Asia, comparing Lincoln to John Brown whom he thought of as "the grandest man of this century." Lincoln was trying to walk "in the footprints of old John Brown" but was not "fit to stand with that rugged old hero."

As Lincoln continued with his speech on Louisiana, Booth turned to his two companions, Lewis Powell and David Herold. "That means nigger citizenship!" Booth growled at them. "Now, by Christ, I'll put him through it. That is the last speech he will ever make."[11]

Booth had his own story to tell about abolitionist John Brown. On November 24, 1859, the flamboyant actor had just come out of a Richmond theater during a rehearsal break when he saw a group of soldiers in gray uniforms marching past. They were the Richmond Grays, a military unit that was leaving by train that morning for Charlestown to assist in the execution of John Brown. In an adventurous mood, Booth asked if he might join the Grays. They said he could and got him a uniform. When one of his theatrical companions asked who would do his part in the play that night, he responded bluntly that he didn't know and didn't care.

For the next week, Booth relished his first and last taste of the military life, until Brown's execution. The moment the platform fell out from under John Brown's feet, Philip Whitlock of the Grays noticed that Booth turned white. When Whitlock asked what was bothering him, Booth said that he needed a good stiff drink.

On Booth's return to Richmond, the theater manager refused to take him back into his company. The Grays prevailed upon the manager to forgive Booth and allow the unpredictable thespian to tread the boards again. Later, Booth told his sister Asia that he thought John Brown was a hero, however much he may have disagreed with Brown's cause. "He was a brave old man," he said; "his heart must have broken when he felt himself deserted."[12]

In the autumn of 1864, Booth planned to kidnap Lincoln and take him to Richmond as a hostage to get Confederate soldiers out of northern prisons. He left a letter with his sister Asia to be opened in the event of his death. In the letter, he boasted that he had "aided in the capture and execution of John Brown." He also wrote that he believed all members of the Republican party deserved the same fate as Brown because the war to preserve the Union had now become a devastating war to end slavery. "The South can make no choice," he added. "It is either extermination or slavery for themselves worse than death to draw from. I know my choice."[13]

On April 12, preparations were under way for a torchlight parade in Alexandria, Virginia. Annie Pierpont was dressed in her best white frock, and had been warned not to damage the embroidered ruffle. To the white dress was added a red skirt and a blue sash. Then, she sat in the bay window of the Pierpont hotel room overlooking the street where the parade would pass.

Her little brother Willie, also dressed in white, stood behind her on a chair waving an American flag. Soldiers marching past their window broke out in cheers, and marching bands played "Home Sweet Home." Willie, in his impatience to view the parade at closer range, made mad dashes for the yard in front of the hotel. His mother Julia always managed to retrieve him, but eventually the nurse was called to put Willie to bed. A young soldier volunteered to take Willie's place behind Annie in the bay window.[14]

On April 14, Good Friday, Chaplain McCabe arrived in Cincinnati where celebrations for the war's end had been continuing all week. "This city has been given over to enthusiastic demonstrations of rapture upon the part of the people," he wrote in his journal; "cannon and fireworks have filled the air with sounds familiar to every soldier's ear, and which cannot fail even in the midst of his rejoicing to bring to memory the terrible field of carnage."

McCabe gloried in the knowledge that this was the day the American flag would fly once more over Fort Sumter, the very same flag removed from the fort four years ago to the day when Major Robert Anderson surrendered the fort to Confederate forces under General Beauregard. Anderson would attend the ceremony. To the chaplain, that flag "with every star remaining" had a "higher and holier meaning attached" to it.[15]

That same morning, at 11 a.m., President Lincoln, General Grant, and his cabinet met. Secretary of State William Seward was recuperating at home from a carriage accident earlier in the week. His son Frederick sat in for him at the meeting. Stanton introduced his plans for reconstruction of the Confederate states, starting with Virginia. The plan included provisions for reasserting federal authority in Virginia and the re-establishment of its state government. Secretary of the Navy Gideon Welles objected to Stanton's proposal because Virginia already had a recognized, Union-loyal state government led by Francis H. Pierpont.

The men moved on to discuss the possible surrender of Confederate forces under General Joseph E. Johnston who was then facing Sherman's army near Greensboro, North Carolina. With Lee's army gone, everyone expected that Johnston would surrender, but so far the telegraph messages indicated that Sherman and Johnston were still negotiating. Grant commented that he expected to hear some word any moment from Sherman.

Lincoln then told the cabinet about a dream he had the previous night. When Welles inquired what kind of dream it was, Lincoln replied, "It relates to your element, the water. I seemed to be in some indescribable vessel and I was moving with great rapidity toward an indefinite shore." The president said he had the dream preceding many of the great victories and consequential events of the war: Sumter, Bull Run, Antietam, Gettysburg, Stone's River, and Vicksburg.

"Stone River was certainly no victory," Grant commented. "Nor can I think of any great results following it."

Lincoln admitted that it had not been a great moment for the Union, but he held that the dream came to him just before a great victory or some important event. "I had this strange dream again last night," he continued, "and we shall, judging from the past, have great news very soon. I think it must be from Sherman. My thoughts are in that direction as are most of yours."

"Perhaps at each of these periods there were possibilities of great change or disaster," Frederick Seward suggested, "and the vague feeling of uncertainty may have led to the dim vision in sleep."

"Perhaps," the president said, "that is the explanation."[16]

The cabinet meeting ended after three hours. General Grant thanked Lincoln for allowing him to attend, and proceeded with some hesitation to a more delicate matter. Earlier that morning, Lincoln had invited the general and his wife to come with him to Ford's Theater that evening. Ford's had scheduled a production of a farce by British playwright Tom Taylor called *Our American Cousin*. It concerned the visit of Asa Trenchard of Brattleboro, Vermont, to upper class relatives in England. English actress Laura Keene would be performing the role of Florence Trenchard, Asa's cousin. Stanton had put pressure on Grant to refuse the invitation, not wishing to encourage Lincoln to appear in public with so many southern sympathizers wandering the streets.

Grant told Lincoln that he could not attend the play that evening. His wife insisted that they take the afternoon train to Philadelphia so that they could see their children, and she wanted no further delay. The president said he thought there would be time to see the children later. Right now, Washington wanted to see the general that had helped preserve the Union.

Just then, Colonel Horace Porter brought in a note from Grant's wife stating her eagerness to be on time for the afternoon train. The general showed the note to Lincoln, and the matter was settled. Grant would not be staying in Washington.[17]

That same day, Booth walked to Ford's Theater to pick up his mail. While talking with theater manager H. Clay "Harry" Ford, a carpenter came in. Ford instructed him to prepare the president's box, as Lincoln and General Grant would be attending the evening's performance. For Ford, this was a stroke of luck. Normally on a Good Friday, a play would draw a very small audience, but tonight, thanks to the president and General Grant, he expected to sell out the house. Booth scurried off to make plans of his own.

As evening approached, a crowd of civilians and soldiers lined the streets around Ford's Theater at 10th Street. They were hoping to get a glimpse of the tall, dark bearded president and his wife as they entered the building.

Near eight o'clock, a closed carriage pulled up next to the front door of the White House. Before stepping outside, Lincoln handed a note to a Congressman granting permission for him and a friend to visit the president the following morning. Turning to his bodyguard, George Crook, Lincoln said, "Goodbye." Afterward, Crook wondered why the president had said "goodbye" instead of the usual "good night."

As the footman helped his wife into the coach, Lincoln made an impromptu speech for the people gathered on the White House lawn. He told them Grant had made a proposal to reduce the cost of the army, thereby reducing the national debt and bringing U.S. currency "up to par, or nearly so, with gold."

Just as Lincoln was entering the carriage, an old friend came out onto the driveway to speak with the president. "Excuse me, now," Lincoln said. "I am going to the theater. Come and see me in the morning."

The carriage rolled out onto Pennsylvania Avenue. When they reached Jackson Place, a block north of the White House, they stopped to let in their two companions for the evening, Major Henry Rathbone and his fiancée Clara Harris. The young couple rode backward chatting with the Lincolns.

Soon, the carriage pulled up to an entrance on the right side of Ford's Theater. The presidential party got out and walked past the cheering throngs. Moving toward the back of the building, they soon found the stairs leading up to the presidential box. John F. Parker, a bodyguard who worked for the Washington police department, escorted the Lincolns and their two associates into the box. The policeman then took up his station outside the door, but grew frustrated with the fact that he could hear the play but not see it. He soon abandoned his position for a seat in the first balcony or dress circle near a door leading to the landing outside the president's box. Eventually, Parker grew bored with the play and left to have a drink at Taltavul's Star Saloon next door.

Around ten o'clock, John Wilkes Booth entered the lobby of Ford's Theater. He walked up a staircase on the left and entered the dress circle, then moved toward the door leading to the president's box, entering it without challenge. Now on the landing and out of sight of the audience, Booth took out his 44 caliber, single-shot derringer and waited for the moment to strike.

Inside the box, Lincoln noticed that Major Rathbone was holding Miss Harris's hand. He reached over and took Mrs. Lincoln's hand.

"What will Miss Harris think of my hanging on to you so?" Mrs. Lincoln asked.

"Why, she will think nothing about it," the president replied.

Booth waited patiently outside the door for Harry Hawk, who played Asa Trenchard, to deliver the funniest line of the play. It came in a section where Trenchard accuses Mrs. Montchessington of wanting to settle all arguments with "sockdologers" or decisive blows. Finally, Hawk recited the line: "Well, I guess I know enough to turn you inside out, old gal—you sockdologizing old man trap."

Booth stepped into the box, pointed his derringer at the back of Lincoln's head, and pulled the trigger. Lincoln's eyes shut and his body slumped over in the rocking chair. Major Rathbone, startled by the loud bang, leapt at Booth. The wily actor drew a knife and tried to stab Rathbone in the chest. The major blocked the blow with his left arm and was cut to the bone. Booth then jumped from the box, landing on the stage near an astounded Harry Hawk. Some in the audience later said Booth shouted, "The South is avenged," before running out the back of the theater. Others insisted Booth had yelled out "Sic semper tyrannis," the Virginia state motto: "Thus shall it ever be for tyrants."

But Lincoln had not yet perished. The first doctor to reach him, an army surgeon, Dr. Charles Leale, removed a clot from the wound and found the president's pulse. That pulse would not cease until 7:22 the following morning.

Close to midnight on April 14, someone knocked loudly on the door of Pierpont's Alexandria residence. Julia Pierpont whispered to her husband, "Ask who's there."

"What's wanted?" Governor Pierpont demanded.

"Open your door, Governor!" replied the familiar voice of an army colonel.

"What's your business, Colonel?"

"I've come to warn you! Open quick!"

Francis Pierpont unlocked the door and flung it open. "What is it? What's happened?"

"I was at Ford's Theater tonight," the officer explained in breathless haste, "and a man sprang into the President's box and shot him. I heard on the street that Secretary Seward had also been shot." Fearing that Governor Pierpont might be one of the next victims, the colonel hastened to Alexandria on the last ferry. "Call out your guard, Governor!" the man warned. "They may be here at any minute. You are in danger."

Ignoring this last remark, Pierpont asked about Lincoln. The colonel, who was now sobbing, choked out the words, "I saw him, Governor. I believe the President is dead."[18]

Although much of what the colonel told Pierpont was inaccurate, the situation was still very serious. Lincoln lived, but just barely. Lewis Powell, armed with a huge Bowie knife, had ineffectively stabbed Seward repeatedly in his bed. Three men attempted to restrain Powell, but he fought them off with the knife. Then he fled the Seward household screaming "I'm mad. I'm mad." The secretary of state, though badly wounded, would live.

Telegraph keys clicked out the terrible news through the night. An army colonel sent the first at midnight to Grant who was then en route to Philadelphia. "The President was assassinated at Ford's Theatre at 10.20 to-night and cannot live," the message ran. "The Secretary of War desires that you return to Washington immediately." A second telegram sent to Grant a half hour later warned the general to "Keep a close watch on all persons who come near you."

At 1:30 a.m., Secretary Stanton telegraphed the news to Major General John A. Dix in New York City. Dix was the military commander of the army in the northeast. At that time, Stanton was still unclear as to the identity of the assassin, but by 3:30 in the morning he was certain. He telegraphed Dix again with the news that John Wilkes Booth had fired the fatal shot.[19]

By dawn, word of the disaster had reached Ohio. Chaplain McCabe, traveling down the Ohio River aboard the steamer *Telegraph*, saw flags flying at half mast in Portsmouth, the steamer's next port of call. He asked one of his fellow travelers about them. When the man told him that Lincoln and Seward had been assassinated, McCabe nearly fell overboard. The chaplain quickly retreated to his stateroom "to feel for the pillars of everlasting strength."

In his journal that day, the chaplain wrote, "Cursed be slavery! for it was that which nerved the assassin's arm. Cursed be slavery! Let it perish from the Earth!"[20]

On April 15, John Hutchinson heard the news in Hudson, Ohio, and immediately took a train to Cleveland. There, he found everyone discussing the tragic circumstances of Lincoln's death. Meetings were held at which angry orators shouted for vengeance. "We gave no concert that night," Hutchinson wrote in his memoirs. "We could not sing, for we had no heart to do it."[21]

Senator Collamer, recently appointed to the prestigious committee charged with maintaining and extending the services of the Library of Congress, was in his home's flower garden in Woodstock, Vermont, on that Saturday afternoon. The senator had intended the garden, which stood between his yellow brick house and the Congregational church next door, to be the perfect place to escape the cares of political office. Before the end of the afternoon, a messenger from the telegraph office arrived looking for the senator, and was directed to the garden's stone walkway which meandered past budding maple trees and through a vine-covered gazebo. "My God!" Collamer exclaimed when he read the message about Lincoln's assassination. "What will happen to the country now?"[22]

y the time Collamer received his telegram, the dreadful news had already reached Boston. Julia Ward Howe wrote in her diary, "A black day in history, though outwardly most fair." Since the death of her youngest child, Samuel Gridley, Jr., in 1863, she had not experienced anything that gave her "so much personal pain." To her, it was even worse that John Wilkes Booth, an actor, had done this horrible thing. "This atrocious act," she wrote, "which was committed in a very theatrical manner, is enough to ruin not the Booth family only, but the theatrical profession."[23]

Her husband called the children together and told them in anguished tones of the president's death. The following day, he and Julia attended a meeting of the Massachusetts State Legislature where Governor Andrew officially recounted what was then known of the events surrounding Lincoln's assassination.

"It is enough for his immortal glory," Andrew told the Massachusetts legislators, "that he faithfully *represented* the People, their confidence in democratic government, their constancy in the hour of adversity, and their magnanimity in the hour of triumph." He explained that Lincoln had not intended to interfere with slavery where it existed, only to check its spread into the western territories. "And yet he proclaimed liberty to three millions of American slaves, and prepared the way for universal emancipation."

The governor also quoted from Shakespeare's Scottish play, *Macbeth*. The lines he chose from Act I, Scene vii, are spoken by Macbeth shortly after his wife urged him to kill Duncan, the king of Scotland, who is a guest at Macbeth's castle. Macbeth is inventing reasons to shun the murder:

> Besides, this Duncan
> Hath borne his faculties so meek, hath been
> So clear in his great office, that his virtues
> Will plead like angels, trumpet-tongued, against
> The deep damnation of his taking-off....[24]

On Wednesday, Mrs. Howe roamed the streets of Boston, gazing blankly at the houses decorated with black and white cloth. It was the day of Lincoln's official funeral in the city. She wandered over to the church of Cyrus Bartol, their neighbor on Chestnut Street. In his funeral oration, Bartol blamed the assassination on the "barbarism of slavery" which, he claimed, had "whispered in the actor's ear!" Lincoln, on the other hand, was "the mildest among all he was set over," and "a waiter on the people, who also waited on the Lord."[25]

On returning home, Julia wrote a long poem about the assassination called "Parricide." In keeping with Bartol's gripping comparison of Booth with his victim, she gave voice to her own feelings about both men. For Booth, she wrote:

> Fair assassin, murder white,
> With thy serpent speed avoid
> Each unsullied household light,
> Every conscience unalloyed.
>> Neither heart nor home
>> Where good angels come
> Suffer thee in nearness to abide.

For Lincoln, she reserved her gentlest words:

> Honor to the heart of love,
> Honor to the peaceful will,
> Slow to threaten, strong to move,
> Swift to render good for ill!
>> Glory crowns his end,
>> And the captive's friend
> From his ashes makes us freemen still.[26]

On learning of Booth's capture and death at the Richard Garrett Farm in Virginia on April 26, Mrs. Howe wrote a companion piece for "Parricide" called "Pardon." The new poem, which promised forgiveness, had a galloping rhythm suggestive of a horse and rider on the run, or a heart wildly beating. The faltering of the beat in every other line suggests that the fugitive will not live long:

> Death brings atonement; he did that whereof ye accuse him,—
>> Murder accurst;
> But, from that crisis of crime in which Satan did lose him,
>> Suffered the worst.[27]

During the time following the assassination, Mrs. Howe's diary reveals the culmination of the domestic crisis caused by her husband's

JEFFERSON DAVIS A PRISONER
PASSING THROUGH MACON, GEORGIA, IN AN AMBULANCE

Davis's captors regaled the ex-Confederate president with taunts of "We'll hang Jeff Davis to a sour apple tree." Davis asked that this behavior cease, but his request fell on deaf ears.

objections to her writing. On Sunday, April 23, the day of their twenty-second wedding anniversary, she complained that she had "never known my husband to approve any act of mine which I myself valued." All her literary works were "contemptible or contraband in his eyes, because it was not his way of doing things."

These complaints reached Dr. Howe's ears. The next day, he told her that "if he had been engaged to Florence Nightingale and had loved her ever so dearly, he would have given her up as soon as she commenced her career as a public woman."

Julia thought little of her husband's attitude. "His sex will not endorse it," she wrote in her journal, and there the matter rested. Mrs. Howe would continue writing poems, essays, and books.[28]

News of Lincoln's death spread more slowly southward. At Durham Station, near Greensboro, North Carolina, General Sherman, negotiating for the surrender of Johnston's Confederate Army, didn't get the news until April 17. It arrived in the form of a telegram from Stanton. When Sherman showed the message to Johnston, the Confederate general's face broke out in large beads of sweat.[29]

The next day, after bolstering the provost guard around the Union camp, Sherman allowed his men to hear of Lincoln's death. One of the men in the Eleventh Iowa said that Lincoln should have been shot three years ago. He was immediately arrested and placed under guard. Another Union veteran shot a North Carolina resident who dared to express satisfaction with the assassination. Other troops attempted to burn down the town of Raleigh. Union Major General John "Black Jack" Logan managed to dissuade them. "Use your common sense," Logan told the mob of soldiers carrying firebrands just outside the town. "The people of Raleigh had no part in the killing. Don't do something you'll be sorry for. Go back to camp."[30]

The reaction of Confederate soldiers in Johnston's worn-out army was even more mixed. Lieutenant John Sergeant Wise, a surviving son of Henry Wise, was with Johnston's army at the time of the surrender. In his memoir of the war, Lieutenant Wise wrote, "We greeted [Lincoln's] death in a spirit of reckless hate, and hailed it as bringing agony and bitterness to those who were the cause of our own agony and bitterness. To us, Lincoln was an inhuman monster, Grant a butcher, and Sherman a fiend."

But among the officers and the more educated men, "the assassination caused a shudder of horror at the heinousness of the act, and at the thought of its possible consequences...."[31] One such officer at Greensboro was General Beauregard, who, upon hearing his men whooping outside his tent, lost his temper. "Shut those men up," he shouted. "If they won't shut up, have them arrested."[32]

Johnston's army surrendered to Sherman on April 26, the same day that Booth was run to ground at the Garrett Farm in northern Virginia.

On Friday morning, April 21, just one week after the assassination, Lincoln's funeral train prepared to leave Washington for the long trip home to Springfield, Illinois. He would not make this final journey alone. The casket of his young son Willie, who had died of typhoid in February of 1862, was also carried onto the seven-car train.[33] The steam-driven procession caused a greater sensation than either John Brown's or Colonel Ellsworth's ever could have. People gathered along the tracks everywhere the train went to pay their last respects to the man who had saved the Union. In the large cities where Lincoln's body would be publicly displayed, there was great rivalry to see who could produce the most elaborate hearse or catafalque, and which of them could host the most dramatic funeral of the twelve held during the journey. Crowds stood in line for hours to view his body. Though some who were Lincoln's enemies went to make sure Lincoln was really dead, the vast majority went to mourn.

It was impossible to stop the train in the smaller towns, but whenever it did stop for water or coal, someone would come to the president's carriage to leave flowers. In York, Pennsylvania, six ladies boarded the train to place a three-foot wreath of red and white roses on the coffin; others could only gaze as the train went by.

Late into the night, people would gather at the small town stations sometimes until three or four in the morning straining to hear the train whistle and bell and to catch sight of the headlamp in the distance. As the train approached, a band would start to play. Ladies in a local civic group would assemble themselves into a tableau (usually one representing the thirty six states in the Union, including Nevada which entered the Union on October 31, 1864). And as the train passed, children would wave flags, women would weep, and veterans would give a last salute to their commander-in-chief. Sometimes the towns would put up banners: "In God We Trust," "We Mourn the Nation's Loss," or even "He Died for Truth, Justice and Mercy." Many towns had a woman dressed up as the Goddess of Liberty. In Cold Spring, New York, a black veiled goddess appeared with a kneeling boy soldier on her right and a kneeling boy sailor on her left.[34]

While the train moved slowly across the country, a bereaved Chaplain McCabe waited for its arrival in Chicago. He had been attending a conference in the city, but when the meeting ended in late April, McCabe remained behind, intending "to witness the funeral pageant of Mr. Lincoln."

On April 28, the chaplain made note in his diary of the local preparations: "The mansions of the wealthy and the cottages of the poor are all clad in these significant emblems of national bereavement. More tears are shed for Mr. Lincoln than for any man that ever lived and died."[35]

On Sunday, April 30, McCabe went to Bryan Hall to hear the address of Speaker of the House Schuyler Colfax. The hall was packed with listeners who were overcome by "a wild, weird, solemn, sorrowful enthusiasm...."

Colfax recalled Lincoln's life and work as politician and president, and stated with angry words how Lincoln did not wish for the blood of his southern enemies, "but their associates thirsted for his...." They allowed him "No last words of affection to weeping wife and children.... No moment's space for prayer to God. But in order that consciousness might end with the instant, the pistol was held close to the skull, that the bullet might be buried in his brain."[36]

At the end of the address, Chaplain McCabe was asked to sing the "Battle Hymn of the Republic." He did so, with some reservations. "It did not seem appropriate to me at first," he commented in his journal, "but, as we sang on, it was the natural expression of our gloomy joy."[37]

The funeral train arrived in Chicago the next day, May 1. Thirty-six schoolgirls dressed in white, each representing a state in the Union, accompanied his hearse as it drove under a huge triple arch near 12th Street and Michigan Avenue. The entire structure was festooned with flags, and an eagle perched at the top of the central arch over a shield bearing the initials A. L. Slogans on the main arch and the two smaller arches to either side read:

REST IN PEACE NOBLE SOUL, PATRIOT, HEART.
Faithful to Right, A Martyr to Justice.
We Honor Him Dead who honored Us while Living.[38]

Chaplain McCabe drifted behind the hearse in a silent river of mourners. Some spoke in whispers as the long lines flowed gently and quietly toward the Cook County courthouse where Lincoln's body would lie in state. "All classes were in that procession," McCabe wrote of the event. "All nations were represented there; all religions too. The Hebrew stood side by side with the Roman Catholic. They forgot in that great moment the strife and hatred of centuries. The son of Africa was there, too, and his mute grief moved me most of all. There, in that coffin, was the hand that had smitten off his fetters. His Moses was dead, dead on the border but still on this side Jordan."[39]

The following day, McCabe was in Springfield to witness the remaining obsequies for Lincoln. On May 3, the day Lincoln's body

Jefferson Davis wearing the clothes in which he was captured. Davis admitted that he was wearing his wife's shawl and waterproof shortly before his arrest, but he discarded them when a cavalry officer rode up to him

arrived in the Illinois capital, the chaplain was invited to serve on a Chicago committee and share their lodgings.

That evening, McCabe attended another lecture on the life of Lincoln and sang Howe's "Battle Hymn" at the conclusion of the address. The chaplain again sang the "Battle Hymn" at the governor's office, with civil and military officers joining in the chorus. "They wanted it sung," McCabe wrote later that day, "because Mr. Lincoln loved it so."[40]

At midnight, Chaplain McCabe went for the last time to gaze on Lincoln in his casket. With no crowds moving through the building at that hour, the chaplain was able to stand for several minutes by the open coffin on the catafalque.

On May 4, McCabe saw Lincoln's body placed to rest in a vault at Oakridge Cemetery. Bishop Matthew Simpson of the Methodist Church gave the burial sermon.

The bishop considered what should be done about the leaders of the rebellion? Simpson believed they should be hanged as traitors, but for the ordinary enlisted men in the Confederate Army, the bishop counseled the extension of the "arms of forgiveness."[41]

The next day, McCabe traveled by train with Bishop Simpson and his wife to Chicago. The war was over, and the chaplain, no longer attached to the U.S. Christian Commission, longed for "the pastoral work." Simpson wanted McCabe to forego the work and go to Philadelphia. McCabe readily agreed. "I have little heart just now to do anything," the former army chaplain wrote in his journal. "Abraham Lincoln is dead! Oh, what a bereavement! It is no comfort to think that his murderer is slain. A thousand worthless lives like his would be no compensation for the death of Abraham Lincoln."[42]

While some in the North felt the Confederate leaders should be forgiven, many others cried for vengeance. By the time of Lincoln's burial, three of Booth's conspirators awaited trial: Lewis Powell, who had unsuccessfully attacked Secretary Seward; David Herold, who had guided Powell to Seward's house; and George Atzerodt, whom Booth had assigned to kill Vice President Johnson. Atzerodt had lacked the courage to do so, but he would hang with Powell and Herold anyway. Mary Surratt, who was probably only guilty of allowing some of the conspirators to meet in her boarding house on H Street in Washington, would also hang.

Four others would be jailed and then quietly released: Dr. Samuel Mudd, who treated Booth's broken leg while he was on the run; Edman "Ned" Spangler, who had found someone to hold Booth's horse shortly before Booth shot the president; and Michael O'Laughlin and Samuel Arnold, who participated in Booth's failed attempt to kidnap Lincoln. But the man whom many felt was most responsible for Lincoln's death, Confederate President Jefferson Davis, was still at large.

This situation changed in the early morning hours, six days after Lincoln's burial, when soldiers of the Fourth Michigan Cavalry under Lieutenant Colonel Benjamin Pritchard closed in on an encampment outside Irwinville, Georgia. A trooper saw a figure dressed in a raglan and shawl rapidly walking away from the encampment. He rode up to the man and pointed his carbine at him. The man, Jefferson Davis, instantly threw off the raglan and shawl, and attempted to throw the officer off his horse. But his wife placed herself between her husband and the carbine, making any escape attempt impossible. And so the former president of the Confederacy was captured.

It was later discovered that the raglan (or loose overcoat) and shawl Davis had been wearing were not his own, but his wife's. Just before the Michigan Cavalry arrived, Davis had hastily dressed in a darkened tent and took his wife's raglan by mistake. Mrs. Davis had given her husband one of her own shawls to wear when he could not find one of his own.

While searching Davis's luggage for the Confederate gold bullion Davis was supposedly carrying, one of the cavalry officers discovered something with which to torment the Confederate president: a new hooped skirt which Mrs. Davis had never worn. Some of the men decided to embellish the story of the capture by insisting that, instead of his wife's overcoat and shawl which might easily have been worn by either sex, Davis had worn this dress.[43]

As Pritchard marched his prisoners northward to Macon, the men in his command spoke profanely in front of Mrs. Davis and her children, and regaled the former president of the Confederacy with their favorite portion of the John Brown song: "We'll hang Jeff Davis to a sour apple tree." Davis appealed to Pritchard about this behavior, and the Michigan colonel promised that he would do what he could to curb his men's tongues. But very little changed. The cavalry officers and enlisted men believed that Jefferson Davis would certainly hang, either for ordering the assassination of Lincoln or for being a traitor to his country, and they felt no obligation to treat him with anything but contempt.[44]

14

"...talking Reconstruction."

On the morning of May 24, 1865, two weeks after the capture of Jefferson Davis, the U.S. Cabinet, now under the guidance of President Andrew Johnson, agreed to let Francis H. Pierpont assume control of the Virginia state government. Governor Pierpont prepared for the journey to Richmond with some reservations. "I do not expect to have the love and sympathy of the Rebels," he confided to a friend, "but by the grace of God, by doing right, I mean to command their respect."[1]

The U.S. Navy loaned Pierpont a captured blockade runner called the *Diamond*. A small, iron-hulled side-wheeler, it had been captured off the coast of Georgia by the U.S.S. *Stettin* while attempting to make her first run on September 23, 1863. The Pierpont family and a host of politicians, reporters, and sightseers boarded the *Diamond* on the morning of May 25 and headed down the Potomac River and out into Chesapeake Bay.[2]

During the long journey, one of the officers asked seven-year-old Annie Pierpont what she and her two brothers, Willie and Sammie, were doing to pass the time. Wishing to impress the young man with her knowledge of U.S. efforts to reconstruct the governments of the southern states, she replied, "Oh, nothing much, just talking Reconstruction." The officer roared with laughter, leaving Annie with a startled look and a bruised ego.[3]

In late afternoon, the ship reached Hampton Roads near the mouth of the James River and within sight of the formidable walls of Fort Monroe. Cannon fire coming from the fort so agitated Annie that she

West Virginians honored Pierpont with this statue placed in Statuary Hall in the U.S. Congress.

ran crying to her mother. Julia assured her that the loud booming was a salute in honor of her father.

The *Diamond* docked just off the fortress, and the passengers left the vessel to tour the star-shaped facility. Brigadier General Nelson Miles asked Governor Pierpont if he would like to see Jefferson Davis, now imprisoned in Casemate B at the fort. Pierpont declined, saying he would much rather see the clothes in which Davis was captured. Miles led the visitors to a closet in his office. There, hanging from a nail was what Anna later described as a "waterproof cloak" of the type worn by women. With it was a shawl and a pair of boots.[4]

After the peek at the closet, the general ushered the visitors into his sitting room, furnished with items taken from the home of Henry Wise in Princess Anne County in late 1863. There sat the ex-governor's piano. A woman in the party decided that it would be a nice joke to play "John Brown's Body" on the instrument. Everyone in the room sang along until someone declared the piano was "thoroughly reconstructed."[5]

The *Diamond* landed at the Rocketts Naval Yard in Richmond at 2:30 p.m. the following day after having a broken shaft repaired. Now that Governor Pierpont was here, the reception committee quickly organized a parade to bring the governor and his party in style to the two-story, white-brick Governor's Mansion on Capitol Square.

Once the Pierponts were installed in the mansion's roomy parlors and salons, the official reception began with a welcome by Francis J. Smith who assured everyone present that there were many Virginians who, during the war, "still clung fondly to the hope that, at no distant day, they would be...restored to that condition which makes men feel free...."

Governor Pierpont told the citizens of Richmond that he had "no idea whatever of occupying any such position [as governor of the state] when I united in opposing the rebellion." He did not serve "with the view of benefiting myself ...but with the sole object of being able to stretch forth my hand and to save all of Virginia that I could."[6]

The early days of Reconstruction in Richmond were difficult. Slavery was gone from America thanks to adoption of the Thirteenth Amendment in December 1865, but President Andrew Johnson, at first highly vindictive toward southern leaders of the Confederacy, suddenly started working to pardon and "reconstruct" them in order to prevent African Americans from gaining political power. Pierpont cooperated

Willie Pierpont nearly started a riot outside the Governor's Mansion in Richmond, Virginia, when he sang "We'll hang Jeff Davis to a sour apple tree," from the upstairs nursery window.

until he realized that the ex-Confederates were passing special laws called "Black Codes" to restrict the rights of former slaves. Although the codes legalized marriages of black people, gave them the right to own property, and to sue in the courts, they also included broad-based vagrancy laws which allowed the local authorities to arrest any unemployed black man and sell him to a landholder or force him to labor on public works without compensation.[7]

One day, Anna invited a troubled black woman into the Governor's Mansion, telling the guards at the gate that she was a friend of the family. The woman brought news of what life was like for former slaves in Reconstruction-Era Virginia, telling Governor Pierpont and his wife that the mayor of Richmond had instituted a pass system for African Americans. Any ex-slave found without a pass could be arrested and placed on a chain gang. But possession of a pass did not prevent summary arrests and cruel enslavement worse than anything they had previously experienced.[8]

Pierpont had the mayor of Richmond arrested and the pass system abolished, but there was a larger problem. Many former slaves were asking the Freedmen's Bureau, which President Johnson wanted to

Although Annie Pierpont and her brothers were fond of singing "John Brown's Body" before a mock battle, Annie feared that she might meet John Brown's ghost in the Governor's Mansion in Richmond.

abolish, for protection against former Confederates. The federal government had promised them "forty acres and a mule," or the chance to own and work lands abandoned by their masters during the war. Instead, Johnson made sure the lands were restored to the original owners who then created a new form of slavery called "sharecropping." Under this new system, the freedmen worked the master's land with the promise of a share in the crops once the harvest came. But the masters also sold their former slaves goods at inflated prices, making sure that the freedmen would incur large debts which they could never pay. If a freedman ran away from his master's land, he could now be returned to his master for non payment of debt.

The reconstructed state governments also contended with a new organization called the Ku Klux Klan, a band of former Confederate soldiers bent on preventing African Americans from exercising political power. They terrorized northern politicians with burning crosses and threatened blacks with violence. Black men who refused to be intimidated were lynched. In the Klan's view, white Europeans had created America, and only whites should be allowed to vote and hold political office.

In an angry letter to Henry Ward Beecher who supported Johnson's policies, Pierpont wrote, "The old masters combine to pay wages on which [the freedmen] cannot live, and raise their children. The legislature passes vagrant laws to compel them to work for these starvation prices.... How long, sir, under the appliances of the low wages and vagrant laws, do you suppose it will be until the freedman will long for his bonds, and curse the hand that freed him?"

In Pierpont's opinion, withdrawal of the military from the southern states would lead to open hostility against the Union within three months, and all efforts to teach blacks in the newly created Freedmen's Schools would cease. "The course taken by President Johnson and Mr. Seward and backed up by you, has retarded the progress of conciliation for ten years. Those lately in open rebellion have been inspired by new hopes of gaining power and control of the government, this has unchained the fierce devilish spirit of rebellion, which is now more bitter than while hostilities were in active progress."[9]

Just as Pierpont had felt himself pushed into the Whig and later the Republican party, the moderate and conservative governor of Virginia was slowly becoming a radical, for it was the so-called "radical Republicans" who were pledged to protect the freedmen, guarantee them civil rights, an education, and economic opportunities, and keep former Confederates out of politics.

Anna Pierpont, sometimes called Nannie, was running her hoop through Capitol Square in the summer of 1866 as her father walked slowly behind her on the gravel walkway under the trees. Suddenly, her hoop crashed into the shins of a gentleman walking up the same path. The gentleman was Henry Wise. Anna apologized to the man just as her father came up and shook his hand and said, "My daughter Nannie, General Wise. I'm glad to introduce you two, for I am planning to send her to Congress. I want her to know everyone worth knowing."

Henry Wise laughed and shook Anna's hand.[10]

"General, I suppose you have been rusticating as I have missed you for some time," Pierpont said.

"Yes," Wise replied. "I have been down to my farm in Princess Ann County; and what do you suppose I found there."

"I do not know; when I was there in 1863 I saw a large number of Freedmen cutting your timber." The timber provided lumber for housing for ex-slaves who flooded into the area during the war. "What did you find, General?" Pierpont asked.

"Why, sir, I found John Brown's daughter teaching a negro school in my mansion house; and they would not permit me to go into my house."

Governor Pierpont started to laugh, but Wise looked him in the eye and asked why he was laughing.

"General, you must excuse me," Pierpont said. "A ludicrous idea struck me. It was this—that in less than seven years after you hung John Brown for his supposed attempt to steal the Negroes from Virginia, his daughter was teaching a negro school in your mansion house and you were a fugitive not permitted to enter it."

"John Brown was a great man, sir," Wise announced, raising his right hand and assuming an air of great dignity, "he was a great man. Yes, John Brown was a hero."[11]

Though this conversation meant little to Anna, she recognized the name of John Brown, the hero immortalized in the song she and her brothers were so fond of singing while preparing for an imaginary battle. "I had no objection to John Brown's body mouldering in the grave," she wrote of the song, "for I didn't know what it meant. I didn't see why if he were comfortably buried, he did not stay where he was put. This thing of a soul marching around, especially at nighttime when it was very dark, surely was disturbing."

Anna worried about the possibility of stumbling across John Brown's ghostly presence in the gallery which ran under the Governor's Mansion. This gallery led to a brick walkway with a tin canopy connecting the mansion to a two-story building used as the mansion's kitchen. She frequently evaded her governess after an evening meal, and dragged her brother Willie through the dark gallery and out under the canopy to the kitchen where she found servants full "of good cheer, and interesting stories, and songs that thrilled one." Still, the thought of meeting John Brown's marching soul in the gallery was "a restraining and educative influence in my young life and almost as depressing to me as his memory seemed to be to the courtly General Wise."[12]

In May of 1867, Anna again got her runaway hoop tangled in the legs of a gentleman walking in Capitol Square. The man was Horace Greeley, in Richmond to attend the trial of Jefferson Davis. Greeley, along with Cornelius Vanderbilt and Gerrit Smith, who had provided money for John Brown's raid on Harper's Ferry, intended to underwrite a $100,000 bond for the release of the former Confederate president.[13] Governor Pierpont introduced his daughter, and Greeley picked her up and kissed her.

When he set her down, she ran off to tell her brothers Sammie and Willie that she had met the man who was going to free Jeff Davis. The boys took exception to this, being particularly fond of singing that part of the John Brown song concerned with hanging "Jeff Davis to a sour apple tree." But the adults could not oblige their offspring. On May 13, Davis was released on bond pending the outcome of his trial for treason in Richmond. The trial never happened, and Davis and his family left Virginia for Canada and England. They eventually returned to settle first in Tennessee and then their native Mississippi.

The morning after Davis's hearing, Mrs. Pierpont, sitting in one of the downstairs rooms at the Governor's Mansion, was startled by the sounds of an angry mob gathered outside. Some in the group were looking up and shaking their fists at a second floor window. Julia dashed up the stairs, where she heard Willie singing at the top of his lungs in the nursery, and was appalled to see her son leaning out the nursery window holding a cord. Tied by the neck to the other end of the cord was a doll. With a delighted smile, Willie was singing, "We'll hang Jeff Davis to a sour apple tree, as we go marching on." Mrs. Pierpont rapidly put an end to the boy's venture into radical Republicanism.[14]

By early 1868, Governor Pierpont was working for the ratification of the Fourteenth Amendment to the U.S. Constitution, guaranteeing full citizenship to all persons born in the United States, including former slaves freed by passage of the Thirteenth Amendment. The new amendment would also make it difficult for former Confederates who had taken oaths of loyalty to the United States before fomenting rebellion against the federal government to regain any measure of political power. President Johnson, an avowed white supremacist, opposed the measure, but for Pierpont, the issue of voting rights was very simple.

"All wealth comes from labor," he explained to his fellow Virginians meeting in convention on February 27, 1868; "and I do not see why the man who digs the earth for a living causing two blades of grass to grow, where but one, or none grew before, is not as much entitled to vote, as the polished loafer, who lives on the hard earnings of his ancestors, never producing a tithe of his subsistence. But, frequently, this class make the loudest objections to the laboring man's vote."[15]

Johnson was already in trouble for replacing Edwin Stanton as secretary of war with General Ulysses S. Grant. This action was in violation of the Tenure of Office Act passed by Congress over Johnson's veto. The president, wishing to test the constitutionality of the act, had fired Stanton, thinking the case would be tried in the Supreme Court. Instead, on March 3, 1868, the House of Representatives passed articles of impeachment against him.

The impeachment proceedings began in the U.S. Senate on March 5.[16] The next day, Pierpont met with senators Waitman T. Willey and Peter G. Van Winkle of West Virginia. Pierpont had recently done a favor for Willey, and told him that he wanted the conviction of President Johnson and the assurance that New Yorkers would not be placed in office in Virginia. "There is not a valuable office in the state," he told the two men, "but half a dozen New Yorkers are after it."[17]

Anna Pierpont attended a few minutes of the impeachment proceedings. She and her friend Fannie convinced a guard to allow them to sit in the gallery at what they thought was a peach party Johnson was throwing in the Senate Chamber.

"I must say, if that was an impeachment, I never cared to attend another," she wrote of the event. "There was nothing to be seen or heard of the least interest. Some very dull gentlemen were making some very dull speeches, and as for peaches, or any other good things to eat, you might as well look for a party in a church!"

The girls soon tired of the affair and slipped out, smiling at the guard and saying, "We are very much obliged. Thank you, sir."[18]

The effort to oust Johnson failed. On May 16 and 26, the Senate took two votes on impeachment. 36 were needed to convict, but only 35 found Johnson guilty. 19 senators pronounced him not guilty, including Peter Van Winkle who was later castigated in the Wheeling *Daily Intelligencer* as "West Virginia's betrayer."[19] President Johnson

At the end of his term as governor of Virginia, Francis Pierpont retired to his home in Fairmont, West Virginia.

was at last free from any further persecution, but the radical Republicans had won a partial victory. With the Congress now able to pass almost any legislation it wanted over Johnson's veto, measures had already been put in place to divide the South into five military districts. Virginia would constitute one district. The second included the Carolinas; the third Georgia, Alabama, and Florida; the fourth Mississippi and Arkansas; and the fifth Texas and Louisiana. On April 4, 1868, Pierpont's term of office expired, and he was replaced as governor of Virginia by a military governor.[20] There was nothing left for him to do except return to his home in Fairmont, West Virginia.

In retirement, Francis Harrison Pierpont saw all his worst fears realized. Although the country had passed the Fourteenth Amendment granting citizenship to blacks and the Fifteenth Amendment giving black males the right to vote, the Congress had compromised with the South over the election of Republican Rutherford B. Hayes as president in 1876. Neither Hayes nor his opponent, Democrat Samuel J. Tilden, had gained enough electoral votes to win, and the election was decided in Congress through a fifteen-man commission and its recommendations regarding disputed electoral votes from Louisiana, Florida, South Carolina, and Oregon. Southern legislators offered to allow Hayes to become president so long as the Congress promised to end Reconstruction and withdraw the U.S. army from the South. The northern representatives agreed, and the South, now free of federal interference, put in place a new set of laws, called "Jim Crow" laws after a character from a black minstrel song, to restrict black voting rights and segregate blacks from white society. It appeared that the struggles of John Brown and other northern abolitionists had been in vain, and that black people, though technically freed from chattel slavery, would have to struggle for a long time to free themselves from these new oppressive laws.

No longer politically active, Pierpont could do nothing in the decades that followed to protect African Americans. He spent his last years with his daughter, Anna Pierpont Siviter, and died at her home in Pittsburgh, Pennsylvania, on March 24, 1899.

15

"Let us live to make men free."

In the pre-dawn hours of February 1, 1870, 50-year-old Julia Ward Howe stepped off the train at Montpelier, Vermont. Carrying her heavy luggage in the freezing air, she felt herself "friendless and forlorn," until she glimpsed a large woman heading for the station waiting room. "Oh, you dear big Livermore!" Julia cried out. Mary Livermore, a woman who had served as a nurse during the Civil War, turned and recognized her friend Julia.[1]

Both women were recent converts to a new cause gaining in popularity and notoriety since the end of the Civil War: women's suffrage. Both had also chosen to shun the radical National Woman Suffrage Association or NWSA (led by Susan B. Anthony and Elizabeth Cady Stanton) which advocated passage of an amendment to the U.S. Constitution allowing women to vote, and openly espoused divorce and birth control. Instead, Howe and Livermore joined the more moderate American Woman Suffrage Association (AWSA) which campaigned for state legislation but remained silent on controversial topics.

In 1870, Vermont was a prime target for a woman's suffrage campaign. In the summer of 1869, a group called the Council of Censors met to review and update the Vermont Constitution, a process undertaken every half century. Jaspar Rand of St. Albans introduced a bill calling for an amendment to the state constitution allowing women to vote. Rand persuaded the council to adopt the measure.[2]

The pending legislation drew a host of supporters to the frigid state capital that winter. Many like Julia were former abolitionists, some of whom had supported John Brown's violent attempt to free slaves. But now that the slaves were freed and granted full citizenship, Brown

---

Dr. Howe, the creator of the Perkins School for the Blind, lived until 1876.

was forgotten, and the abolitionists considered supporting other social issues. William Lloyd Garrison took a train from Boston to lend his aid, and the Hutchinson Family Singers, led by Abby Hutchinson Patten, planned a series of concerts promoting woman's suffrage and temperance.

That morning, there were so many "strong-minded" women gathered around the pot-bellied stove in the waiting room at the train station in Montpelier that they attracted the attention of a lean man in need of a shave and a haircut. "If my wife even wanted to vote," the man told the women, "I wouldn't live with her one hour." Livermore and the others chose to ignore the remark, concluding that they themselves would not remain even a second with such a man.[3]

Mrs. Howe spoke at a conference held the day after her arrival. "We need not tell those present why women should be enfranchised," she told the audience. "They know the partial laws, the unequal judgments, the inferiority of education, the inequality in the distribution of labor, and the greater inequality in the distribution of wages." She insisted that "one-half of the human race has been negatived by the other half" and that women had been "educated to waste themselves on indifferent things."[4]

The Montpelier conference met with stiff opposition. One Vermont woman wrote a letter to the *Vermont Watchman and State Journal* protesting the action to grant suffrage to women. "It touches our sense of the ludicrous," she wrote, "to see people coming to the hard working women of Vermont to tell us that we are dying of ennui; that if we do not want the suffrage, it is because we are 'simpering to please the men;' because we care for nothing higher than 'making pretty things to wear.'" The anonymous writer concluded that she and the other women of Vermont "certainly do not ask for any Moses that we saw here last week to lead us to any Canaan of Woman Suffrage."[5]

Mrs. Howe journeyed to Vermont on two other occasions, once on February 21 with William Lloyd Garrison to attend a meeting in Rutland, and with Mary Livermore in March to Burlington where the feeling toward woman suffrage was openly hostile.

Their effort had no affect on the outcome. In June all but one delegate to the Vermont Constitutional Convention voted against the measure. The Vermont press claimed that the suffrage campaign had failed because of the presence of "outside agitators."[6] Curiously, that same year in March saw ratification of the Fifteenth Amendment to

In 1870, Abby Hutchinson Patten led the Hutchinson Family Singers in Vermont to promote womens' suffrage.

the U.S. Constitution prohibiting discrimination in voter registration on the basis of race, color, or previous condition of servitude.

By the time of Julia's Vermont campaign for women's suffrage, Dr. Samuel Gridley Howe had accomplished his last great philanthropic act, the formation of the Clarke Institute for the Deaf in Northampton, Massachusetts. He had worked fifteen years to create a school which would emphasize use of the manual alphabet as opposed to sign language, and would teach the deaf how to speak. But once this project was accomplished he longed for something more to do.

For the next four years, Howe toiled on a government commission investigating the possibility of annexing Santo Domingo as a territory of the United States. A revolution wrecked American hopes of expansion in the Caribbean. Meanwhile, Howe's health deteriorated rapidly due to a cancerous brain tumor.[7]

The doctor clung to life for more than a year while Julia labored for women's suffrage, world peace, and the promotion of the New England Women's Club. In November of 1875, she suspended these activities when she discovered her beloved Chev was dying. Howe, knowing that he could not last much longer, divulged to his wife of many years that he had been unfaithful to her.

On November 23, 1875, Julia wrote in her diary: "I have had some sad revelations from dear Chev of things about some of my own sex which really astonish me. From these I learn that women are not only sensual but lustful and that men are attracted rather than shocked by this trait. The privacy of offices, or at least their remoteness from domestic visitation, is eagerly made available by these women for the vilest purposes.... If thought has a grave may this ghost be laid and appear no more."

For a long time, she had speculated about those occasions when her husband had gone to the Perkins Institute at night, refusing to allow her to accompany him. Now she knew, but wished that she had been spared this knowledge of the "depth and vulgarity of evil in the human heart."[8]

Once Howe had confessed his indiscretions, he became much more affectionate toward Julia. Julia's diary entry for December 8 records "a most touching and comforting talk with dear Chev, in which I felt once more all the moral beauty which had been my faith and delight in him." But less than a month later, on January 4, 1876, Howe had a sudden attack which left him bedridden. Five days after the attack, the remainder of Howe's life was reckoned in hours. About 8:30 on the morning of January 9, 1876, Laura Bridgman arrived to say good-bye to the man who had brought her out of darkness. "I asked [Laura] if she did not wish to kiss him for good bye," Julia wrote in her diary that day, "she said yes, did so." Around 12:20 p.m., Samuel Gridley Howe died.[9]

After Howe's funeral and burial two days later, James Freeman Clarke conversed with Julia about John Brown and other abolitionists they had known. Julia replied, "I have been thinking of that beautiful company in which the Doctor is." Clarke asked, "Who?" Julia mentioned Theodore Parker, one of John Brown's secret backers; along with Senator Charles Sumner, and Howe's lawyer John A. Andrew.[10]

"Let us live to make men free."

After the war, John Hutchinson fought with Julia Ward Howe over the wording of the last verse of the "Battle Hymn of the Republic." John preferred to sing "Let us live to make men free."

Through the long years following her husband's death, Julia devoted time to her many causes. She also wrote occasional poems, including verses celebrating the lives of Robert E. Lee and Abraham Lincoln. To Julia, Lee was "A gallant foeman in the fight,/ A brother when the fight was o'er." She recalled that Lee had "The blessed torch of learning bore" while serving as president of Washington College in Virginia. The poem about Lincoln briefly traced the sixteenth president's life from "A cabin of the western wild," through the war years of "Distrustful days and sleepless nights," to the "treacherous shot" that ended his life.[11] She also remembered John Brown ("martyr, our pioneer") in a poem entitled "Kansas." In those verses, she identified herself with the people who, like Brown, had "breasted the wilderness, lone and drear" for the sake of liberty.[12]

Old friends and supporters visited or wrote Julia when they found the time. John Hutchinson called on her frequently in her later years. The two commonly argued over a change John had made in her "Battle Hymn." Hutchinson had never liked the line, "As he died to make men holy, let us die to make men free." Instead, he sang "let us *live* to make men free." On one occasion, when John had brought his granddaughter Katie Campbell for a visit, Julia, in frustration, turned to the little girl and asked, "Katie, will you sing it as I wrote it?" "Yes," Katie said with a smile.[13]

Charles Cardwell McCabe, who became a bishop in the Methodist Church in 1896, wrote to Mrs. Howe requesting a copy of her "Battle Hymn." He told her the story of singing the poem while in Libby Prison on learning of Meade's victory at Gettysburg. "I have sung it a thousand times since," he wrote, "and shall continue to sing it as long as I live. No hymn has ever stirred the nation's heart like 'The Battle Hymn of the Republic.'"[14] She sent the promised autograph copy in September 1904, apologizing for the "wavering of my aged hand."[15]

More than two years later, on December 10, 1906, Bishop McCabe stopped in Torrington, Connecticut, near the birthplace of John Brown. He was raising money to pay off the $10,000 mortgage on a church. That evening, he gave for the last time his lecture on "The Bright Side of Life in Libby Prison."

On his way home from this event, he suffered an apoplectic stroke while walking from Grand Central Station in New York City to the Twenty-third Street ferry. He was rushed to the New York City Hospital by ambulance. Dr. George P. Mains of the Methodist Book Concern

"Let us live to make men free."

Kate Campbell, the granddaughter of John Hutchinson, promised Julia Ward Howe that she would not change the wording of the "Battle Hymn of the Republic."

went to the hospital to find the ailing bishop, whose right side was paralyzed.

"This is the end with me," the bishop told Mains.

"I hope not, Bishop," Mains responded.

"Yes," McCabe said, "this is the end; but it is all right. Let nobody be disturbed about it."

Mains asked if McCabe was suffering any pain.

"No," he said, and then used his left hand to lift up his right. "This seems like another man's hand; it does not seem like my own hand." He asked Mains to communicate with his wife in Germantown, Pennsylvania, but was unable to recall the exact address. Mains asked if they had a telephone. McCabe said they did.

Mrs. McCabe arrived at her husband's bedside that evening at 8:00, but there was very little anyone could do for the 70-year-old bishop. For more than a week, he stood between this life and the next. Death took him at 5:20 a.m. on December 19.[16]

Just as Mrs. Howe lost one great champion of her "Battle Hymn," another appeared on the scene: President Theodore Roosevelt. In 1908, the president went riding with his aides Captain Fitzhugh Lee and Captain Archie Butt. They had just heard a concert of the Arion Singing Society, and Roosevelt had asked them to sing Dan Emmett's "Dixie." The president and his aides agreed that "Dixie" "had won its way until it was the tune which would bring everybody to his feet with a yell in any audience in any part of the country...." Unfortunately it lacked proper words. Captain Butt suggested that Mrs. Howe's "Battle Hymn of the Republic" was "the very finest and noblest battle hymn possest by any Nation of the world...." Roosevelt, who had always liked the hymn, proposed to start a movement to make it the official U.S. national anthem.

On June 15, 1908, he wrote to his friend Joel Chandler Harris, creator of Uncle Remus, to ask him what he thought of the idea. "...I hoped that sooner or later all Americans would grow to realize that in this 'Battle Hymn of the Republic' we had what really ought to be a great National treasure," the president told Harris, "something that all

In 1908, President Theodore Roosevelt attempted to make Howe's "Battle Hymn" into the U.S. national anthem. Southerners refused to support the idea.

Americans would grow to know intimately...."[17] Harris, then near death, wrote, "Acquiescence in President Roosevelt's proposition would mark to a greater degree than almost anything else could the fact that this is indeed a united country."[18]

While most Southerners chose to remain silent on the issue, one anonymous correspondent to *The New York Times* berated President Roosevelt for suggesting that a song written by an "Abolitionist agitator" could ever be our national anthem, and reminded him that the tune for the "Battle Hymn" was associated with John Brown, the man who had nearly caused a slave insurrection in Virginia. The writer recommended that when "the old wounds in this country are thoroughly healed, if we are to have a National hymn let it be one in the glory of peace."[19]

In early October 1910, Julia Ward Howe, now 91, rode by train to Smith College to receive an honorary degree. Wearing her mortarboard over her white lace cap, Julia was brought in a wheelchair and lifted onto the platform at the front of the hall where she would receive the honor. She was the last to receive a degree that day, and as she wheeled forward to receive it, a chorus supported by an organ sang the "Battle Hymn of the Republic."

After the ceremony, Julia returned to Oak Glen, her home outside Newport, Rhode Island. A few days afterward, she went by carriage to her club, the Papetrie, and insisted that the top be left down when she rode back to her home. The weather was mild that evening, and she desired to view the simultaneous setting of the sun and rising of the full moon. By the next morning, she had developed a cold which rapidly became bronchitis and then pneumonia. She died early Monday morning, October 17.[20]

Two days later, a train brought her body from Newport to Boston for a funeral held at the Church of the Disciples. All that day, public schools around the city held memorial services. Students recited her poems and sang the "Battle Hymn of the Republic."[21]

Theodore Roosevelt continued writing tributes to Mrs. Howe long after her death. In 1912, the former president wrote, "I pin my faith to woman suffragists of the type of the late Julia Ward Howe." In 1916, he said that Julia "preached that stern and lofty courage of soul which shrinks neither from war nor from any other form of suffering and hardship and danger if it is only thereby that justice can be served."[22] Three years later, Congress proposed the passage of a Nineteenth Amendment to the U.S. Constitution allowing women to vote. It was ratified the following year, just ten years after Julia's death.

President Roosevelt had loved Mrs. Howe's "Battle Hymn" so much that, when plans were made for the dedication of the New York State Roosevelt Memorial on January 19, 1936, the organizers of the

In 1896, Chaplain McCabe became a bishop in the Methodist Church.

event hired African American tenor Roland Hayes to sing it. Hayes's performance was so moving that the audience's applause brought him twice to the front of the stage.[23]

Although Mrs. Howe's poem has proved popular over the years, it has also caused occasional controversy. When Franklin Delano Roosevelt selected it for a Thanksgiving Day service at the White House during his third term, he discovered that, to avoid offending Southerners, he had to remove its warlike third and fourth verses.[24]

The "Battle Hymn" created an even greater problem in 1965 for Richard P. Condie, director of the Mormon Tabernacle Choir. He wanted to include it in the inaugural program for President Lyndon Baines Johnson. A few members of the Joint Congressional Committee on Inaugural Ceremonies, led by Democratic Senator H. Everett Jordan of North Carolina, insisted that Howe's hymn was "a Union song." Condie explained that the choir had already sung it in New Orleans and Atlanta, and Southerners had responded positively to it. "Some people might not like it," the director admitted, "but it's connected with our country and it has a stirring message—that's the point." The committee backed down, and the piece was performed on January 20 after Johnson's inaugural address.[25]

Ten days later on the opposite side of the Atlantic Ocean, the strains of the "Battle Hymn" echoed without controversy in St. Paul's Cathedral, London, for the funeral of Winston Churchill, the man who had served as prime minister of Great Britain during the darkest hours of World War II. Churchill's family requested the music in honor of Winston's American mother. Like Julia Ward Howe, Lady Randolph Churchill came from a prominent New York City family.[26]

On March 25, 1965, Martin Luther King Jr. employed Howe's "Battle Hymn" during a dramatic speech in Montgomery, the state capital of Alabama. He addressed a host of civil rights activists from a flatbed truck armed with microphones and loudspeakers. Behind him a Confederate battle flag flew under the Alabama state flag on the capitol dome. An imposing statue of Jefferson Davis loomed over King's audience. From time to time, Governor George Wallace peered out the venetian blinds on his office window to watch the large crowd.

King inquired how long the assemblage thought it would take to achieve racial equality and justice in America. "How long? Not long. Because mine eyes have seen the glory of the coming of the Lord...."[27]

Three years later, King utilized Howe's verses again in Memphis, Tennessee, during a strike of black sanitation workers. Standing before a gathering of two thousand at Mason Temple, he announced that someone had threatened to kill him. He said he was "not concerned about that now." God had allowed him to climb to the mountain top and see the Promised Land. "So, I'm happy tonight," he assured his listeners. "I'm not fearing *any* man. Mine eyes have seen the glory of the coming of the Lord."[28]

It was King's final tribute to Julia Ward Howe. The following day, April 4, 1968, a sniper gunned him down at his motel.

FROM A PHOTOGRAPH.

John Brown

Epilog

"His soul is marching on!"

Along with Howe's "Battle Hymn", the memory of John Brown's raid on Harper's Ferry has been kept alive in the twentieth century, thanks to a succession of films and TV shows and documentaries. In 1940, Hollywood first assayed the Brown legend with a film entitled *Santa Fe Trail*. The movie, which dealt with Brown's days in Kansas, bore little resemblance to the history of the territory, and made only passing references to the Santa Fe Trail. Movie makers tried a second time in 1955 with a movie about Brown and his sons, *Seven Angry Men*. While this new film depicted Brown's bloody Kansas activities with greater accuracy than its predecessor, it reduced the raid on Harper's Ferry to a pointless gun battle. However, it did include brief scenes of Brown's trial taken from the trial transcripts.

On TV, Brown was shown in his jail cell and at his execution in the opening episode of the miniseries *The Blue and the Gray*, first aired in 1982. Three years later, the ABC network offered a miniseries about the Civil War based on John Jakes's best selling novel, *North and South*. Brown, played by Johnny Cash, appeared in scenes portraying the Harper's Ferry raid. In 1990, Ken Burns's *Civil War* series gave viewers a brief glimpse of the events of the raid.

Poets and songwriters have also kept Brown's memory fresh. In 1928, Stephen Vincent Benét completed work on an epic poem called *John Brown's Body*, winner of the 1929 Pulitzer Prize for poetry. African American poet Robert Hayden included a set of verses about Brown in his collection, *American Journal*. And in response to the growing civil rights movement of the 1960's, Len Chandler resurrected Brown's ghost in a song parody of "John Brown's Body" called "Move on Over":

> You conspire to keep us silent in the field and in the slum
> You promise us the vote then sing us We Shall Overcome
> But John Brown knew what freedom was and died to win us some
> That's why we keep marching on.[1]

State and national parks also commemorate Brown's abolitionist activities. The hardscrabble farm near Lake Placid where Brown and his sons are buried was turned into a New York state park in 1895. More than fifty thousand people visit the farm from late May to late October every year, and the number is growing. Fort Warren on George's Island, the birthplace of the song "John Brown's Body," was transformed into a state park after Massachusetts purchased the facility from the federal government in 1958. Ferrys docked near Boston's Aquarium annually transport over one hundred thousand tourists to the fort. The town of Harpers Ferry was declared a national monument during World War II. As many as two million people have toured the park in a single year.

The growing interest in Brown has caused some scholars to compare the instigator of the Harper's Ferry insurrection with contemporary revolutionaries and radical social activists like Timothy McVeigh, sentenced to death for the Oklahoma City bombing; David Koresh, founder of the Branch Davidian compound in Waco, Texas; and suicide advocate Dr. Jack Kevorkian. Some activists are even willing to claim Brown as a role model. Michael Bray, a Lutheran minister convicted in 1986 for fire bombing an abortion clinic, cites John Brown's raid as an example of "righteous violence."[2]

But what did Brown's "righteous violence" accomplish? It did not directly cause the Civil War, although it contributed to the tension between North and South. Historians now generally acknowledge, however, that the raid caused Southerners to take more seriously the training of local militia companies. This being the case, it might be argued that the raid prolonged the Civil War. Given President Lincoln's ambivalence toward the idea of freeing slaves, one wonders if any slaves would have been emancipated by executive order if the war had only lasted a few months or years.

Was John Brown a saint, as some insist, because he played an integral role in destroying chattel slavery in the United States? Or was he a demon whose "righteous violence" caused a backlash of white anger and prejudice against African Americans? Whatever else might be said about Brown, he must be seen as a product of the violent times in which he lived. He was raised in a country committed to a contradiction: a country that espoused the idea that "All men are created equal," but also legitimized the institution of slavery in its Constitution. His Bible admonished him to "remember them that are in bonds as bound with them." His association with African Americans taught him that he was not their superior but their equal. And his conscience told him that he must take steps to end the afflictions of slavery. In the end, Brown is neither angel nor devil, only a man with a tormented soul which is still marching on.

Selected Poetry of Julia Ward Howe

BATTLE HYMN OF THE REPUBLIC
(RECONSTRUCTION OF FIRST DRAFT VERSION)

Mine eyes have seen the glory of the coming of the Lord.
He is trampling out the wine press where the grapes of wrath are stored,
He hath loosed the fateful lightning of his terrible swift sword,
    His truth is marching on.

I have seen him in the watchfires of an hundred circling camps
They have builded him an altar in the evening dews and damps,
I can read his righteous sentence by the dim and flaring lamps
    His day is marching on.

I have read a burning gospel, writ in fiery rows of steel,
As ye deal with my contemners, so with you my grace shall deal
Let the Hero, born of woman crush the serpent with his heel,
    Our God is marching on.

He has sounded out the trumpet that shall never call retreat,
He has waked the earth's dull bosom with a high ecstatic beat,
O be swift my soul to answer him, be jubilant, my feet.
    Our God is marching on.

In the whiteness of the lilies he was born across the sea
With a glory in his bosom that shines out in you and me,
As he died to make men holy, let us die to make men free,
    Our God is marching on.

He is coming like the glory of the morning on the wave
He is wisdom to the mighty, he is honor to the brave
So the world shall be his footstool, and the soul of wrong his slave
    Our God is marching on.

BATTLE HYMN OF THE REPUBLIC
FINAL VERSION PUBLISHED IN THE ATLANTIC MONTHLY, FEB. 1862

Mine eyes have seen the glory of the coming of the Lord:
He is trampling out the vintage where the grapes of wrath are stored;
He hath loosed the fateful lightning of His terrible swift sword:
His truth is marching on.

I have seen Him in the watch-fires of a hundred circling camps;
They have builded Him an altar in the evening dews and damps;
I can read His righteous sentence by the dim and flaring lamps:
His day is marching on.

I have read a fiery gospel writ in burnished rows of steel:
"As ye deal with my contemners, so with you my grace shall deal;
Let the Hero, born of woman, crush the serpent with his heel,
Since God is marching on."

He has sounded forth the trumpet that shall never call retreat;
He is sifting out the hearts of men before His judgment-seat:
Oh, be swift, my soul, to answer Him! be jubilant, my feet!
Our God is marching on.

In the beauty of the lilies Christ was born across the sea,
With a glory in his bosom that transfigures you and me:
As he died to make men holy, let us die to make men free,
While God is marching on.

THE HEART'S ASTRONOMY

This evening, as the twilight fell,
My younger children watched for me;
Like cherubs in the window framed,
I saw the smiling group of three.

While round and round the house I trudged,
Intent to walk a weary mile,
Oft as I passed within their range,
The little things would beck and smile.

They watched me, as Astronomers,
Whose business lies in heaven afar,
Await, beside the slanting glass,
The re-appearance of a star.

Not so, not so, my pretty ones,
Seek stars in yonder cloudless sky;
But mark no steadfast path for me,
A comet dire and strange am I.

Now to the inmost spheres of light
Lifted, my wondering soul dilates;
Now, dropped in endless depth of night,
My hope God's slow recall awaits.

Among the shining I have shone,
Among the blessing have been blest;
Then wearying years have held me bound
Where darkness deadness gives, not rest.

Between extremes distraught and rent,
I question not the way I go;
Who made me, gave it me, I deem,
Thus to aspire, to languish so.

But Comets, too, have holy laws,
Their fiery sinews to restrain,
And from their outmost wanderings
Are drawn to heaven's dear heart again.

And ye, beloved one, when ye know
What wild, erratic natures are,
Pray that the laws of heavenly force
Would help and guide the Mother star.

THE FIRST MARTYR

My five-year's darling, on my knee,
Chattered and toyed and laughed with me:
"Now tell me, mother mine," quoth she,
    "Where you went i' the afternoon."
"Alas! my pretty little life,
I went to see a sorrowing wife,
    Who will be widowed soon."

"Now, mother, what is that?" she said,
With wondering eyes and restless head:
"Will, then, her husband soon be dead?
    Tell me, why must he die?
Is he like flowers the frost doth sear,
Or like the birds, that, every year,
    Melt back into the sky?"

"No, love: the flowers may bloom their time,
The birdlings sing their merry chime,
Till bids them seek another clime
    The Winter sharp and cold;
But he who waits with fettered limb,
Nor God nor Nature sends for him,—
    He is not weak nor old.

"He lies upon a prison bed
With sabre gashes on his head:
And one short month will see him led
    Where vengeance wields the sword.
Then shall his form be lifted high,
And strangled in the public eye
    With horrible accord."

"But, mother, say, what has he done?
Has he not robbed or murdered one?"
"My darling, he has injured none.
    To free the wretched slaves
He led a band of chosen men,
Brave, but too few; made captives them,
    And doomed to felon graves."

"O mother! let us go this day
To that sad prison, far away;
The cruel governor we'll pray
    To unloose the door so stout.
Some comfort we can bring him, sure:
And is he locked up so secure,
    We could not get him out?"

"No, darling: he is closely kept."
Then nearer to my heart she crept,
And, hiding there her beauty, wept
    For human misery.
Child! it is fit that thou shouldst weep;
The very babe unborn would leap
    To rescue such as he.

O babe unborn! O future race!
Heir of our glory and disgrace,
We cannot see thy veiled face;
    But shouldst thou keep our crime,
No new Apocalypse need say
In what wild woe shall pass away
    The falsehood of the time.

OUR COUNTRY

On primal rocks she wrote her name,
Her towers were reared on holy graves,
The golden seed that bore her came
Swift-winged with prayer o'er ocean waves.

The Forest bowed his solemn crest,
And open flung his sylvan doors;
Meek Rivers led the appointed Guest
To clasp the wide-embracing shores;

Till, fold by fold, the broidered Land
To swell her virgin vestments grew,
While Sages, strong in heart and hand,
Her virtue's fiery girdle drew.

O Exile of the wrath of Kings!
O Pilgrim Ark of Liberty!
The refuge of divinest things,
Their record must abide in thee.

First in the glories of thy front
Let the crown jewel Truth be found;
Thy right hand fling with generous wont
Love's happy chain to furthest bound.

Let Justice with the faultless scales
Hold fast the worship of thy sons,
Thy commerce spread her shining sails
Where no dark tide of rapine runs.

So link thy ways to those of God,
So follow firm the heavenly laws,
That stars may greet thee, warrior-browed,
And storm-sped angels hail thy cause.

O Land, the measure of our prayers,
Hope of the world, in grief and wrong!
Be thine the blessing of the years,
The gift of faith, the crown of song.

OUR ORDERS

Weave no more silks, ye Lyons looms,
        To deck our girls for gay delights!
The crimson flower of battle blooms,
        And solemn marches fill the night.

Weave but the flag whose bars to-day
        Drooped heavy o'er our early dead,
And homely garments, coarse and gray,
        For orphans that must earn their bread!

Keep back your times, ye viols sweet,
  That poured delight from other lands!
Rouse there the dancer's restless feet:
  The trumpet leads our warrior bands.

And ye that wage the war of words
  With mystic fame and subtle power,
Go, chatter to the idle birds,
  Or teach the lesson of the hour!

Ye Sibyl Arts, in one stern know
  Be all your offices combined!
Stand close, while Courage draws the lot,
  The destiny of human kind.

And if that destiny could fail,
  The sun should darken in the sky,
The eternal bloom of Nature pale,
  And God, and Truth, and Freedom die!

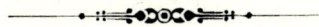

PARRICIDE

ABRAHAM LINCOLN—APRIL 14, 1865

O'er the warrior gauntlet grim
Late the silken glove we drew,
Bade the watch-fires slacken dim
In the dawn's auspicious hue.
  Stayed the armèd heel;
  Still the clanging steel;
Joys unwonted thrilled the silence through.

Glad drew near the Easter tide;
And the thoughts of men anew
Turned to Him who spotless died
For the peace that none shall rue.

Out of mortal pain
This abiding strain
Issued: "Peace, my peace, I give to you."

Musing o'er the silent strings,
By their apathy opprest,
Waiting for the spirit-wings,
To be touched and soul-possessed,
  "I am dull," I said:
  "Treason is not dead;
Still in ambush lurks that shivering guest."

Then a woman's shriek of fear
Smote us in its arrowy flight;
And a wonder wild and drear
Did the hearts of men unite.
  Has the seed of crime
  Reached its flowering-time,
That it shoots to this audacious height?

Then, as frosts the landscape change,
Stiffening from the summer's glow,
Grew the jocund faces strange,
Lay the loftiest emblem low:
  Kings are of the past,
  Suffered still to last;
Those twin crowns the present did bestow.

Fair assassin, murder white,
With thy serpent speed avoid
Each unsullied household light,
Every conscience unalloyed.
  Neither heart nor home
  Where good angels come
Suffer thee in nearness to abide.

Slanderer of the gracious brow,
The untiring blood of youth,
Servant of an evil vow,
Of a crime that beggars ruth,
  Treason was thy dam,
  Wolfing, when the Lamb,
The Anointed, met thy venomed tooth.

With the righteous did he fall,
With the sainted doth he lie;
While the gibbet's vultures call
Thee, that, 'twixt the earth and sky,
    Disavowed of both
    In their Godward troth,
Thou mayst make thy poor amend, and die.

If it were my latest breath,
Doomed his bloody end to share,
I would brand thee with his death
As a deed beyond despair.
    Since the Christ was lost
    For a felon's cost,
None like thee of vengeance should beware.

Leave the murderer, noble song,
Helpless in the toils of fate:
To the just thy meeds belong,
To the martyr, to the state.
    When the storm beats loud
    Over sail and shroud,
Tunefully the seaman cheers his mate.

Never tempest lashed the wave
But to leave it fresher calm;
Never weapon scarred the brave
But their blood did purchase balm.
    God hath writ on high
    Such a victory
As uplifts the nation with its psalm.

Honor to the heart of love,
Honor to the peaceful will,
Slow to threaten, strong to move,
Swift to render good for ill!
    Glory crowns his end,
    And the captive's friend
From his ashes makes us freemen still.

PARDON

WILKES BOOTH—APRIL 26, 1865

Pains the sharp sentence the heart in whose wrath it was uttered,
    Now thou art cold;
Vengeance, the headlong, and Justice, with purpose close muttered,
    Loosen their hold.

Death brings atonement; he did that whereof ye accuse him,—
    Murder accurst;
But, from that crisis of crime in which Satan did lose him,
    Suffered the worst.

Harshly the red dawn arose on a deed of his doing,
    Never to mend;
But harsher days he wore out in the bitter pursuing
    And the wild end.

So lift the pale flag of truce, wrap those mysteries round him,
    In whose avail
Madness that moved, and the swift retribution that found him,
    Falter and fail.

So the soft purples that quiet the heavens with mourning,
    Willing to fall,
Lend him one fold, his illustrious victim adorning
    With wider pall.

Back to the cross, where the Saviour uplifted in dying
    Bade all souls live,
Turns the reft bosom of Nature, his mother, low sighing,
    Greatest, forgive!

ROBERT E. LEE

READ AT THE RICHMOND CELEBRATION OF THE HUNDREDTH ANNIVERSARY OF GENERAL LEE'S BIRTH

A gallant foe in the fight,
    A brother when the fight was o'er,
The hand that led the host with might
    The blessed torch of learning bore.

No shriek of shell nor roll of drums,
    No challenge fierce, resounding far,
When reconciling Wisdom comes
    To heal the cruel wounds of war.

Thought may the minds of men divide,
    Love makes the hearts of nation one;
And so, thy soldier grave beside,
    We honor thee, Virginia's son.
January 19, 1907.

ABRAHAM LINCOLN

READ BY MRS. HOWE AT THE LINCOLN CENTENARY MEETING IN SYMPHONY HALL, BOSTON, FEBRUARY 12, 1909

Through the dim pageant of the years
A wondrous tracery appears:
A cabin of the western wild
Shelters in sleep a new-born child.

Nor nurse, nor parent dear can know
The way those infant feet must go;
And yet a nation's help and hope
Are sealed within that horoscope.

Beyond is toil for daily bread,
And thought, to noble issues led,
And courage, arming for the morn
For whose behest this man was born.

A man of homely, rustic ways,
Yet he achieves the forum's praise,
And soon earth's highest meed has won,
The seat and sway of Washington.

No throne of honors and delights;
Distrustful days and sleepless nights,
To struggle, suffer, and aspire,
Like Israel, led by cloud and fire.

A treacherous shot, a sob of rest,
A martyr's palm upon his breast,
A welcome from the glorious seat
Where blameless souls of heroes meet;

And, thrilling through unmeasured days,
A song of gratitude and praise;
A cry that all the earth shall heed,
To God, who gave him for our need.

KANSAS

Sing us a song of the grand old time,
Of John Brown, martyr, our pioneer.
Tell how, in view of a nation's crime,
We breasted the wilderness, lone and drear.
Bible and rifle in hand we went,
To rear in the desert our flag and tent.

For a wicked bugle note had called
The men who would hold their fellow slave;
When, at its falseness unappalled,

Came forth a company clean and brave,
Unfettered by customs old and ill,
With the freeman's mind and the freeman's will.

Some who started in manhood's bloom
Short time abode and never returned,
But most of us stayed as we found room,
And fairly the Pilgrim's guerdon earned.
With nights of watching and days of toil,
We saved from dishonor a virgin soil.

Firm on our shoulder the Duties sate
That grow with the growth of human kind,
No worship of Fortune, nor creed of Fate,
But the leadership of the well-taught mind.
Where the wild man left but briar and thorn,
We planted the field, and gathered the corn.

And so, we builded our cities fair,
For our fathers' tongue and our fathers' faith.
The church spire hallowed our place of prayer,
The school bell uttered its blessed breath,
And he who crosses our bound shall find
That he leaves no gain of the age behind.

With many a weary task 'twas done,
With murder lurking in thicket and grove,
With backs that ached 'neath a burning sun,
With homes that sheltered but thrift and love.
We lightened our labor with speech and song,
And the women worked with us, right along!
Now, half a hundred years have sped
To make the desert a blooming state;
We thank our God for honest bread,
For duteous children and loving mate,
But most, that the Fathers went out to see
The land redeemed for liberty.

Notes

PROLOG: "I TREMBLE FOR MY COUNTRY...."

1. Willard Sterne Randall, *Thomas Jefferson: A Life* (New York: Henry Holt and Company, 1993), 266-267.

2. Peter Force, ed., *American Archives: Consisting of a Collection of Authentick Records, State Papers, Debates, and Letters and Other Notices of Publick Affairs*, 4th ser., vol. 3 (Washington: M. St. Clair Clarke and Peter Force, December, 1840), 1385. Brackets in this quotation appear in the original document.

3. Jared Sparks, *The Writings of George Washington; Being His Correspondence, Addresses, Messages, and Other Papers, Official and Private*, vol. 3 (Boston: Little Brown, and Company, 1858), 218.

4. *Journals of the Continental Congress, 1774-1789*, vol. 4, 1776, Jan. 1-June 4 (Washington: GPO, 1906), 60.

5. Many of Dunmore's liberated slaves were relocated to Sierre Leone in 1787 along with a large number of British Africans culled from London's poor and white women who were either poor or had worked as domestic servants. They intended to colonize the country and set up trade with England and other British colonies. Under the patronage of Granville Sharp, one of a growing number of abolitionists in Great Britain, the colonists built a settlement called Granville Town.

6. John Locke, *An Essay Concerning the True Original Extent and End of Civil Government*, in *Great Books*, vol. 35 (Chicago: Encyclopedia Britannica, Inc., 1987), 25.

7. Quoted in Randall, loc. cit., 276-277.

8. Quoted in Matthew T. Mellon, *Early American Views on Negro Slavery: From the Letters and Papers of the Founders of the Republic* (New York: The New American Library, 1969), 98.

9. Albert Ellery Bergh, ed., *The Writings of Thomas Jefferson*, vol. 18 (Washington, D.C.: The Thomas Jefferson Memorial Association, 1907), 169-170.

10. Quoted from "A Declaration of the Rights of the Inhabitants of the State of Vermont" in the 1777 Vermont Constitution as found in William Doyle, *The Vermont Political Tradition: And Those Who Helped Make It* (Barre, Vermont: Northlight Studio Press, 1984), 236.

11. The full text of Captain Allen's freedom letter for Dinah Mattis is found in E. P. Walton, ed., *Records of the Governor and Council*, vol. 1 (Montpelier, Vermont: Steam Press of J. & J. M. Poland, 1873), 93.

12. John Codman Hurd, *The Law of Freedom and Bondage in the United States*, 2 vols. (New York: Negro Universities Press, 1968), 1:28.

13. Ibid., 1:35.

14. Thomas Jefferson, *Notes on the State of Virginia*, as found in *Jefferson's Writings* (New York: The Library of America, 1984), 266-267, 264.

15. Ibid., 289, 270.

16. Randall, loc. cit., 362-363.

17. See "Chap. 113: An Act to Continue in Force 'An Act to Protect the Commerce of the United States and Punish the Crime of Piracy' and also to Make Further Provision for Punishing the Crime of Piracy," in Richard Peters, ed., *The Public Statutes at Large of the United States of America*, vol. 3 (Boston: Charles C. Little and James Brown, 1846), 600-601. For the full story of Gordon's capture and execution see James A. Rawley, "Captain Nathaniel Gordon, the Only American Executed for Violating the Slave Trade Laws" in *Civil War History: A Journal of the Middle Period*, published by the Kent State University Press, vol. 39, no. 3 (September, 1993).

18. Letter from Jefferson to Benjamin Banneker, dated Aug. 30, 1791, as found in Jefferson, *Writings*, 982-983.

19. Letter from Jefferson to Henri Gregoire, dated Feb. 25, 1809, as found in Jefferson, *Writings*, 1202.

20. Letter from Jefferson to Jared Sparks, dated Feb. 4, 1824, as found in Jefferson, *Writings*, 1486-1487.

21. Letter from Jefferson to John Holmes, dated Apr. 22, 1820, as found in Jefferson, *Writings*, 1434-1435.

22. Randall, loc. cit., 590-591, 594.

23. David Hackett Fischer, *Albion's Seed: Four British Folkways in America* (New York: Oxford University Press, 1989), 132-133.

24. Kenneth M. Stampp, *The Peculiar Institution: Slavery in the Antebellum South* (New York: Alfred A. Knopf, 1972), 54-56.

25. Ibid., 296-307.

26. Fischer, loc. cit., 347.

27. Irving Sablosky, *American Music* (Chicago; The University of Chicago Press, 1969), 70-72.

28. James McPherson, *Battle Cry of Freedom: The Civil War Era* (New York: Ballantine Books, 1988), 105-107. For the full history of both López expeditions see Tom Chaffin, *Fatal Glory: Narciso López and the First Clandestine U.S. War Against Cuba* (Charlottesville: University Press of Virginia, 1996).

29. Benjamin C. Howard, *Reports of Cases Argued and Adjudged in the Supreme Court of the United States: December Term, 1856*, vol. 19 (Washington: W. H. & O. H. Morrison, Law Publishers and Booksellers, 1859), 407, 410.

30. Roy P. Basler, ed., "The Dred Scott Decision: Speech at Springfield, Illinois, June 26, 1857," *Abraham Lincoln: His Speeches and Writings* (New York: Da Capo Press, Inc., 1946), 361-362.

CHAPTER 1: "THE BEES WILL BEGIN TO SWARM...."

1. Unless otherwise indicated, the story of this meeting is taken from Frederick Douglass, *Life and Times of Frederick Douglass: His Early Life as a Slave, His Escape from Bondage, and His Complete History* (New York: Collier Books, 1962), 318-320. Although Douglass

reported that John Brown's alias was John Smith, I have discovered from source documents used in Villard's biography of Brown that this could not have been true. From the moment of Brown's arrival in Chambersburg, he started signing his name as I. Smith. See Brown's letter to Kagi of June 30, 1859, in Oswald Garrison Villard, *John Brown: A Biography, 1800-1859* (Garden City, New York: Doubleday, Doran & Company, Inc., 1910), 402.

2. For more details concerning Douglass's informal education, see Chapter 7, Frederick Douglass, *Narrative of the Life of Frederick Douglass* (New York: New American Library, 1968), 52-58.

3. Letter from John Brown to Henry L. Stearns, July 15, 1857, reprinted in *A John Brown Reader: A Story of John Brown in His Own Words, in the Words of Those Who Knew Him, and in the Poetry and Prose of the Literary Heritage* (New York: Abelard-Schuman, 1959), 38.

4. Richard O. Boyer, *The Legend of John Brown: A Biography and History* (New York: Alfred A. Knopf, 1973), 314.

5. Stephen B. Oates, *To Purge This Land with Blood: A Biography of John Brown* (Amherst, Massachusetts: The University of Massachusetts Press, 1984), 42-43.

6. Villard, loc. cit., 57-59.

7. Oates, loc. cit., 65.

8. Edwin N. Cotter, Jr., "John Brown at North Elba: Questions and Answers" (Lake Placid, New York: John Brown Farm, n.d.), 2.

9. Edwin N. Cotter, Jr., "John Brown in the Adirondacks," *Adirondack Life* (Summer, 1972), 9.

10. Ibid., 9.

11. Ibid., 9.

12. *John Brown Reader*, 76.

13. Oates, loc. cit., 170-171.

14. Villard, loc. cit., 317-318.

15. Oates, loc. cit., 261-265.

16. James D. Horan, *The Pinkertons: The Detective Dynasty That Made History* (New York: Crown Publishers, 1967), 40-42.

17. Villard, loc. cit., 408.

18. The Diagram Group, *Weapons: An International Encyclopedia from 5000 BC to 2000 AD* (New York: St. Martin's Press, 1990), 133. I am grateful to the rangers at Harpers Ferry and William Eagan of the Green Mountain Civil War Round Table based in White River Junction, Vermont, for setting me straight about how these Sharps carbines work. Up to this point, historians have mistakenly reported that the Sharps Model 1855 is a "repeater" but this is not true. Mr. Eagan did tell me that this gun had an optional capping mechanism which repeated but that it also used regular metal caps. I have seen nothing to indicate whether Brown's men used this repeated capping system or not during the raid.

19. Oates, loc. cit., 286.

20. Ibid., 287-289.

21. Villard, loc. cit., 430.

22. This section comes directly from the testimony of Dr. John D. Starry, *United States Senate, 36th Congress, 1st Session*, S. Rept. 278 (Washington: GPO, 1860), serial 1040, 23-27 (hereafter cited as Senate Rept. 278.) In this report, testimony is paginated separately from the documents at the front of the report. From Starry's description of the placement of his room and what he could see from the window, it seems likely that his room was either above a jewelry store or a barber shop, and that the window faced the B. & O. railroad office just opposite. The jewelry store, being the larger of the two buildings, is the most likely candidate. For further information, consult Dave Gilbert, *A Walker's Guide to Harpers Ferry, West Virginia* (Harpers Ferry, WV: Harpers Ferry Historical Association, 1991), 22, 30.

23. Villard, loc. cit., 436-437.

24. Ibid., 438-439.

25. Ibid., 441.

26. Testimony of Henry Hunter as found in *The Life, Trial and Execution of Captain John Brown Known as "Old Brown of Ossawatomie": Compiled from Official and Authentic Sources* (New York: Da Capo Press, 1969), 76. The trial transcript here cited gives the figure avenging Thompson's death at "80,000,000,000," a sheer impossibility. Villard states that the actual trial transcript gives a figure of "80,000,000," but that the actual figure quoted by Thompson was more likely "80,000." Most modern historians give the figure at this lower and more reasonable rate.

27. Villard, loc. cit., 446-447.

28. Ibid., 447.

29. Sinn story taken from his testimony in *Life, Trial and Execution*, 80-81, and Villard, loc. cit., 447-448.

CHAPTER 2: "No man sent me here."

1. Colonel Lee's involvement in putting down the Harpers Ferry raid is recorded in Douglas Southall Freeman, *R. E. Lee: A Biography*, 4 vols. (New York: Charles Scribner's Sons, 1935), 1:394-399, and in his letter on the incident dtd. Oct. 19, 1859 in Senate Rept. 278, 40-43.

2. See Richard Harwell, *Lee: An Abridgment in One Volume of the Four-volume R. E. Lee by Douglas Southall Freeman* (New York: Collier Books, 1991), 79, for a brief explanation of all Lee's brevets earned in Mexico.

3. Freeman, loc. cit., 1:395, reports 500 insurgents. Villard, *John Brown*, 449, reports 700.

4. The death of Oliver Brown is described in the testimony of John Allstadt's son as found in Villard, loc. cit., 448.

5. From the recollections of John E. P. Daingerfield in "John Brown at Harper's Ferry: The Fight at the Engine House, as Seen by One of His Prisoners," *The Century Magazine*, vol. 30, no. 2 (June, 1885), 267. The two men who expressed concern about committing treason are identified in Villard, loc. cit., 449.

6. Quoted from Senate Rept. 278, 43-44.

7. Daingerfield, loc. cit., 267.

8. The assault on the Engine House is described in Villard, loc. cit., 452-454. There are two descriptions of how the doors were opened. Lt. Green claims the doors were smashed in and splintered creating a "ragged hole low down in the right hand door...." (Villard, loc. cit., 453.) But John Daingerfield claimed that he loosened the fastenings on the doors, thereby allowing the wagons to be pushed back creating an opening for the continuation of the assault. (See Daingerfield, "John Brown at Harper's Ferry," 267.) Since a ladder makes a poor battering ram at best, and it is known the doors were fastened with ropes which would minimize the effectiveness of any blows administered to them, it appears that the Daingerfield version may be correct. Dr. John T. Atwood, Jr., of Marie Selby Gardens, Sarasota, Fla., has, however, suggested that the oak doors could have been rotted by the rains and damp fogs which plague the area, thereby giving some credence to Green's tale. This is a topic which will probably be open to debate for some time.

9. This incident is recorded in a letter of C. W. Tayleure written to John Brown, Jr., quoted in Villard, loc. cit., 454-455.

10. Ibid., 467; and Oates, loc. cit., 301.

11. Villard, loc. cit., 444.

12. Craig M. Simpson, *A Good Southerner: The Life of Henry A. Wise of Virginia* (Chapel Hill: The University of North Carolina Press, 1985), 110-111.

13. Ibid., 6.

14. Barton H. Wise, *The Life of Henry A. Wise of Virginia, 1806-1876* (New York: The MacMillan Company, 1889), 159.

15. Ibid., 160.

16. Ibid., 126-128.

17. The interview with Brown was originally recorded by a reporter for the *New York Herald*, and is excerpted in Villard, loc. cit., 456-463.

18. Joseph Barry, *The Strange Story of Harper's Ferry with Legends of the Surrounding Country* (Shepherdstown, WV: Shepherdstown Register, Inc., 1979), 66-67; Freeman, *R. E. Lee*, 1:401-402.

CHAPTER 3: "A COMET DIRE AND STRANGE AM I."

1. *Boston Transcript*, October 18, 1859; Julia Ward Howe, *Reminiscences, 1819-1889* (New York: Houghton Mifflin and Co., 1899), 255.

2. Letter from Theodore Parker to Francis Jackson, Rome, Nov. 24, 1859, quoted in John Weiss, *Life and Correspondence of Theodore Parker, Minister of the Twenty-eighth Congregational Society, Boston*, vol. 2 (London: Longman, Green, Longman, Roberts, and Green, 1863), 171.

3. The Law Library in Montpelier has one of Dr. Howe's books for the blind in its special collection. It is my guess that the State of Vermont may have acquired the book during one of Howe's many excursions in the U. S. and Canada promoting schools for the blind. I would further conclude that samples of Howe's books can likely be found in the collections of most Ante-bellum States.

4. J. W. Howe, loc. cit., 81-82.

5. Milton Meltzer, *A Light in the Dark: The Life of Samuel Gridley Howe* (New York: Thomas Y. Crowell Co., 1964), 118-119.

6. Harold Schwartz, *Samuel Gridley Howe: Social Reformer, 1801-1876* (Cambridge, Mass.: Harvard University Press, 1956), 112.

7. Meltzer, loc. cit., 168-169.

8. Julia Ward Howe, *Passion Flowers* (Boston: Ticknor & Fields, 1854), 100-102.

9 Schwartz, loc. cit., 152-153.

10. Meltzer, loc. cit., 177-180.

11. Jeffery Rossbach, *Ambivalent Conspirators: John Brown, the Secret Six, and a Theory of Slave Violence* (Philadelphia: University of Pennsylvania Press, 1982), 36-37.

12. J. W. Howe, *Reminiscences*, 253-254.

13. This section about Brown's trial is taken entirely from the trial transcript as recorded in *The Life, Trial and Execution*, 55-95.

14. For a full account of the incident, see Barry, loc. cit., 25-27.

15. Oates, *loc. cit.*, 316.

16. On August 12, 1791, a slave rebellion began in Santo Domingo on the island of Hispaniola of which Haiti is a part. The slaves managed to gain control of large parts of the island then governed by France. Two years later, slavery was officially abolished in Santo Domingo. The French Assembly followed this act by abolishing slavery in all French held territory on February 4, 1794. They also granted full French citizenship to all former slaves. This was done because the Assembly wanted to protect their territories and felt that former slaves granted full citizenship would make good guardians. This successful slave rebellion sent shivers through the slave-holding South. Many Southerners feared a similar rebellion would end slavery in America.

17. Rossbach, loc. cit., 224-225.

18. Ibid., 229.

19. Oates, loc. cit., 313. Oates gives the date that Howe and Stearns fled to Canada as October 25, but this cannot be correct. Rossbach states that the two men left some time after Mary Brown's visit to Boston. Howe's own letter on the subject of his flight and his involvement with Brown which is dated November 14, 1859, suggests that the flight took place either just before or after the letter was written.

20. Letter quoted from *The New York Times*, Nov. 16, 1859, 8.

21. Julia Ward Howe to her sister Annie dated Sunday, November 6, 1859, quoted in Laura E. Richards and Maud Howe Elliott, *Julia Ward Howe, 1819-1910* (Boston and New York: Houghton Mifflin Company, 1916), 177.

22. Julia Ward Howe, *Later Lyrics* (Boston: Lee and Shepard, 1865), 12-14.

23. Villard, loc. cit., 508-509; Oates loc. cit., 334-335.

24. Richard Warch and Jonathan Fanton, eds., *John Brown* (Englewood Cliffs, NJ: Prentice-Hall, Inc., 1973), 104, 107.

CHAPTER 4: "BLOW YE THE TRUMPET, BLOW!"

1. Letter of Victor Hugo to the *London Star* as found in *The New York Times*, Friday, December 23, 1859, 2; Matthew Josephson, *Victor Hugo: A Realistic Biography of the Great Romantic* (Garden City, NY: Doubleday, Doran & Co., Inc., 1942), 432-433.

2. Scenes at the execution of John Brown taken from Stephen B. Oates, loc. cit., 351-352; Edward Stone, *Incidents at Harper's Ferry* (Englewood Cliffs, NJ: Prentice-Hall, Inc., 1956), 157-158; the story of John Brown's pulse being taken is not found in Oates's book, but can be found in other sources, particularly Warch and Fanton, loc. cit., 103.

3. *Barre Gazette*, Friday, December 9, 1859, 3.

4. Dorothy Canfield Fisher, "One Side of My Great-grandmother's Character," *Memories of Arlington, Vermont* (New York: Duell, Sloan and Pearce, 1957), 84-85.

5. John Wallace Hutchinson, *Story of the Hutchinsons (Tribe of Jesse)*, 2 vols. (Boston: Lee and Shepard, 1896), 1:365.

6. *Barre Gazette*, Friday, December 9, 1859, 2.

7. Oates, loc. cit., 356. Watson and Oliver were eventually buried at North Elba. Oliver's body, along with those of other raiders, arrived for burial in 1899. Watson's arrived in 1882 by a much more circuitous route. During the Civil War, an army officer discovered Watson's body at the medical college in Winchester and removed it north where he gave it to a lodge he belonged to. For years, the lodge used the body for its secret rituals. But upon hearing that Mary Brown, who then resided in California, would be traveling through his area in 1882, the officer moved the body to a doctor's office and arranged for Mrs. Brown's son, John Jr., to identify it. This done, Mary took Watson's body to North Elba for burial. This information was graciously provided by Edwin N. Cotter, Jr., Superintendent of the John Brown Farm in Lake Placid, New York.

8. Mary C. Crawford, *The Romance of Old New England Churches* (Boston: L. C. Page & Co., 1904), 341-342.

9. Bill of sale for John Brown's Coffin and other services dtd. Dec. 5th, 1859, in the collection of Edwin N. Cotter, Jr., John Brown Farm, Lake Placid, New York.

10. Loyal C. Kellogg, a newly appointed Vermont Supreme Court judge, wrote in his diary for December 5, 1859, that he saw "Wendell Phillips and Mrs Brown, widow of John Brown, at the Bardwell House this evening—they accompanying the corpse of John Brown, who was executed at Charlestown, Virginia, on Friday last on their way to North Elba, Essex County, New York, for burial." The Kellogg diaries are found at the Vermont Historical Society, Montpelier, Vermont.

11. Oates, loc. cit., 357.

12. Joshua Young, "The Funeral of John Brown," *New England Magazine*, reprint (April, 1904), 9. Unless otherwise specified, this section on the funeral of John Brown is taken from this article, 9-13.

13. Crawford, loc. cit., 342.

14. Robert E. Senghas, "Joshua Young: Burlington Abolitionist" (Burlington, Vt.: First Unitarian Universalist Society, December 6, 1981), 1.

15. Joshua Young, *God Greater Than Man: A Sermon Preached June 11th, after the Rendition of Anthony Burns* (Burlington, Vt.: Samuel B. Nichols, 1854), 20-21.

16. *The Burlington Free Press* (Weekly ed.), June 4, 1858, 2.

17. Minutes of meeting held Dec. 11, 1858, Papers of the First Unitarian Church, Special Collections, Bailey/Howe Library, University of Vermont, Burlington, Vt.

18. Joshua Young's resignation dtd. Nov. 28, 1858, Papers of the First Unitarian Church.

19. Here, Young is quoting from the Bible, Judges 6:20. Sisera fought against the Israelite leader Barak, who defeated Sisera's army. Sisera escaped, only to die at the hands of Jael, the wife of Heber. The confrontation is described in the fourth chapter of Judges.

20. Oates, loc. cit., 357.

21. Text can be found in *The Methodist Hymnal: Official Hymnal of the Methodist Church* (Nashville, Tenn.: The Methodist Publishing House, 1964, 1966), hymn 100. It is easy to see why John Brown loved this particular hymn so much. Wesley based the hymn on passages from Leviticus (25:8-17) which mention the great year of "jubile" during which the people were supposed to "proclaim liberty throughout all the land." Among other things, masters freed their servants during this year.

22. *New York Daily Tribune*, December 12, 1859, 6.

23. *A John Brown Reader*, 283.

24. Letter of John H. Metcalf published in *The Burlington Free Press*, March 15, 1902, 4.

25. Letter of Joshua Young to the First Cong. Society of Burlington, Vt., dtd. April 27th, 1862, Papers of the First Unitarian Church. Young's own description of his treatment after officiating at Brown's funeral is found in Young, "The Funeral of John Brown," 14. Elizabeth Dow, Special Collections librarian at the Bailey/Howe Library, University of Vermont, has an interesting theory about Young's second resignation concerning the Winooski Cotton Mill which had no trouble getting southern cotton from the British during the Civil War. Ms. Dow speculates that the illicit shipments might have come from blockade runners shipping out from Savannah, Georgia, Mobile, Alabama, or even better, Galveston, Texas. The runners would drop their loads off in Bermuda where they would be transferred to British merchant vessels headed for Canada. The vessels would then enter the Canadian interior on the St. Lawrence River and head down the Richelieu River just above Montreal. This river flows directly into Lake Champlain which would give them access to the harbor at Burlington, Vermont. If Reverend Young had learned of these illegal shipments, he would not have been able to keep his mouth shut about them. It is also possible that some members of his congregation may have had connections either with the Winooski mill or the illicit cotton trade. But so far, no records have been uncovered to prove Dow's theory. Historian David J. Blow, who has a list of people who voted to accept Young's resignation in 1862, has failed to connect any of them with the cotton trade. Blow says that no records were ever kept of foreign imports at Burlington Harbor during that period, and that Young's sermons for that period cannot be found. We leave it to future historians to discover the truth of these matters. My thanks to Elizabeth Dow and David J. Blow for discussing this theory with me.

26. Josephson, loc. cit., 433.

27. *A John Brown Reader*, 155.

28. *Vermont Journal*, December 10, 1859, 2.

29. Ibid.

CHAPTER 5: "...ALL THE WILD BEASTS OF EPHESUS."

1. Letter of Clark H. Chapman to Jacob Collamer, Dec. 16, 1859, Collamer Papers, Special Collections, Bailey/Howe Library, University of Vermont, Burlington, Vt.

2. Letter of Jacob Collamer to Clark H. Chapman, Dec. 19, 1859, Collamer Papers.

3. Letter of Clark H. Chapman to Jacob Collamer, Dec. 24, 1859, Collamer Papers.

4. Letter of Clark H. Chapman to Jacob Collamer, Jan. 24, 1860, Collamer Papers.

5. Mary Louise Kelly, *Jacob Collamer* (Woodstock, Vt.: The Woodstock Historical Society, 1944), 3. Unless otherwise indicated, all material in this section on Collamer's early life and political career up to the time of the John Brown raid comes from Kelly, 3-7.

6. O. M. Tinkham, "Jacob Collamer," *The Vermonter*, Vol. 5, No. 12 (July, 1900), 234. Although Mary Louise Kelly maintains that Jacob Collamer introduced the postage stamp to America while serving as Postmaster General under President Taylor, I find this hard to believe. According to the *Postal Service Guide to U.S. Stamps*, the first issues, the 5 cent Benjamin Franklin and 10 cent Washington, came out in 1847, two years before Collamer served in Taylor's Cabinet. He may have had something to do with the innovation while serving in the U.S. Congress. Kelly does write that Collamer used one of the first stamps on a letter to his brother, claiming that if the "new system worked, the stamp would some day be quite valuable." According to the *Postal Service Guide for 1987*, a used 5 cent Franklin is worth $650. A used Washington is worth $2000.

7. Jacob Collamer, "Views of the Minority," August 11, 1856, *United States Senate, 34th Congress, 1st Session*, vol. 2, Report of the Committee on Territories, S. Rept. 282 (Washington: A. O. P. Nicholson, Senate Printer, 1856), serial 837, 16.

8. Found in the address of Alexander H. Stephens of Georgia, *Addresses on the Presentation of the Statue of Jacob Collamer* (Washington: s.n., 1881), 15.

9. Senate Rept. 278, 28-30.

10. Schwartz, loc. cit., 243. Letter of Howe to Sumner, Jan. 15, 1860, quoted in Schwartz, loc. cit., 244. Original in Howe Papers, Houghton Library.

11. Schwartz, loc. cit., 245.

12. My thanks to Betty K. Koed of the Senate Historical Office for helping me determine the setting of the committee meetings.

13. This section is taken from the testimony of Dr. Howe in Senate Rept. 278, 156-179.

14. Letter from Howe to Higginson, Feb. 16, 1860, Higginson Papers, Rare Books Collection, Boston Public Library; cited by courtesy of the Trustees of the Boston Public Library.

15. Testimony of George L. Stearns, Senate Rept. 278, 225-245.

16. Journal of the Select Committee, Senate Rept. 278, 35-36.

17. Walter Harding, *The Days of Henry Thoreau: A Biography* (New York: Dover Publications, Inc., 1982), 423-424.

18. Senate Rept. 278, 18.

19. Ibid., 24-25.

CHAPTER 6: "TAKE A LESSON FROM JOHN BROWN."

1. Wise, *Life of Henry A. Wise*, 264-265. By extension of Wise's argument about free and slave settlers in Kansas, it can be seen how 32 free settlers could easily survive on the 1,280 acres needed for the two slave owners. There is no way slave owners could hold a majority in direct competition with free settlers under such conditions. Popular sovereignty would always result in the creation of a free state.

2. Hutchinson, loc. cit., 1:371.

3. Irwin Silber, ed., *Songs of the Civil War* (New York: Columbia University Press, 1960), 97.

4. From a speech given either on November 30 or December 1, 1859, at Elwood, Kansas, as found in Roy P. Basler, ed., *The Collected Works of Abraham Lincoln*, vol. 3 (New Brunswick, N.J.: Rutgers University Press, 1953), 496 (hereafter cited as Basler, *Collected Works*.)

5. Ibid., 3:502.

6. Basler, *Abraham Lincoln: His Speeches and Writings*, 529.

7. Letter of Wise to Davis, Feb. 22, 1861, from the Confederate papers relating to Army Officers, RG 109, in the National Archives, as quoted in William C. Davis, *"A Government of Our Own": The Making of the Confederacy*, (New York: The Free Press, 1994), 323.

8. Bruce Catton, *The Coming Fury*, (New York: Washington Square Press, 1961), 334.

9. *Proceedings of the Virginia State Convention of 1861*, vol. 4 (Richmond, Virginia: Virginia State Library, 1965), 6.

10. Wise, *Life of Henry A. Wise*, 275-276.

11. John D. Imboden, "Jackson at Harper's Ferry in 1861," in R. U. Johnson and C. C. Buel, eds., *Battles and Leaders of the Civil War*, vol. 1 (New York: The Century Company, 1887-1888), 111-113.

12. Wise, *Life of Henry A. Wise*, 276-277.

13. *Proceedings of the Virginia State Convention of 1861*, 4: 124. At this point, Wise is gravely exaggerating the situation. As will be seen later, Harper's Ferry was not then being reinforced by Washington, nor could it be. As for the sinking of ships at the Gosport Naval Yard, history tells us that did not happen until April 22, Monday of the following week, and it was done by members of the Union Navy.

14. Ibid., 4: 126-131.

15. Ibid., 4: 144.

16. Ibid., 4: 146-147.

17. Merritt Roe Smith, *Harpers Ferry Armory and the New Technology: The Challenge of Change* (Ithaca, NY: Cornell University Press, 1977), 318-319; and Barry, *The Strange Story of Harper's Ferry*, 97-98.

18. Roger Jones, "Affair at Harper's Ferry, Va.", Doc. 103, as found in Frank Moore, ed., *The Rebellion Record: A Diary of American Events*, supplement-1st vol. (New York: D. Van Nostrand, 1869), 754.

19. Catton, loc. cit., 336.

20. *The Papers of Jefferson Davis*, vol. 7 (Baton Rouge: Louisiana State University Press, 1992), 184.

21. Edward A. Pollard, *Lee and His Lieutenants* (Augusta, Georgia: Southern Publishing Company, 1870), 563.

CHAPTER 7: "THERE IS A JUST GOD WHO RIDES UPON THE WHIRLWIND."

1. Gordon Battelle to F. H. Pierpont, April 23, 1861, Francis Harrison Pierpont Papers, A&M 9, West Virginia and Regional History Collection, West Virginia University, Morgantown, WV.

2. Phil Conley, ed., *The West Virginia Encyclopedia* (Charleston, WV: West Virginia Publishing Company, 1929), 376.

3. Ibid., 373.

4. Ibid., 377.

5. Ibid., 377-378.

6. Anna Pierpont Siviter, *Recollections of War and Peace, 1861-1868* (New York: G. P. Putnam's Sons, 1938), 76-77.

7. Ibid., 78.

8. Ibid., 75.

9. Charles Ambler, *Francis H. Pierpont: Union War Governor of Virginia and Father of West Virginia* (Chapel Hill: The University of North Carolina Press, 1937), 36-37.

10. Dialogue taken from a letter of Julia Pierpont to F. H. Pierpont dated May 17, 1861. Pierpont Papers, A&M 9.

11. Ibid., and Siviter, loc. cit., 80.

12. Siviter, loc. cit., 52-53.

13. Article 4, Section 4, Guarantees to the States, *U.S. Constitution*. Mort Gerberg, in his book, *The U.S. Constitution for Everyone* (New York: Perigree Books, 1987), 33, maintains that no action has ever been taken to enforce this regulation. In light of the history of western Virginia, this assertion seems false.

14. Virgil A. Lewis, *How West Virginia Was Made* (West Virginia: William G. Conley, 1909), 166-169.

15. Ibid., 171-173.

16. United States War Department, *The War of the Rebellion: A Compilation of the Official Records of the Union and Confederate Armies*, ser. 1, vol. 2 (Washington: GPO, 1880), serial 3113, 713.

17. Ibid., 723-724.

18. Ambler, loc. cit., 379.

CHAPTER 8: "JOHN BROWN'S BODY LIES A MOULDERIN' IN THE GRAVE."

1. Letter of Samuel Gridley Howe to Governor John A. Andrew dated April 13, 1861, Andrew Papers, Massachusetts Historical Society, Boston, Mass.

2. Henry Greenleaf Pearson, *The Life of John A. Andrew, Governor of Massachusetts, 1861-1865*, 2 vols. (Boston: Houghton, Mifflin, 1904), 1:202.

3. MDC Ranger Mark Anderson pointed out these features to me on the day I visited Fort Warren. I am greatly indebted to him for giving me a guided tour of the fort and providing me with maps of the island.

4. Pearson, loc. cit., 1:203; and Boyd B. Stutler, *Glory, Glory, Hallelujah!: The Story of "John Brown's Body" and "Battle Hymn of the Republic"* (Cincinnati: C. J. Krehbiel Company, 1960), 15.

5. Edward Rowe Snow, *The Romance of Boston Bay* (Boston: The Yankee Publishing Company, 1944), 169-170.

6. Louis C. Elson, *The History of American Music* (New York: The Macmillan Company, 1925), 157.

7. Charles Dunbar, ed., *The Union Harp and Revival Chorister: Being a Collection of Hymns and Tunes, Designed More Particularly for the Social Means of Grace* (Cincinnati: H. M. Rulison, Queen City Publishing House, 1858), 6, 265-266.

8. Snow, loc. cit., 170.

9. O. C. Bosbyshell, "Origin of 'John Brown's Body,'" *Grand Army Scout and Soldier's Mail*, Philadelphia, November 3, 1883.

10. Stutler, *Glory, Glory, Hallelujah!*, 16-17.

11. Boyd B. Stutler, "John Brown's Body," *Civil War History IV* (September, 1958), 256.

12. Ibid., 254.

13. Stutler, *Glory, Glory, Hallelujah!*, 23-24.

14. Stutler, "John Brown's Body," 254.

15. Richard K. Patterson, "The Greatest Little Man I Ever Met," *American History Illustrated* (December, 1971), 30-32.

16. Ibid., 32-33.

17. Ibid., 34.

18. Ibid., 35.

19. Ruth Painter Randall, *Colonel Elmer Ellsworth: A Biography of Lincoln's Friend and First Hero of the Civil War* (Boston: Little, Brown and Company, 1960), 266.

20. Ibid., 252.

21. Ibid., 254.

22. The story of Ellsworth's death in Alexandria is taken from Randall, *Colonel Elmer Ellsworth*, 256-263, and Patterson's article.

23. Stutler, "John Brown's Body," 255, 257.

24. Stutler, *Glory, Glory, Hallelujah!*, 28, 30.

25. Benjamin F. Cook, *History of the Twelfth Massachusetts Volunteers (Webster Regiment)* (Boston: Twelfth (Webster) Regiment Association, 1882), 19.

26. Ibid., 21.

27. Stutler, *Glory, Glory, Hallelujah!*, 27.

28. Cook, loc. cit., 22; and letter from Franklin Sanborn to Florence Howe Hall dated 1916 quoted in Florence Howe Hall, *The Story of the Battle Hymn of the Republic* (New York: Harper & Brothers, 1916), 59-60.

29. Richard Grant White, *Poetry Lyrical, Narrative, and Satirical of the Civil War* (New York: The American News Company, 1866), viii; George Templeton Strong, *Diary of the Civil War, 1860-1865* (New York: The Macmillan Company, 1962), 205. John Wycliffe was a fourteenth century English scholar and philosopher who openly opposed the Pope of Rome. During the reign of Richard II, John Ball, a follower of Wycliffe, led a revolt against the King, now called the Peasant's Revolt, in 1381 to resist the imposition of a poll tax. At his trial for treason, Ball openly admitted he was a follower of Wycliffe. Ball was hanged along with some 200 other rebels. Wycliffe died of natural causes on the evening of December 31, 1384, and was buried at Lutterworth. But he was so hated by the Catholic clerics that Bishop Fleming, under orders from Pope Martin V, dug up Wycliffe's body in 1428 and burned it.

CHAPTER 9: "MINE EYES HAVE SEEN THE GLORY...."

1. *New York Times*, May 19, 1861.

2. Richard Grant White, *National Hymns, How They Are Written and How They Are Not Written: A Lyric and National Study for the Times* (New York: Rudd & Carleton, 1861), 19, 22.

3. *New York Times*, May 19, 1861.

4. J. W. Howe, *Reminiscences*, 273.

5. Julia Ward Howe, *From Sunset Ridge: Poems Old and New* (New York: Houghton, Mifflin Company, 1899), 3.

6. White, *National Hymns*, 97.

7. Ibid., 98.

8. *New York Times*, August 8, 1861, 3.

9. J. W. Howe, *From Sunset Ridge*, 5.

10. J. W. Howe, *Reminiscences*, 274.

11. Ibid., 270.

12. Ibid., 271-272.

13. Deborah Pickman Clifford, *Mine Eyes Have Seen the Glory: A Biography of Julia Ward Howe* (Boston: Little, Brown and Co., 1979), 143-144; Stutler, *Glory, Glory, Hallelujah!*, 36; J. W. Howe, *Reminiscences*, 274-275.

14. J. W. Howe, *Reminiscences*, 275.

15 Ibid., 254.

16. Clifford, *loc. cit.*, 146-147.

17. The main part of this story is derived from two sources: Carol Brink's *Harps in the Wind: The Story of the Singing Hutchinsons*, (New York: The Macmillan Company, 1947), 205-211; and John Wallace Hutchinson's more detailed account in *Story of the Hutchinsons* 1:380-393. Other sources are noted as necessary.

18. Quoted in Dorothy Meserve Kunhardt and Philip B. Kunhardt Jr., *Twenty Days: A Narrative in Text and Pictures of the Assassination of Abraham Lincoln and the Twenty Days and Nights That Followed—The Nation in Mourning, The Long Trip Home to Springfield* (New York: Harper & Row, 1965), 136.

19. Silber, loc. cit., 286.

20. Cook, loc. cit., 39.

21. Barry, loc. cit., 119-120.

22. Elisha Hunt Rhodes of the 2nd Rhode Island records in his diary for August 10, 1864: "We left Harpers Ferry this morning and marched to this camp passing through Charlestown. This is the place where John Brown was hung and we had each band and drum corps play 'John Brown's Body Lies Mouldering in the Grave.' 'But His Soul Goes Marching On' as we passed through the streets of the town. The men joined in singing the hymn much to the disgust of the people." (See Robert Hunt Rhodes, ed. *All for the Union: The Civil War Diary and Letters of Elisha Hunt Rhodes* (New York: Vintage Books, 1985), 170.) Private Wilbur Fisk of the 2nd Vermont Infantry also writes in a letter of September 4, 1864, of his experiences in northern Virginia: "Charlestown has the notoriety of being the place where John Brown was tried and hung. The jail where he was confined, and the court-house where he was tried, have the appearance of being roughly treated from some cause or other. Large holes were punched through the brick walls of both buildings, and from the street they looked as if they had been given over to ruin and decay. When the brigade came through there the last time, the band played the John Brown song, to the edification of that man's executioners. It just suited the boys to hear that air played there. They were determined to give the people there the benefit of it, and if the band hadn't played it they had agreed to sing it, and sing it as soldiers who know how. If they had done so I imagine the citizens would have thought that the ghost of John Brown was actually 'marching on.'" (See Emil & Ruth Rosenblatt, eds., *Hard Marching Every Day: The Civil War Letters of Private Wilbur Fisk, 1861-1865* (Lawrence, Kansas: University Press of Kansas, 1992), 253.

23. [12th Massachusetts Regiment Annual Booklet] (November, 1915). My thanks to Edmund Hands, historian and archivist for the 12th Mass. re-enactors for providing this information.

24. Stutler, "John Brown's Body," 254; Richard Crawford, ed., *The Civil War Songbook: Complete Original Sheet Music for 37 Songs* (New York: Dover Publications, 1977), 10.

25. The Kansas State Historical Society in Topeka has correspondence written in 1885 from George A. Huron claiming that he made up the line in the Spring of 1862 while campaigning against Jackson in the Shenandoah Valley. But this claim has its detractors.

26. Cook, loc. cit., 61.

27. Ibid., 63.

28. Ira Berlin, Barbara J. Fields, et al., *Freedom: A Documentary History of Emancipation: 1861-1867: The Destruction of Slavery*, series 1, vol. 1 (New York: Cambridge University Press, 1987), 70-72.

29. Henry Clay Work, "Kingdom Coming," as found in Crawford, 146-148. For those readers who are fans of the Boston Pops, this tune is used for a piece called "The Doodletown Pipers." There are two modern recordings of the song, one by the 97th Regimental String Band which uses the original text with the offensive term "darkies," and one by Bobby Horton who substitutes "black folks" for "darkies." I personally prefer to perform the piece as an instrumental and mention the content of the text by way of introduction.

CHAPTER 10: "'PROPHETS AND KINGS' HAVE WAITED FOR THIS DAY...."

1. Laura E. Richards, ed., *Letters and Journals of Samuel Gridley Howe*, vol. 2 (Boston: Dana Estes & Company, 1906), 500-501.

2. Basler, *Collected Works*, vol. 5, 144-146.

3. See Stephen B. Oates, *With Malice Toward None: The Life of Abraham Lincoln* (New York: New American Library, 1977), 338, 358.

4. Basler, *Collected Works*, vol. 5, 318-319.

5. Ibid., 372-373.

6. John G. Nicolay and John Hay, *Abraham Lincoln: A History*, 10 vols. (New York: The Century Co., 1904), 6:358-359.

7. Carl Sandburg, *Abraham Lincoln: The Prairie Years and The War Years*, 3 vols. (New York: Dell Publishing, 1968), 2:206-207. This volume is cited only once and is not to be confused with the longer set of works cited below. Sandburg wrote three sets of volumes about Lincoln, the shortest is one volume, the one cited here is in 3 volumes, and the one cited below is divided into two parts: *The Prairie Years* in 2 volumes and *The War Years* in 4.

8. Basler, *Collected Works*, vol. 5, 434.

9. Albert Gallatin Browne, Jr., *Sketch of the Official Life of John A. Andrew, As Governor of Massachusetts* (New York: Hurd and Houghton, 1868), 74.

10. Ibid., 76.

11. Nicolay, Hay, loc. cit., 167.

12. Pearson, loc. cit., vol. 2, 51.

13. Basler, *Abraham Lincoln: His Speeches and Writings*, 679, et seq.

14. Carl Sandburg, *Abraham Lincoln: The War Years*, 4 vols. (New York: Harcourt, Brace & Company, 1939), 2:8.

15. Ambler, *Francis H. Pierpont*, 184.

16. Ibid., 184-185; and Basler, *Collected Works of Lincoln*, 6:28.

17. Sandburg, *Abraham Lincoln: The War Years*, 2:10.

18. Gay Wilson Allen, *Waldo Emerson* (New York: Penguin Books, 1981), 618; Frank Preston Stearns, *The Life and Public Services of George Luther Stearns* (Philadelphia: J. B. Lippincott Company, 1907), 275-276.

19. Charlotte L. Forten, "New Year's Day on the Islands of South Carolina, 1863," as found in Lydia Maria Child, *The Freedmen's Book* (Boston: Ticknor and Fields, 1866), 254.

20. Ibid., 255; Thomas Wentworth Higginson, *Army Life in a Black Regiment* (Boston: Lee and Shepard, 1890), 41.

21. Higginson, loc. cit., 41.

22. Schwartz, loc. cit., 261.

23. Ibid., 261; Samuel Gridley Howe, *The Refugees from Slavery in Canada West: Report to the Freedmen's Inquiry Commission* (Boston: Wright & Potter, 1864), 92-93.

24. Stephen Jay Gould, *The Mismeasure of Man* (New York: W. W. Norton & Company, 1981), 45.

25. Ibid., 48.

26. Ibid., 50. Modern scientists now know that just the opposite is true. Racial interbreeding usually results in a condition known as "hybrid vigor." Although this is no rule of thumb, there are some outstanding examples of this in the black community in America. For example, concert pianist Andre Watts is so accomplished that he is sought out by major orchestras and recital halls all over the globe.

27. Howe, *The Refugees from Slavery in Canada West*, 103-104.

28. *How West Virginia Was Made*, 332-334.

29. Ambler, loc. cit., 192; Siviter, loc. cit., 94-95; *The Fairmont Times* (Friday, August 3, 1951), 11.

30. Letter from F. H. Pierpont to Julia Pierpont dated August 23, 1863. Pierpont Papers, A&M 9.

31. John S. Mosby, *Gray Ghost: The Memoirs of Colonel John S. Mosby* (New York: Bantam Books, 1992), 202.

32. Siviter, loc. cit., 128.

33. Jeffry D. Wert, *Mosby's Rangers* (New York: Simon & Schuster, 1990), 98.

34. Henry Clay Work, "Song of a Thousand Years" (Chicago: Root & Cady, 1862).

35. Silber, loc. cit., 25.

CHAPTER 11: "I SEEM DOOMED TO RAISE MONEY."

1. Charles C. McCabe, "The Bright Side of Life in Libby Prison," quoted in Frank Milton Bristol, *The Life of Chaplain McCabe* (New York: Fleming H. Revell Company, 1908), 124.

2. Ibid., 125.

3. Charles Downer Schwartz and Ouida Davis Schwartz, *A Flame of Fire: The Story of Troy Annual Conference* (Rutland, VT: Academy Books, 1982), 185.

4. Bristol, loc. cit., 72.

5. McCabe, loc. cit., 128.

6. I. N. Johnston, *Four Months in Libby, and the Campaign Against Atlanta* (Cincinnati: R. F. Thompson, 1864), 48.

7. McCabe, loc. cit., 125-126.

8. Ibid., 128-130.

9. Bristol, loc. cit., 95-96.

10. McCabe, loc. cit., 133-135; Edward P. Smith, *Incidents of the United States Christian Commission* (Philadelphia: J. B. Lippincott & Co., 1869), 398-399.

11. McCabe, loc. cit., 137-138; John Y. Foster, *New Jersey and the Rebellion* (Newark, N.J.: Martin R. Dennis, 1868), 868-871.

12. Richmond *Daily Dispatch*, July 6, 1863.

13. Smith, *Incidents of the United States Christian Commission*, 396; McCabe, loc. cit., 135.

14. McCabe, loc. cit., 135-136; Smith, *Incidents of the United States Christian Commission*, 396-397.

15. McCabe, loc. cit., 138.

16. Ibid., 126.

17. Ibid., 132.

18. Letter from McCabe to his wife Rebecca dated July 22, 1863, quoted in Bristol, loc. cit., 97.

19. Letter from McCabe to his wife Rebecca dated August 28, 1863, quoted in Bristol, loc. cit., 101.

20. Johnston, loc. cit., 49-50.

21. Letter from McCabe to his wife Rebecca dated September 25, 1863, quoted in Bristol, loc. cit., 108.

22. McCabe, loc. cit., 141-142.

23. Ibid., 142.

24. Bristol, loc. cit., 111.

25. McCabe, loc. cit., 142-143. Blue mass in various forms was considered a cure-all for a variety of afflictions, especially fevers. The trouble was that, since it contained mercury, it could also leave a patient with a debilitating condition afterward due to heavy metal poisoning. Louisa May Alcott, for example, received injections of calomel, another medicine using mercury, when she contracted typhoid during the war. The injections left her debilitated for life, but just active enough to write some of the finest stories and novels to see print.

26. Ibid., 143-145.

27. Bristol, loc. cit., 115.

28. Ibid., 117.

29. Bristol, loc. cit., 164.

30. *Evening Star*, Washington, D. C., Wednesday, February 3, 1864; Letter from Chaplain McCabe to his wife Rebecca dated February 3, 1864, quoted in Bristol, 198-200.

31. Bristol, loc. cit., 203.

CHAPTER 12: "A WAR-TIME AURORA BOREALIS"

1. Letter of Henry Wise to his wife Mary, Wise Family Papers, Virginia Historical Society, Richmond, Virginia.

2. B. R. Curtis, "The United States, Appellants, v. The Libellants and Claimants of the Schooner Amistad," *Reports of Decisions in the Supreme Court of the United States, with Notes, and a Digest*, vol. 14 (Boston: Little, Brown and Company, 1855), 156 et seq.; "American Missionary Association, Its History," *American Missionary*, vol. 12, no. 5 (May, 1868), 97.

3. Letter of John Oliver to Rev. S. S. Jocelyn, Portsmouth, Va., Feb. 7, 1863, A. M. A. correspondence at the Amistad Center, Tulane University, New Orleans, Louisiana.

4. Letter from Lucy Chase found in *Dear Ones at Home* edited by Henry Lee Swint (Nashville: Vanderbilt University Press, 1966), 79-85.

5. Letter of Rev. W. S. Bell to S. S. Jocelyn, Wise Farm, Va., Nov. 19th, 1863; letter of Rev. W. S. Bell to W. E. Whiting, Wise Farm near Norfolk, Va., Dec. 10th, 1863, A. M. A. correspondence.

6. Letters of Rev. W. S. Bell published in *American Missionary*, vol. 8 (February, 1864), 37-38.

7. Willis A. Hodges to Catherine Hodges, Sept. 15, 1864, copy in the Alexander A. Moore Collection of the Brooklyn Historical Society, "Nelson-Hodges Papers," Addenda, V-VIII.

8. This section is taken from Ellen Wise Mayo, "A Wartime Aurora Borealis," *Cosmopolitan*, vol. 22, no. 2 (June, 1896), 134-141. There is some disagreement as to when these events took place. Ellen says they happened in February of 1864. Barton Haxall Wise says March of the same year. The principal events occurred in connection with Judson Kilpatrick's failed cavalry raid on Richmond on March 1, 1864. It is my guess that Henry Wise arrived in Richmond on Monday, February 29. Kilpatrick and Dahlgren left on the raid on February 28. Dahlgren never made it into Richmond, but Kilpatrick was before the defenses north of the city on the morning of March 1.

9. This story is taken from Siviter, loc. cit., 129-132. Siviter claims that these events happened on June 30, 1864, but that is impossible. It is more likely they happened on July 11, 1864, as Early's Army attempted to breech the outer defenses around Washington. Siviter also writes of her three-year-old sister being alive at this time. That also is not true since Mary Augusta Pierpont died on June 18, 1864. Therefore, Mary, or Mamie as she was called, does not appear in this account of the story, although I have kept the rest of Siviter's memoir intact.

10. Bristol, loc. cit., 157, 232.

11. Louis W. Koenig, "The Most Unpopular Man in the North," *Civil War Chronicles*, vol. 3, no. 1 (Summer, 1993), 23.

12. Shelby Foote, *The Civil War: A Narrative*, 3 vols. (New York: Vintage Books, 1986), 3:551-552.

13. Ambler, loc. cit., 252-253.

14. Burke Davis, *Sherman's March* (New York: Random House, 1980), 23.

15. William Tecumseh Sherman, *Memoirs of General William T. Sherman*, 2 vols. (Boston: Lee & Shepard. 1875), 2:178-179.

16. Ibid., 1:148-149.

17. Davis, *Sherman's March*, 32.

18. Ibid., 45-46.

19. Ibid., 46.

20. Ibid., 33.

21. Ibid., 93-94.

22. United States War Department, *The War of the Rebellion: A Compilation of the Official Records of the Union and Confederate Armies*, ser. 1, vol. 44 (Washington: GPO, 1895), serial 3240, 836-837.

23. Ibid., 841.

24. Ibid., 847.

25. United States War Department, *The War of the Rebellion: A Compilation of the Official Records of the Union and Confederate Armies*, ser. 1, vol. 47, pt. 2 (Washington: GPO, 1895), serial 3410, 37-41.

26. Ibid., 36-37.

27. Ibid., 210.

28. Stephen B. Oates, *With Malice Toward None: The Life of Abraham Lincoln* (New York: New American Library, 1977), 439-441; Stephen B. Oates, "The Slaves Freed," *Civil War Chronicles*, vol. 2, no. 3 (Winter, 1993), 59.

29. Foote, loc. cit., 3:898, 901-902.

CHAPTER 13: "FAIR ASSASSIN, MURDER WHITE...."

1. Freeman, loc. cit., 4:96-97; John Sergeant Wise, *The End of an Era* (New York: Thomas Yoseloff, 1965), 433-435.

2. Horace Porter, *Campaigning with Grant* (New York: The Century Company, 1906), 458-459; Jerry Korn, *Pursuit to Appomattox: The Last Battles* (Alexandria, Virginia: Time-Life Books, 1987), 133.

3. Wise, *Life of Henry A. Wise*, 369-370.

4. Siviter, loc. cit., 149.

5. Foote, loc. cit., 3:962-963; Siviter, loc. cit., 138-139.

6. Entry for Monday, April 10th, 1865, in Julia Ward Howe's diary, Howe Family Papers (*44M-314(814)), Houghton Library, Harvard University, Cambridge, Mass. Citation of this material made by permission of the Houghton Library, Harvard University.

7. Frank P. Cauble, *The Proceedings Connected with the Surrender of the Army of Northern Virginia, April, 1865* (Appomattox, Virginia: Appomattox Court House National Historical Park, 1962), 164-165; Alice Rains Trulock, *In the Hands of Providence: Joshua L. Chamberlain and the American Civil War* (Chapel Hill: The University of North Carolina Press, 1992), 309.

8. Joshua Lawrence Chamberlain, *The Passing of the Armies: An Account of the Final Campaign of the Army of the Potomac, Based upon Personal Reminiscences of the Fifth Army Corps* (New York: Bantam Books, 1993), 201-202.

9. Sandburg, *Abraham Lincoln: The War Years* 4:219-220; Gene Smith, *American Gothic: The Story of America's Legendary Theatrical Family—Junius, Edwin, and John Wilkes Booth* (New York: Simon & Schuster, 1992), 131.

10. Basler, *Abraham Lincoln: His Speeches and Writings*, 799.

11. Sandburg, *Abraham Lincoln: The War Years*, 4:318; Smith, *American Gothic*, 132.

12. Smith, *American Gothic*, 79-80; Sandburg, *Abraham Lincoln: The War Years*, 4:312.

13. Louis J. Weichmann, *A True History of the Assassination of Abraham Lincoln and of the Conspiracy of 1865* (New York: Alfred A. Knopf, 1975), 50-51.

14. Siviter, loc. cit., 149-151.

15. Bristol, loc. cit., 204-205.

16. Jim Bishop, *The Day Lincoln Was Shot* (New York: Harper & Brothers, 1955), 121-127; Gideon Welles, *Diary of Gideon Welles, Secretary of the Navy under Lincoln and Johnson* (Boston: Houghton Mifflin Company, 1911), 280-283; Sandburg, *Abraham Lincoln: The War Years*, 4:265-266.

17. Bishop, loc. cit., 146.

18. Siviter, loc. cit., 152-153.

19. Clara E. Laughlin, *The Death of Lincoln: The Story of Booth's Plot, His Deed and the Penalty* (Newport, Vt.: Vt. Civil War Enterprises, n.d.), 301.

20. Bristol, loc. cit., 205-206.

21. Hutchinson, loc. cit., 1:427.

22. Story told to the author by Byron G. Kelly and Margaret G. Kelly, both descendants of Jacob Collamer.

23. J. W. Howe's Diary, April 15, 1865, Howe Family Papers, Houghton Library.

24. Richards & Elliott, *Julia Ward Howe*, 1:220-221; Pearson, loc. cit., 2:246.

25. J. W. Howe's Diary, April 19, 1865, Howe Family Papers, Houghton Library; *Sermons Preached in Boston on the Death of Abraham Lincoln* (Boston: J. E. Tilton and Company, 1865), 53, 55.

26. Julia Ward Howe, *From Sunset Ridge*, 17-19.

27. Ibid., 20.

28. J. W. Howe's diary, April 23 & April 24, 1865, Howe Family Papers, Houghton Library.

29. Davis, *Sherman's March*, 259.

30. Ibid., 261.

31. Wise, *The End of an Era*, 454-455.

32. Foote, loc. cit., 3:998.

33. Sandburg, *Abraham Lincoln: The War Years*, 4:393.

34. Sandburg, *Abraham Lincoln: The War Years*, 4:401; For a more detailed description of the events occurring during Lincoln's final journey home, see parts 3, 5, and 6 of Kunhardt, *Twenty Days*.

35. Bristol, loc. cit., 210.

36. *Memorial Record of the Nation's Tribute to Abraham Lincoln* (Washington, D.C.: W. H. & O. H. Morrison, 1865), 216.

37. Bristol, loc. cit., 211.

38. Champ Clark, *The Assassination: Death of the President* (Alexandria, Va.: Time-Life Books, 1987), 127.

39. Bristol, loc. cit., 211-212.

40. Ibid., 212-213.

41. The complete oration is found in *Memorial Record of the Nation's Tribute to Abraham Lincoln*, 228-237; Bristol, loc. cit., 213-214.

42. Bristol, loc. cit., 214-215.

43. Varina Jefferson Davis, *Jefferson Davis: Ex-President of the Confederate States of America: A Memoir* (New York: Belford Company, Publishers, 1890), 638-641.

44. William C. Davis, *Jefferson Davis: The Man and His Hour* (New York: HarperCollins, 1991), 640.

CHAPTER 14: "TALKING RECONSTRUCTION."

1. Siviter, loc. cit., 154, 156.

2. Stephen R. Wise, *Lifeline of the Confederacy: Blockade Running During the Civil War* (University of South Carolina Press, 1988), 296; *Official Records of the Union and Confederate Navies in the War of the Rebellion*, ser. 1, vol. 14 (Washington: GPO, 1902), serial 4353, 670-671; Ambler, loc. cit., 262. Despite the fact that Ambler says Pierpont left Alexandria on May 24, I find from the newspapers of the time that the journey actually took place later that week. The main problem with the newspaper reports is that they are somewhat contradictory about when and where Pierpont's party was during the trip and when they arrived in Richmond. The Wheeling *Daily Intelligencer* for June 1, 1865, says that the *Diamond* arrived at the Virginia capital at 2:30 p.m. on Friday May 26. But the Wheeling *Daily Intelligencer* for May 27, 1865, p. 3, says that Pierpont's party was at Fort Monroe on the 26th until 5:00 p.m. From Mrs. Siviter's narrative, it is clear that the journey to Richmond took at least two days. Therefore, I conclude that the trip started on May 25 and was completed on May 26. My thanks to the U.S. Department of the Navy for providing me with information about the *Diamond*.

3. Siviter, loc. cit., 155.

4. If this part of Mrs. Siviter's story proves true, the garments she saw were not the ones Davis was wearing just before he was captured, but clothes procured elsewhere. Lt. Col. Pritchard had already taken the real "disguise" to Washington under orders from Secretary of War Edwin Stanton. In fact, Pritchard presented Mrs. Davis's waterproof and shawl along with a pair of spurs belonging to Mr. Davis to Stanton on May 25. The "feminine" clothes that Anna says she saw probably came from Jefferson Davis's own wardrobe which had been confiscated by General Miles the moment that Davis was incarcerated at Fort Monroe. Waterproofs and shawls were the closest thing to unisex garments in nineteenth century America. We do not think less of President Lincoln for having used a shawl on occasion, and we certainly should not think less of Jefferson Davis for having used one of his wife's shawls just before his capture. See *War of the Rebellion*, series 1, vol. 49, pt. 1 (Washington: GPO, 1897), serial 3532, 538. My thanks to David J. Johnson of the Casemate Museum, Fort Monroe, Virginia, for valuable help in sorting out the mystery regarding the so-called "Jeff Davis disguise."

5. Siviter, loc. cit., 157-160.

7. Wheeling *Daily Intelligencer*, May 30, 1865, and June 1, 1865.

8. Kenneth M. Stampp, *The Era of Reconstruction, 1865-1877* (New York: Vintage Books, 1965), 79-80.

9. Siviter, loc. cit., 208 et seq.

10. Ambler, loc. cit., 315-316.

11. Siviter, loc. cit., 217.

12. Undated note in the Pierpont Papers, A&M 9. While it is not true that Annie Brown ever taught at the Wise Farm in Princess Anne County, it is true that she was there briefly in December of 1863 before moving west to California with her family. From other sources, it is clear that Wise believed that she might be teaching at Rolleston. In a letter of Lucy Chase dated November 19, 1866, is the following passage: "He [Wise] asked [General Brown] if it was true that John Brown's daughter was teaching in his house, adding, 'John Brown was one of the greatest men who ever lived in this country or in any other but it was my duty to hang him.'" See Swint, *Dear Ones at Home*, 211.

13. Siviter, loc. cit., 231-233; William Seale, *Virginia's Executive Mansion: A History of the Governor's House* (Richmond, Va.: Virginia State Library and Archives, 1988), 28, 42. My thanks to Dr. John C. Tyson of the Virginia State Library and Archives for providing information about the Governor's Mansion.

14. Edward J. Renehan, Jr., *The Secret Six: The True Tale of the Men Who Conspired with John Brown* (New York: Crown Publishers, 1995), 1.

15. Siviter, loc. cit., 344-345.

16. Speech of Gov. Pierpont at Virginia Convention, Feb. 27, 1868, as found in the Pierpont Papers, A&M 9.

17. Stampp, *The Era of Reconstruction*, 149-151.

18. Ambler, loc. cit., 303.

19. Siviter, loc. cit., 351-352.

20. Stampp, *The Era of Reconstruction*, 152-153; John F. Kennedy, *Profiles in Courage* (New York: Pocket Books, 1963), 125-126.

21. Stampp, *The Era of Reconstruction*, 144; Siviter, loc. cit., 354-355.

CHAPTER 15: "LET US LIVE TO MAKE MEN FREE."

1. Deborah P. Clifford, "An Invasion of Strong-minded Women: The Newspapers and the Woman Suffrage Campaign in Vermont in 1870," *Vermont History*, vol. 43, no. 1 (Winter, 1975), 1; J. W. Howe, *Reminiscences*, 381.

2. Clifford, "An Invasion of Strong-minded Women," 2-3.

3. Ibid., 1-2.

4. *Vermont Watchman and State Journal*, February 9, 1870.

5. Ibid.

6. Clifford, "An Invasion of Strong-Minded Women," 8-9, 12-13, 16-17.

7. Clifford, *Mine Eyes Have Seen the Glory*, 190-200; Laura E. Richards, *Samuel Gridley Howe* (New York: D. Appleton-Century Company, 1935), 256-260.

8. Ibid., 203.

9. Ibid., 203-204; Julia Ward Howe, diary entry for January 9th, 1876, Howe Family Papers, Houghton Library.

10. Julia Ward Howe, diary entry for January 11, 1876, Howe Family Papers, Houghton Library.

11. Julia Ward Howe, *At Sunset* (Boston: Houghton Mifflin Company, 1910), 62, 3-4.

12. J. W. Howe, *At Sunset*, 26-27..

13. Brink, loc. cit., 203.

14. Bristol, loc. cit., 195.

15. Julia's letter to Bishop McCabe is tipped into Bristol.

16. Bristol, loc. cit., 400-402.

17. Theodore Roosevelt, "President Roosevelt Presents a Suggestion to You," *Uncle Remus's—The Home Magazine*, vol. 23, no. 6 (August, 1908), 5-6; Elise K. Kirk, *Music at the White House: A History of the American Spirit* (Chicago: University of Illinois Press, 1986), 171.

18. Joel Chandler Harris, "Write Us What You Think About It," *Uncle Remus's—The Home Magazine*, vol. 23, no. 6 (August, 1908), 6.

19. "Not Our National Anthem," *New York Times*, July 29, 1908, 6. Neither the president nor the unknown author of the letter got his wish. On March 31, 1931, the "Star Spangled Banner," a song describing the bombardment of Fort McHenry by the British during the War of 1812, was selected as our national anthem, due in part to the nation's growing fascination with baseball. By 1931, every major league game began with the singing of Francis Scott Key's patriotic poem.

20. Clifford, *Mine Eyes Have Seen the Glory*, 275-276.

21. *The Woman's Journal*, vol. 41, no. 43 (Saturday, October 22, 1910), 183.

22. Albert Bushnell Hart and Herbert Ronald Ferleger, eds., *Theodore Roosevelt Cyclopedia* (New York: Roosevelt Memorial Association, 1941), 234.

23. William J. Hart, *Unfamiliar Stories of Familiar Hymns* (Boston: W. A. Wilde Company, 1940), 214-215.

24. Kirk, loc. cit., 225.

25. Nan Robertson, "'Battle Hymn of the Republic' Will Be Sung at the Inaugural," *New York Times*, Friday, January 8, 1965, 11.

26. David Ewen, ed., *American Popular Songs: From the Revolutionary War to the Present* (New York: Random House, 1966), 33.

27. James Melvin Washington, ed., *A Testament of Hope: The Essential Writings of Martin Luther King, Jr.* (San Francisco: Harper & Row, 1986), 230; Martin Luther King, Jr., *The Speeches of Martin Luther King* (Oak Forest, Ill.: MPI Home Video, 1990).

28. Stephen B. Oates, *Let the Trumpet Sound: The Life of Martin Luther King, Jr.* (New York: New American Library, 1982), 485-486.

EPILOG: "HIS SOUL IS MARCHING ON!"

1. Wanda Willson Whitman, ed., *Songs That Changed the World* (New York: Crown Publishers, 1969), 36.

2. Michael Bray, *A Time to Kill: A Study Concerning the Use of Force and Abortion* (Portland, Oregon: Advocates for Life Publications, 1994), 79-82, 87-89.

Bibliography

MANUSCRIPT SOURCES

BOSTON, MASSACHUSETTS
    Boston Public Library
        Thomas Wentworth Higginson Papers
        Massachusetts Historical Society
        Andrew Letterbook
        Andrew Papers

BROOKLYN, NEW YORK
    Brooklyn Historical Society
        Nelson-Hodges Papers transcribed by Alexander A. Moore

BURLINGTON, VERMONT
    Bailey/Howe Library, University of Vermont
        Jacob Collamer Papers
        First Congregational Society Papers

CAMBRIDGE, MASSACHUSETTS
    Houghton Library, Harvard University
        Howe Family Papers

CHARLESTON, WEST VIRGINIA
    West Virginia Division of Culture and History
        Boyd B. Stutler Collection.

LAKE PLACID, NEW YORK
    John Brown Farm
        John Brown Collection

MONTPELIER, VERMONT
    Vermont Historical Society
        Loyal C. Kellogg Diaries

MORGANTOWN, WEST VIRGINIA
    West Virginia and Regional History Collection
        Calendar of Pierpont Family Papers

New Orleans, Louisiana
    Amistad Research Center, Tulane University
        Correspondence of the American Missionary Association

Richmond, Virginia
    Virginia Historical Society
        Wise Family Papers

Topeka, Kansas
    Kansas State Historical Society
        John Brown Song Collection
        Richard J. Hinton Papers

Newspapers and Serials

American Missionary
The Atlantic Monthly
Barre Gazette (Barre, Mass.)
Boston Transcript
The Burlington Free Press (Burlington, Vt.)
The Congressional Globe
Daily Dispatch (Richmond, Va.)
Daily Intelligencer (Wheeling, W.V.)
Evening Star (Washington, D.C.)
The Fairmont Times (Fairmont, W.V.)
Harper's Weekly
Grand Army Scout and Soldier's Mail (Philadelphia, Pa.)
New York Daily Tribune
New York Times
Rutland Daily Herald (Rutland, Vt.)
Uncle Remus's—The Home Magazine
Vermont Journal
Vermont Standard (Woodstock, Vt.)
Vermont Watchman and State Journal
The Washington Post
The Woman's Journal

Books, Pamphlets, Videotapes, and Magazine Articles

Addresses on the Presentation of the Statue of Jacob Collamer. Washington: s.n., 1881.

Allen, Gay Wilson. *Waldo Emerson*. New York: Penguin Books, 1981.

Ambler, Charles. *Francis H. Pierpont: Union War Governor of Virginia and Father of West Virginia*. Chapel Hill: The University of North Carolina Press, 1937.

Barry, Joseph. *The Strange Story of Harper's Ferry with Legends of the Surrounding Country*. Shepherdstown, W.V.: Shepherdstown Register, Inc., 1979.

Basler, Roy P. *Abraham Lincoln: His Speeches and Writings*. New York: Da Capo Press, Inc., 1946.

_____. *The Collected Works of Abraham Lincoln*. New Brunswick, NJ: Rutgers University Press, 1953.

Berlin, Ira, Barbara J. Fields, et al. *Freedom: A Documentary History of Emancipation: 1861-1867: The Destruction of Slavery*, series 1, vol. 1. New York: Cambridge University Press, 1987.

Bishop, Jim. *The Day Lincoln Was Shot*. New York: Harper & Brothers, 1955.

Boyer, Richard O. *The Legend of John Brown: A Biography and History*. New York: Alfred A. Knopf, 1973.

Bray, Michael. *A Time to Kill: A Study Concerning the Use of Force and Abortion*. Portland, Oregon: Advocates for Life Publications, 1994.

Brink, Carol. *Harps in the Wind: The Story of the Singing Hutchinsons*. New York: The Macmillan Company, 1947.

Bristol, Frank Milton. *The Life of Chaplain McCabe*. New York: Fleming H. Revell Company, 1908.

Browne, Albert Gallatin, Jr. *Sketch of the Official Life of John A. Andrew, As Governor of Massachusetts*. New York: Hurd and Houghton, 1868.

Catton, Bruce. *The Coming Fury*. New York: Washington Square Press, 1961.

Cauble, Frank P. *The Proceedings Connected with the Surrender of the Army of Northern Virginia, April, 1865*. Appomattox, Va.: Appomattox Court House National Historical Park, 1962.

Chamberlain, Joshua Lawrence. *The Passing of the Armies: An Account of the Final Campaign of the Army of the Potomac, Based upon Personal Reminiscences of the Fifth Army Corps*. New York: Bantam Books, 1993.

Child, Lydia Maria. *The Freedmen's Book*. Boston: Ticknor and Fields, 1866.

Chronicle of America. Mt. Kisko, NY: Chronicle Publications, [1989?].

Clark, Champ. *The Assassination: Death of the President*. Alexandria, Va.: Time-Life Books, 1987.

Clifford, Deborah Pickman. "An Invasion of Strong-minded Women:

The Newspapers and the Woman Suffrage Campaign in Vermont in 1870," *Vermont History,* vol. 43, no. 1. Winter, 1975.

_____. *Mine Eyes Have Seen the Glory: A Biography of Julia Ward Howe.* Boston: Little, Brown and Co., 1979.

Conley, Phil, ed. *The West Virginia Encyclopedia.* Charleston, WV: West Virginia Publishing Company, 1929.

Cook, Benjamin F. *History of the Twelfth Massachusetts Volunteers (Webster Regiment).* Boston: Twelfth (Webster) Regiment Association, 1882.

Cotter, Edwin N., Jr. "John Brown at North Elba: Questions and Answers." Lake Placid, NY: John Brown Farm, n.d.

_____. "John Brown in the Adirondacks," *Adirondack Life.* Summer, 1972.

Crawford, Mary C. *The Romance of Old New England Churches.* Boston: L. C. Page & Co., 1904.

Crockett, Walter Hill. *Vermont: The Green Mountain State.* New York: The Century History Company, Inc., 1923.

Daingerfield, John E. P. "John Brown at Harper's Ferry: The Fight at the Engine House, as Seen by One of His Prisoners," *The Century Magazine,* vol. 30, no. 2. June, 1885.

Davis, Burke. *Sherman's March.* New York: Random House, 1980.

Davis, Varina Jefferson. *Jefferson Davis: Ex-President of the Confederate States of America: A Memoir.* New York: Belford Company, Publishers, 1890.

Davis, William C. *"A Government of Our Own": The Making of the Confederacy.* New York: The Free Press, 1994.

_____. *Jefferson Davis: The Man and His Hour.* New York: HarperCollins Publishers, 1991.

Diagram Group. *Weapons: An International Encyclopedia from 5000 BC to 2000 AD.* New York: St. Martin's Press, 1990.

Douglass, Frederick. *Life and Times of Frederick Douglass: His Early Life as a Slave, His Escape from Bondage, and His Complete History.* New York: Collier Books, 1962.

_____. *Narrative of the Life of Frederick Douglass.* New York: New American Library, 1968.

Doyle, William. *The Vermont Political Tradition: And Those Who Helped Make It.* Barre, Vt.: Northlight Studio Press, 1984.

Dunbar, Charles, ed. *The Union Harp and Revival Chorister.* Cincinnati: H. M. Rulison, Queen City Publishing House, 1858.

Elson, Louis C. *The History of American Music.* New York: The Macmillan Company, 1925.

Ewen, David, ed. *American Popular Songs: From the Revolutionary War to the Present.* New York: Random House, 1966.

Fischer, David Hackett. *Albion's Seed: Four British Folkways in America.* New York: Oxford University Press, 1989.

Fisher, Dorothy Canfield. *Memories of Arlington, Vermont.* New York:

Duell, Sloan and Pearce, 1957.

Foote, Shelby. *The Civil War: A Narrative*, three vols. New York: Vintage Books, 1986.

Force, Peter, ed. *American Archives*. Washington: M. St. Clair Clarke and Peter Force, 1840.

Foster, John Y. *New Jersey and the Rebellion*. Newark, N.J.: Martin R. Dennis, 1868.

Freeman, Douglas Southall. *R. E. Lee: A Biography*, four vols. New York: Charles Scribner's Sons, 1935.

Gould, Stephen Jay. *The Mismeasure of Man*. New York: Vintage Books, 1956.

Gerberg, Mort. *The U.S. Constitution for Everyone*. New York: Perigree Books, 1987.

Gilbert, Dave. *A Walker's Guide to Harpers Ferry, West Virginia*. Harpers Ferry, W. V.: Harpers Ferry Historical Association, 1991.

Hance, Dawn D. *The History of Rutland, Vermont, 1761-1861*. Rutland, Vt.: Academy Books, 1991.

Hall, Florence Howe. *The Story of the Battle Hymn of the Republic*. New York: Harper & Brothers, 1916.

Harding, Walter. *The Days of Henry Thoreau: A Biography*. New York: Dover Publications, Inc., 1982.

Harris, Marvin. *The Rise of Anthropological Theory: A History of Theories of Culture*. New York: Thomas Y. Crowell Company, 1968.

Hart, Albert Bushnell and Herbert Ronald Ferleger, eds. *Theodore Roosevelt Cyclopedia*. New York: Roosevelt Memorial Association, 1941.

Hart, William J. *Unfamiliar Stories of Familiar Hymns*. Boston: W. A. Wilde Company, 1940.

Harwell, Richard. *Lee: An Abridgment in One Volume of the Four-volume R. E. Lee by Douglas Southall Freeman*. New York: Collier Books, 1991.

Heffner, Richard D. *A Documentary History of the United States*. New York: Mentor, 1991.

Higginson, Thomas Wentworth. *Army Life in a Black Regiment*. Boston: Lee and Shepard, 1890.

Hitchcock, H. Wiley. *Music in the United States: A Historical Introduction*. Englewood Cliffs, NJ: Prentice Hall, Inc., 1974.

Horan, James D. *The Pinkertons: The Detective Dynasty That Made History*. New York: Crown Publishers, 1967.

Howe, Henry. *Historical Collections of Virginia*. Charleston, S.C.: Wm. R. Babcock, 1856.

Howe, Julia Ward. *At Sunset*. Boston: Houghton Mifflin Company, 1910.

_____. *From Sunset Ridge: Poems Old and New*. New York: Houghton, Mifflin Company, 1899.

_____. *Later Lyrics*. Boston: Lee and Shepard, 1865.

_____. *Passion Flowers*. Boston: Ticknor & Fields, 1854.

_____. *Reminiscences 1819-1889*. New York: Houghton

Mifflin and Co., 1899.

Howe, Samuel Gridley. *The Refugees from Slavery in Canada West: Report to the Freedmen's Inquiry Commission.* Boston: Wright & Potter, 1864.

Hurd, John Codman. *The Law of Freedom and Bondage in the United States,* two vols. New York: Negro Universities Press, 1968.

Hutchinson, John Wallace. *Story of the Hutchinsons (Tribe of Jesse),* two vols. Boston: Lee and Shepard, 1896.

Jefferson, Thomas. *Thomas Jefferson Writings.* New York: The Library of America, 1984.

Johnson, R. U., and C. C. Buel, eds. *Battles and Leaders of the Civil War,* four vols. New York: The Century Company, 1887-1888.

Johnston, I. N. *Four Months in Libby, and the Campaign Against Atlanta.* Cincinnati: R. F. Thompson, 1864.

Jones, Roger. "Affair at Harper's Ferry, Va.," *The Rebellion Record: A Diary of American Events,* supplement-first vol. New York: D. Van Nostrand, 1869.

Journals of the Continental Congress, 1774-1789. Washington, D.C.: GPO, 1906.

Josephson, Matthew. *Victor Hugo: A Realistic Biography of the Great Romantic.* Garden City, NY: Doubleday, Doran & Co., Inc., 1942.

Kelly, Mary Louise. *Jacob Collamer.* Woodstock, Vt.: The Woodstock Historical Society, 1944.

Kennedy, John F. *Profiles in Courage.* New York: Pocket Books, 1963.

King, Martin Luther, Jr. *The Speeches of Martin Luther King.* Oak Forest, Ill.: MPI Home Video, 1990.

Kirk, Elise K. *Music at the White House: A History of the American Spirit.* Chicago: University of Illinois Press, 1986.

Koenig, Louis W. "The Most Unpopular Man in the North," *Civil War Chronicles,* vol. 3, no. 1. Summer, 1993.

Kolchin, Peter. *American Slavery, 1619-1877.* New York: Hill and Wang, 1993.

Korn, Jerry. *Pursuit to Appomattox: The Last Battles.* Alexandria, Va.: Time-Life Books, 1987.

Kunhardt, Dorothy Meserve and Phillip B. Kunhardt. *Twenty Days: A Narrative in Text and Pictures of the Assassination of Abraham Lincoln and the Twenty Days and Nights That Followed—The Nation in Mourning, The Long Trip Home to Springfield.* New York: Harper & Row, 1965.

Laughlin, Clara E. *The Death of Lincoln: The Story of Booth's Plot, His Deed and the Penalty.* Newport, Vt.: Vermont Civil War Enterprises, n.d.

Lewis, Virgil A. *How West Virginia Was Made.* West Virginia: William G. Conley, 1909.

The Life, Trial and Execution of Captain John Brown Known as "Old Brown of Ossawatomie": Compiled from Official and Authentic Sources. New York: Da Capo Press, 1969.

Locke, John. *An Essay Concerning the True Original Extent and End of Civil*

Government. Chicago: Encyclopedia Britannica, Inc., 1987.

Lomax, Alan. *The Folk Songs of North America in the English Language*. Garden City, NY: Doubleday & Company, Inc., 1960.

Martin, Albro. *Railroads Triumphant: The Growth, Rejection, and Rebirth of a Vital American Force*. New York : Oxford University Press, 1992.

Mayo, Ellen Wise. "A Wartime Aurora Borealis," *Cosmopolitan*, vol. 22, no. 2. June, 1896.

McCutcheon, Mark. *The Writer's Guide to Everyday Life in the 1800s*. Cincinnati: Writer's Digest Books, 1993.

Mellon, Matthew T. *Early American Views on Negro Slavery: From the Letters and Papers of the Founders of the Republic*. New York: The New American Library, 1969.

Meltzer, Milton. *A Light in the Dark: The Life of Samuel Gridley Howe*. New York: Thomas Y. Crowell Co., 1964.

Memorial Record of the Nation's Tribute to Abraham Lincoln. Washington, D.C.: W. H. & O. H. Morrison, 1865.

The Methodist Hymnal: Official Hymnal of the Methodist Church. Nashville, Tenn.: The Methodist Publishing House, 1964, 1966.

Miller, Francis Trevelyan, ed. *The Photographic History of the Civil War*, ten vols. New York: The Review of Reviews Co., 1911, 1912.

Mosby, John S. *Gray Ghost: The Memoirs of Colonel John S. Mosby*. New York: Bantam Books, 1992.

The New Oxford Book of American Verse. New York: Oxford University Press, 1976.

Oates, Stephen B. *Let the Trumpet Sound: The Life of Martin Luther King, Jr*. New York: New America Library, 1982.

_____. "The Slaves Freed," *Civil War Chronicles*, vol. 2, no. 3. Winter, 1993.

_____. *To Purge This Land with Blood: A Biography of John Brown*. Amherst, Mass.: The University of Massachusetts Press, 1984.

_____. *With Malice Toward None: The Life of Abraham Lincoln*. New York: New American Library, 1977.

The Papers of Jefferson Davis. Baton Rouge, La.: State University Press, 1992.

Patterson, Richard K. "The Greatest Little Man I Ever Met," *American History Illustrated*. December, 1971.

Pearson, Henry Greenleaf. *The Life of John A. Andrew, Governor of Massachusetts, 1861-1865*, two vols. Boston: Houghton, Mifflin, 1904.

Pollard, Edward. *Lee and His Lieutenants*. Augusta, Ga.: Southern Publishing Company, 1870.

Porter, Horace. *Campaigning with Grant*. New York: The Century Company, 1906.

Randall, Ruth Painter. *Colonel Elmer Ellsworth: A Biography of Lincoln's Friend and First Hero of the Civil War*. Boston: Little, Brown and Company, 1960.

Randall, Willard Sterne. *Thomas Jefferson: A Life*. New York: Henry Holt and Company, 1993.

Rawley, James A. "Captain Nathaniel Gordon, the Only American Executed for Violating the Slave Trade Laws," *Civil War History*, vol. 39, No. 3. Kent State University Press, September, 1993.

Reese, George H., ed. *Proceedings of the Virginia State Convention of 1861, February 13- May 1*, four volumes. Richmond, Va.: Virginia State Library, 1965.

Reid, Whitelaw. *Ohio in the War: Her Statesmen, Her Generals, and Soldiers*. Cincinnati: Moore, Wilstach & Baldwin, 1868.

Renehan, Edward J., Jr. *The Secret Six: The True Tale of the Men Who Conspired with John Brown*. New York: Crown Publishers, 1995.

Rhodes, Robert Hunt, ed. *All for the Union: The Civil War Diary and Letters of Elisha Hunt Rhodes*. New York: Vintage Books, 1985.

Richards, Laura E. and Maud Howe Elliott. *Julia Ward Howe, 1819-1910*. Boston: Houghton Mifflin Company, 1916.

Richards, Laura E. *Letters and Journals of Samuel Gridley Howe*, in two vols. Boston: Dana Estes & Company, 1906.

_____. *Samuel Gridley Howe*. New York: D. Appleton-Century Company, 1935.

Rosenblatt, Emil and Ruth, eds. *Hard Marching Every Day: The Civil War Letters of Private Wilbur Fisk, 1861-1865*. Lawrence, Kansas: University Press of Kansas, 1992.

Rossback, Jeffery. *Ambivalent Conspirators: John Brown, the Secret Six, and a Theory of Slave Violence*. Philadelphia: University of Pennsylvania Press, 1982.

Ruchames, Louis, ed. *The John Brown Reader*. New York: Abelard-Schuman, 1959.

Sablosky, Irving. *American Music*. Chicago: The University of Chicago Press, 1969.

Sandburg, Carl. *Abraham Lincoln: The Prairie Years and the War Years*, three vols. New York: Dell Publishing, 1968.

_____. *Abraham Lincoln: The War Years*, four vols. New York: Harcourt, Brace & Company, 1939.

Schwartz, Charles Downer and Ouida Davis Schwartz. *A Flame of Fire: The Story of Troy Annual Conference*. Rutland, Vt.: Academy Books, 1982.

Schwartz, Harold. *Samuel Gridley Howe: Social Reformer, 1801-1876*. Cambridge, Mass.: Harvard University Press, 1956.

Seale, William. *Virginia's Executive Mansion: A History of the Governor's House*. Richmond, Va.: Virginia State Library and Archives, 1988.

Senghas, Robert E. "Joshua Young: Burlington Abolitionist." Burlington, Vt.: First Unitarian Universalist Society, December 6, 1981.

Sermons Preached in Boston on the Death of Abraham Lincoln. Boston: J. E. Tilton and Company, 1865.

Sherman, William Tecumseh. *Memoirs of General William T. Sherman*, two vols. Boston: Lee & Shepard, 1875.

Simpson, Craig M. *A Good Southerner: The Life of Henry A. Wise of Virginia*. Chapel Hill: The University of North Carolina, 1985.

Siviter, Anna Pierpont. *Recollections of War and Peace, 1861-1868*. New York: G. P. Putnam's Sons, 1938.

Smith, Edward P. *Incidents of the United States Christian Commission*. Philadelphia: J. B. Lippincott & Co., 1869.

Smith, Gene. *American Gothic: The Story of America's Legendary Theatrical Family—Junius, Edwin, and John Wilkes Booth*. New York: Simon & Schuster, 1992.

Smith, Merritt Roe. *Harpers Ferry Armory and the New Technology: The Challenge of Change*. Ithaca, NY: Cornell University Press, 1977.

Snow, Edward Roe. *Historic Fort Warren*. Boston: The Yankee Publishing Company, 1944.

_____. *The Romance of Boston Bay*. Boston: The Yankee Publishing Company, 1944.

Sparks, Jared. *The Writings of George Washington*. Boston: Little, Brown, and Company, 1858.

Stampp, Kenneth M. *The Era of Reconstruction, 1865-1877*. New York: Vintage Books, 1965.

_____. *The Peculiar Institution: Slavery in the Ante-Bellum South*. New York: Vintage Books, 1956.

Stearns, Frank Preston. *The Life and Public Services of George Luther Stearns*. Philadelphia: J. B. Lippincott Company, 1907.

Stone, Edward, ed. *Incident at Harper's Ferry*. Englewood Cliffs, NJ: Prentice-Hall, Inc. 1956.

Strong, George Templeton. *Diary of the Civil War, 1860-1865*. New York: The Macmillan Company, 1962.

Stutler, Boyd B. *Glory, Glory, Hallelujah!: The Story of "John Brown's Body" and "Battle Hymn of the Republic"*. Cincinnati: C. J. Krehbiel Company, 1960.

_____. "John Brown's Body," *Civil War History* IV. September, 1958.

Swint, Henry Lee, ed. *Dear Ones at Home*. Nashville, Tenn.: Vanderbilt University Press, 1966.

Swint, Henry Lee. *The Northern Teacher in the South, 1862-1870*. New York: Octagon Books, Inc., 1967.

Tinkham, O. M. "Jacob Collamer," *The Vermonter*, vol. 5, no. 12. July, 1900.

Trulock, Alice Rains. *In the Hands of Providence: Joshua L. Chamberlain and the American Civil War*. Chapel Hill: The University of North Carolina Press, 1992.

United States Senate. *34th Congress, 1st Session*, vol. 2. Report of the Committee on Territories (S. Rpt. 282). Washington: A. O. P.

Nicholson, Senate Printer, 1856. Serial 837.

United States Senate. *36th Congress, 1st Session.* [Report on the Invasion at Harper's Ferry] (S. Rpt. 278). Washington: GPO, 1860. Serial 1040.

Villard, Oswald Garrison. *John Brown: A Biography, 1800-1859.* Garden City, NY: Doubleday, Doran, & Company, Inc., 1910.

Walton, E. P., ed. *Records of the Governor and Council.* Montpelier, Vt.: Steam Press of J. & J. M. Poland, 1873.

Warch, Richard and Jonathan Fanton, eds. *John Brown.* Englewood Cliffs, NJ: Prentice-Hall, Inc., 1973.

Ward, Geoffrey C. with Ric and Ken Burns. *The Civil War: An Illustrated History.* New York: Alfred A. Knopf, 1990.

Washington, James Melvin, ed. *A Testament of Hope: The Essential Writings of Martin Luther King, Jr.* San Francisco: Harper & Row, 1986.

Weichmann, Louis J. *A True History of the Assassination of Abraham Lincoln and of the Conspiracy of 1865.* New York: Alfred A. Knopf, 1975.

Weiss, John. *Life and Correspondence of Theodore Parker, Minister of the Twenty-eighth Congregational Society, Boston,* two vols. London: Longman, Green, Longman, Roberts, and Green, 1863.

Wells, Gideon. *Diary of Gideon Welles, Secretary of the Navy under Lincoln and Johnson.* Boston: Houghton Mifflin Company, 1911.

Wert, Jeffry D. *Mosby's Rangers.* New York: Simon & Schuster, 1990.

Whipple, J. Rayner. "'John Brown's Body Lies a Mouldering in the Grave': The Popular Civil War Song Which Originated at Fort Warren, Boston Harbor," *Old-Time New England,* vol. 32, no. 4. April, 1942.

White, Richard Grant. *National Hymns, How They Are Written and How They Are Not Written: A Lyric and National Study for the Times.* New York: Rudd & Carleton, 1861.

_____. *Poetry Lyrical, Narrative, and Satirical of the Civil War.* New York: The American News Company, 1866.

Whitman, Wanda Willson, ed. *Songs That Changed the World.* New York: Crown Publishers, 1969.

Wise, Barton H. *The Life of Henry A. Wise of Virginia, 1806-1876.* New York: The Macmillan Company, 1889.

Wise, John Sergeant. *The End of an Era.* New York: Thomas Yoseloff, 1965.

Wise, Stephen R. *Lifeline of the Confederacy: Blockade Running During the Civil War.* S.l.: University of South Carolina Press, 1988.

Young, Joshua. "The Funeral of John Brown," *New England Magazine,* reprint. April, 1904.

_____. *God Greater Than Man: A Sermon Preached June 11th, after the Rendition of Anthony Burns.* Burlington, Vt.: Samuel B. Nichols, 1854.

MUSIC SCORES AND RECORDINGS

Crawford, Richard, ed. *The Civil War Songbook: Complete Original Sheet Music for 37 Songs.* New York: Dover Publications, Inc., 1977.

Dale, Clamma. *Unforgotten: An Album of Healing.* New York: DAL Productions Ltd., 1995.

Erbsen, Wayne. *Southern Soldier Boy: 16 Authentic Tunes of the Civil War.* Asheville, N.C.: Native Ground, 1992.

Glass, Paul and Louis C. Singer. *Singing Soldiers: A History of the Civil War in Song.* New York: Da Capo, 1975.

Silber, Irwin. *Songs of the Civil War.* New York: Columbia University Press, 1960.

Songs of the Civil War, produced by Jim Brown, Ken Burns, and Don DeVito. New York: Sony Music Entertainment, Inc., 1991.

Songs of the Civil War: First Recordings from Original Editions. New York: New World Records, 1976.

Work, Henry Clay. "Song of a Thousand Years." Chicago: Root & Cady, 1862.

Recordings and information are also available from the following:

Bobby Horton
3430 Sagebrook Lane
Birmingham, AL 35243

97th Regimental String Band
P.O. Box 2208 P6
Largo, Florida 33779-2208

The (Henry Clay) Work Gang
Andy Meier, Coord.
1101 Route 5 (in Canaan)
East Chatham, NY 12060-9717

ACKNOWLEDGMENTS

No book of this sort could ever get off the ground without the aid
of many hands along the way. My thanks go first to Dolores Frascoia,
Larry Dane Brimner, Ralph Fair, Jayne Bush, Greg Keilty, and Betty
Bandel, without whose initial encouragement this work would never
have seen daylight.

Digging into the past requires the services of libraries with
extensive historical materials and devoted reference librarians. Here,
my thanks extend immediately to Marjorie Zunder, Paul Donovan,
and the staff of the Law Library in Montpelier, Vermont; Linda Willis
and the gang at the Vermont Midstate Regional Library in Berlin; the
staff of the Norman Williams Library in Woodstock, Vermont; and
Sharon Bartram and the volunteers of the Brown Public Library in
Northfield.

Special collections are a necessity when one is attempting to piece
together obscure moments in history. I have derived invaluable aid in
this respect from Debra Basham at the West Virginia Division of Culture
and History; Edwin N. Cotter, Jr., superintendent of the John Brown
Farm in Lake Placid, New York; Harold Forbes of the West Virginia &
Regional History Collection at West Virginia University, Morgantown;
Virginia H. Smith of the Massachusetts Historical Society; Bob Knecht
at the Kansas State Historical Society in Topeka; Laura V. Monti and
the staff of special collections at the Boston Public Library; Andrew
Simons and the staff of the Amistad Research Center at Tulane
University; Clara M. Lamers of the Brooklyn Historical Society;
Elizabeth M. Gushee and the staff of the Virginia Historical Society;
the staff of the Houghton Library at Harvard University; Edmund
Hands, historian and archivist for the 12th Mass. re-enactors; D.
Gregory Sanford and the staff for the archives of the secretary of the
state of Vermont; Paul Carnahan and the staff of the Vermont Historical
Society in Montpelier; the staff of special collections at the Bailey/Howe
Library at the University of Vermont; and the staffs of U.S. Senator
James Jeffords and U.S. Representative Bernard Sanders of Vermont.

Additional thanks must go to the following individuals: Jack
Anderson, William Eagan, Steve Soper, and Dr. David Cross of the
Green Mountain Civil War Round Table; Bonnie Mathews of the

Central Library of Virginia Beach; Mary Reid Barrow of the *Virginia Pilot* newspaper; Stephen Mansfield of Virginia Wesleyan College; Dennis Frye and the staff of the Harpers Ferry National Park; Robert K. Krick, chief historian of the Fredericksburg and Spotsylvania National Military Park; Betty K. Koed of the Senate Historical Office; Glenn E. Helm, reference librarian for the U.S. Naval Historical Center; David J. Johnson of the Casemate Museum at Fortress Monroe; Mark Anderson, Charlie Boyd and the MDC park rangers at Fort Warren; Rev. Robert E. Senghas; research librarian Elizabeth Dow; historian David J. Blow; Dr. John T. Atwood Jr. of Marie Selby Gardens; Rev. Wayne Jones, Sr., pastor of the Northfield Methodist Church; Jack LaDuke of WCAX, Channel 3 News; my musical accomplices Bob Small, Sue Reid, Priscilla and Euclid Farnham, Elaine Howe, and Claire ManFREDonia; our sound engineer, David Gunn; authors Deborah P. Clifford, Edwin Bearss, and Howard Coffin; John Kingston; my editor Dennis Báthory-Kitsz; my publishers James and Ingrid Wilson; and my supportive friends Alden Kent, Douglas McAdam, Diane Iverson, and Dr. Mary Tomanio.

Index

Sharp, Granville, British abolitionist, 287

Sharps carbines, 29, 31, 289

Shaw, Robert Gould, Union colonel of Fifty-fourth Massachusetts, 174

Shenandoah River, at Harper's Ferry, 31

Shepherd, Hayward, Harper's Ferry baggage master, shot by Brown's men, 32, and Fontaine Beckham, 34

Shepherdstown, Maryland, militia alerted, 33

Sheridan, Philip, Union general, victory at Cedar Creek, 209

Sherman, Roger, on committee to declare independence, 1

Sherman, William Tecumseh, Union major general, *photos*, 196, 208; captures and burns, Atlanta, Georgia, 209-210; at Louisiana military academy, 210; march to the sea, 210-212; and recruitment of freed slaves, 212-214; and Lincoln's death, 233-234; accepts Johnston's surrender, 234

"Ship on Fire," *see* songs

ships and naval vessels:

   Amistad, Cuban coastal slave ship, 25, 198-199

   Diamond, blockade runner, 241-242; note on date of trip to Richmond, 307

   Pawnee, U.S.S., at Union invasion of Alexandria, Virginia, 135

   Robert McClelland, U.S. revenue cutter, taken by Confederates, 147

   Stettin, U.S.S., captures blockade runner, 241

   Telegraph, steamboat, 229

   Washington, Naval brig, and *Amistad*, 198

Shuckburg, Richard, British doctor, and "Yankee Doodle", 147

Sierra Leone, colonization of British freedmen in, 187

Simpson, Matthew, bishop of Methodist Church, gives Lincoln's burial sermon, 238

Sinn, Thomas, captain of Frederick, Md., militia, negotiates with John Brown, 36-37

Siviter, Anna Pierpont, 119; and Early's raid, 205-206; and torchlight parade, 224; visits Fort Monroe, 241-242, 307; and "Black Codes" 243; *photo*, 244; and Henry Wise, 245; and John Brown's ghost, 246; and Horace Greeley, 247; attends Johnson impeachment, 248; father spends last years with, 250

Sixth Massachusetts Regiment, attacked on streets of Baltimore, 149

slave states, and Missouri Compromise, 11; competition with free states, 11-12; use of filibusters to invade Cuba, 12; competition over Kansas territory, 12-14

slave trade, outlawed, 5; Nathaniel Gordon hanged for engaging in, 5

slavery, *xiii*; American system described, 8-9

Smith, Francis J., welcomes Pierpont to Richmond, 242

Smith, Gerrit, Brown supporter, offers Brown land in North Elba, 24; chairs committee on Kansas, 26; *photo*, 50; committed to asylum, 51; summoned to appear before senate committee, 90; and release of Jefferson Davis on bond, 247

Smith, Isaac, John Brown alias, 14, 21, 36, 40, 288-289

Smith, William "Baldy" Union general, attacks Wise at Petersburg, 204

"Song of a Thousand Years," *see* songs

songs:

   "Blow Ye the Trumpet, Blow," Methodist hymn, 76

   "Clear the Tracks," by Hutchinson Family Singers, 11

   "Dixie's Land," by Dan Emmett, 260

   "Hail Columbia," by philip Phylo, Mrs. Pierpont sings, 120; considered unsuitable as national anthem, 147-148

   "John Brown's Body," created at fort in Boston Harbor, x, xiv; Vermont Brigade sings in Charlestown, x; transformed into Howe's "Battle Hymn," x; *ill.* of first published broadside, 80; creation of song, 130-132, 138-139; performance in Boston, 139-140; sung in New York City, 140; sung by Hutchinson Family Singers in Virginia, 160; Twelfth Massachusetts sings "John Brown's Body" at Charlestown, Virginia, 161;

Edited & designed by Dennis Báthory-Kitsz, The Transitive Empire.
Set in classic Aldine Roman and Italic, with U.S. Currency decoratives.

9 780965 932622